To Mari & Mike Dosney

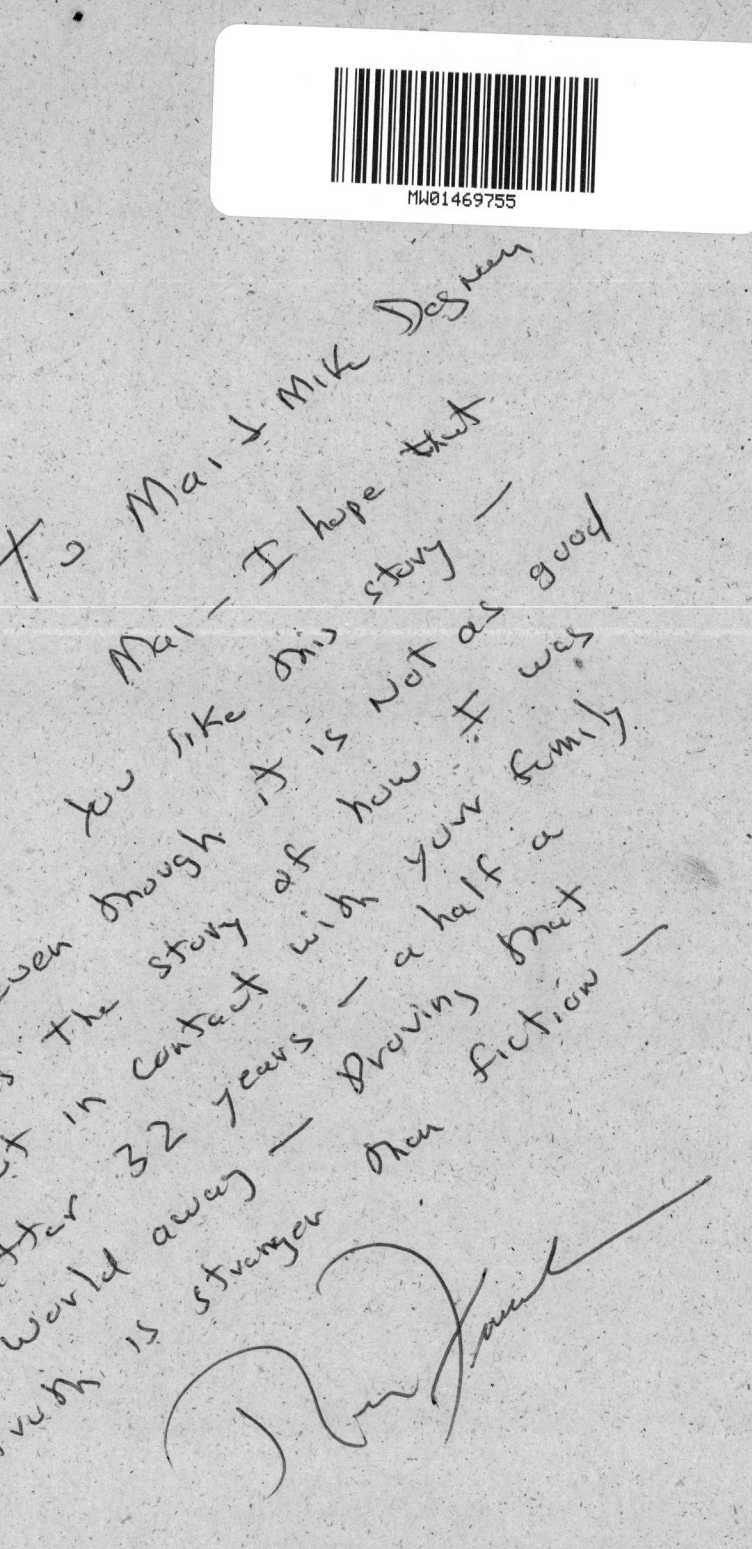

Mari — I hope that you like this story — even though it is not as good as the story of how it was put in contact with your family after 32 years — a half a world away — proving that Truth is stranger than fiction —

Ron [signature]

7/99

And nothing but the truth

And nothing but the truth

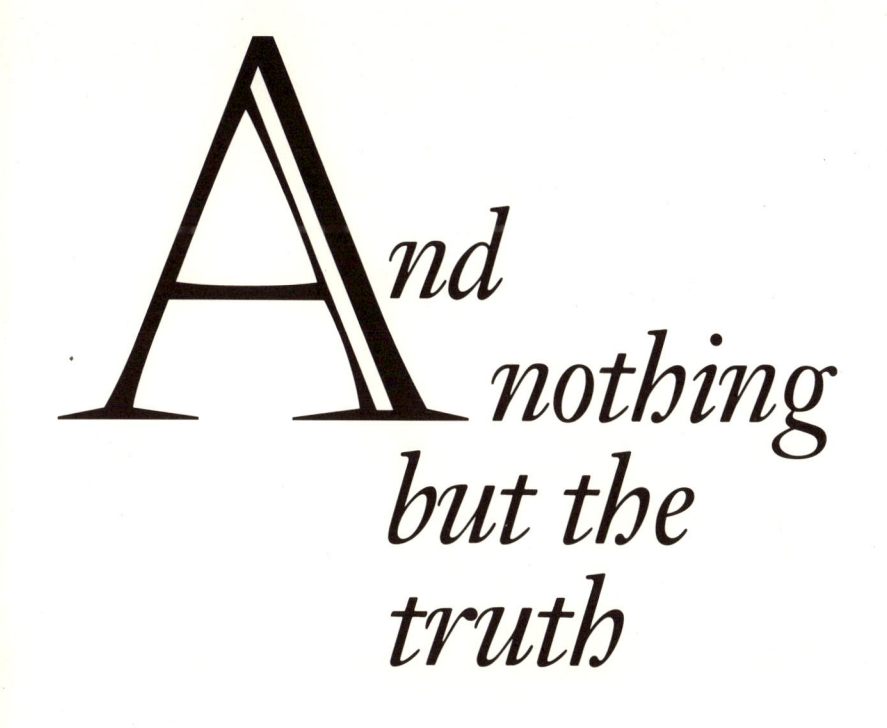

A novel by

Ron Friedman

GEORGE T. BISEL

Copyright © 1995
George T. Bisel Company
710 South Washington Square
Philadelphia, PA 19106
All rights reserved

ISBN 1-887024-00-X

*Charles Perrow, James Petrikin,
and Eben Jones are historical persons.
All of the events and all other characters
depicted in this book are fictitious and
any resemblance of these characters to
any person or persons living or dead is
strictly coincidental.*

To my wife SUSIE,

    without whose love

    and encouragement

    this story could not

    have been written

Do you swear by Almighty God, the searcher of all hearts, that the information you give will be the whole truth and nothing but the truth, or so you shall answer to God on the last Great Day?

Witness Oath,

Court of Common Pleas,

Centre County, Pennsylvania,

1827

1

"Eben Jones is dead."

"Of course, he's dead," I replied with a poorly disguised touch of sarcasm. "He'd be over 180 years old by now."

"That's not what I mean, dear," Sallie lifted her head slightly from the pillow and stretched sleepily. "You're always trying to make something out of nothing. Your imagination . . . you know, you get sidetracked . . . you find mysteries in everything. If you want to figure something out, try thinking about how you're going to hang the drapery rod in the front room this weekend . . . don't waste your time thinking about a slave who is dead, gone, and forgotten."

I slid into the bed and snuggled closer so that our sides touched lightly. Sally did not respond to my advance and within a few minutes she was breathing rhythmically and deeply. She sighed once and turned her back toward me with a finality that only husbands can fully appreciate.

I turned off the light but could not sleep. Of course, Sallie was right. The glands in my head that regulated my imagination were hyperactive. They always have been. I should have been planning how to hang the drapery rod. After all, Eben Jones was dead and gone.

Five months before, outside the Boalsburg, Pennsylvania, Post Office, I saw a handbill advertising an estate sale. The bill stated that an auction would dispose of old coins, tokens, letters, deeds, and "other items of note too numerous to mention."

I love Americana, especially old documents, and I remember making a mental note of the date and time and trying to figure out how I might be able to dodge the weekend chores Sallie had planned for me. Sallie disapproves of my using the word Americana which she defines as junk. When I acquire Americana it becomes expensive junk to her.

[1

Although I love all Americana, I try to limit myself to paper Americana only because it is easier to store and handle. Sallie is especially happy that my addiction to Americana does not include trunks or furniture. I buy paper Americana, when and where I can, restrained only by the tight budget that Sallie imposes upon me. Each scrap of paper is a minute slice of history for me, tangible evidence from the past of people and the events in their lives. I am always fascinated by the thought of the people who created the words of each document and letter. All other traces of them are gone, forgotten by descendants who never knew them. Headstones in overgrown cemeteries and pieces of paper are all that are left of these faceless people whose lives have been reduced to my musings about the papers they left behind. I wonder what they would think if they knew that generations later their creations would be collected, treasured, and handled so reverently.

I decided to slip out of the house on that Saturday afternoon. Any guilt I had for postponing the chores evaporated when I informed Sallie of my plans. She did not seem too upset, although she reminded me of my addiction and requested that I try to control myself. She also advised me that we were to meet Uncle Rudy at the cabin in Spruce Creek later that afternoon.

I found the auction fairly typical. The crowd was not animated, and the bidding was subdued until several Civil War souvenirs were put on the block. The bidding was strong as mini-balls, letters, cartridge cases, and swords were sold. Afterward, the crowd thinned out considerably and the auctioneer seemed to tire. An interesting old deed from the Penn Family to a tract of 200 acres of land was shown. I successfully acquired it as well as a small poster extolling the virtues of Andrew Jackson as a Presidential candidate.

Over my budget and with the two pieces in hand, I was about to leave. I was already in serious jeopardy, having promised to accompany Sallie to her uncle's cottage by 3 P.M. The man next to me, whom I knew to be a stamp dealer in the next town, had a list of the lots to be sold. He leaned toward me and said that the next item was of particular interest.

"A slave document," he whispered to me. "It's an interesting piece. If I can steal it, I will. Blacks always pay top . . . I mean, *top* dollar for anything 'slave.' Are you going to bid?"

I assured him that I would not bid until he dropped out.

"If I can't get it for $25, I'll drop out. It's a nice piece, but it's out of my line."

I must admit that he piqued my interest, and when the bidding reached $35, I joined in. I did not recognize the other bidder, but she seemed intent on getting the document. At $75.00 she hesitated, cast an evil glance in my direction, and did not offer another bid. I went to the cashier to claim my prize.

As I left the auction, a momentary depression overwhelmed me. I conjured up a vision of the deceased former owner carefully accumulating his collection, visiting auctions, flea markets, curiosity shops. I could see him carefully handling each piece, wondering who had held each item, just as I do with my collection. Now his collection, acquired lovingly over decades was once again scattered to the four winds. One year from now, or five decades from now would my collection suffer the same humiliation? I tried to block the thought out of my mind and to direct my attention toward Spruce Creek and Uncle Rudy.

Now as I lay awake, I knew Sallie was right that Eben Jones was dead and gone. But she was wrong when she said he was forgotten. At least one person — me — knew of his existence. But the fact that he had existed was *all* I knew.

The November wind rose and fell outside, and sleep slowly swept over me gently pushing Eben Jones and the auction into the recesses of my mind.

2

"You're late." Marie's greeting was most unwelcome, and I cast as disapproving a look as I could muster in her direction as I removed my topcoat. She pretended not to notice and turned toward her computer, seeming completely unconcerned. She often would test me like this on Monday morning. When I offered no excuse or verbal resistance to her comment, she continued.

"Mrs. Puebella called about her will."

"Wants to change it again?"

Marie nodded. "Mrs. Williston's husband was arrested again on Saturday night. The arraignment is this afternoon at one at Central Court."

"Tell me, Marie is Mrs. Williston's . . ."

"Her account is current," she interrupted.

Of course that was the question I was about to ask, but somehow it always rankled me that Marie could anticipate me so easily. I decided to display some independence.

"No, Marie, I was going to ask whether Mrs. Williston's phone number is on my Rolodex."

She suppressed a grin, knowing well that I was making it up, but she did not press her advantage. "I need your help in transcribing something. Please bring your pad and come to the library."

I set the letter on the mahogany conference table before her.

"What is it?"

"A letter written in 1827."

"Is it important?"

"It was to Eben Jones."

"What beautiful penmanship. That's certainly a lost art." Marie cast an eye in my direction.

"Lovingston, Nelson County, Virginia, September 4, 1827." Marie read the letter hurriedly, then re-read it more slowly.

"Well, Marie, what do you think?"

"It's interesting . . . fascinating really. Can you imagine what it must have been like with slavery? But what does it all mean?"

"I don't know exactly. It's a plea for help from an attorney in Virginia to James Petrikin. I think Petrikin was an attorney here in the county in the early 1800s. The Petrikin family name figures prominently in the land titles I've worked on. There's a building at Bellefonte known as Petrikin Hall . . . late 1800s."

We were interrupted by the phone ringing.

"Back to reality," Marie said wistfully as she went to answer it.

As I stared at the letter for what seemed only a moment, my mind drifted.

4]

3

"Squire Petrikin . . ." the man in coarsely woven clothes called. He shut the door behind him.

Petrikin rose from his seat by the window, placing the book he had been reading on the desk, and went to the anteroom of his offices.

"Ah, the afternoon post . . . what news have you to share with me this beautiful autumn afternoon? I would bet that you are paid to stop by the newspaper before you start your rounds. Save me the cost of the paper by telling me also, Brownell."

"Sir, the horseman reports that the Juniata is very high by Lewistown."

"No, no, I mean news," the attorney said with a laugh.

"Gossip, sir?"

"Please, Brownell, it is not polite to gossip. I am inquiring only if there is news of a more personal nature other than news of a general nature such as the depth of the river by Lewistown."

"I catch your meaning, sir. You wish to hear the latest gossip, but seeing as how you are an upstanding man before the bar, you prefer not to hear gossip, only personal news."

"Ah, Brownell, you certainly have God's own gift for seeing through a man's words and getting to the heart of his intent. Have you ever considered reading law?"

"Be a lawyer, sir, and have to rely upon the postman for gossip? Never!"

Both men laughed. Brownell sorted through a group of letters in his leather pouch and proffered two to Petrikin.

Petrikin nodded, walked Brownell to the door, and watched as the postman passed through the gate continuing his rounds.

"The autumn sun is getting lower," thought Petrikin. "Soon it will be the dead of winter. There is much to do before then. There is never enough time."

He walked back into the inner office and resumed his seat by the window. He examined the two letters closely. Taking a knife from the table nearby, he opened the first.

"Ah. A new case. A creditor of the forge over at Colerain on Spruce Creek in Huntingdon County... not promising. The iron trades are off this season."

He opened the second letter. He read it carefully, then re-read it ever more slowly. He looked up from the letter, out the window and up the hill to the county courthouse building. He stood and placed the letter on the table. He took a seat at the table and stared at the letter.

Petrikin sat lost in thought until the outer door opened and he heard heavy footsteps.

"Anyone here? James, are you about?"

"Henry," Petrikin called, "That you?"

"Yes, my fellow, what keeps you in the office this afternoon? I expected to see you in court. Judge Burnside was in rare form. His honor disposed of half the November term cases on the civil docket. Lawyers were scurrying here and there. Surely you must have had some matters before His honor." The older, more portly man entered the office.

"Nothing of importance," the younger man responded without a hint of interest.

"No matter, no matter. Why so solemn?"

"It is truly a cruel world, Henry. Here, read this letter I received today from an attorney in Nelson County, Virginia," Petrikin offered Henry the letter.

The older man started reading the letter. He halted abruptly.

"I need read no more, James. I only read so far as the first line — 'willing to aid in the humane undertaking of establishing the freedom of Eben Jones...' The translation of the words 'humane undertaking' is the Latin word *gratis*. James, there is no money in this matter. It is purely political. Slavery is a Southern problem. We abolished it here in the Commonwealth some thirty years ago."

"Remember last year — November, I think — there were those officers from Virginia here? They had gone into Penns Valley and

6]

captured two negroes. They came through town making a great show of their captives in heavy chains. People from all over town turned out. I am haunted still by the look of humiliation and disgrace upon the faces of those negroes."

Henry seated himself near the fireplace, making himself comfortable and unbuttoning his outer coat.

He paused, then responded.

"I remember well the incident about which you speak. I was in court that day . . . you know, the Widow Prough . . . no matter. The Virginians appeared in court with their arrest warrants.

"They were respectful, but the judge did not seem to take too kindly to them. He mentioned that they certainly had come a long way from their native territory to the woods of Pennsylvania looking for runaway slaves. He questioned them about why they should come hundreds of miles just for two slaves. They showed him their written authority. I suspected that they were not officers as we know them here but men who chased down people under the color of the law, no better than pirates with letters of marque."

"The judge reviewed their authority and their warrants. I suspected that the judge would have jailed the negroes and held them until the next court of quarter sessions in January and sorted the matter out then. I always thought that the judge was unsympathetic to the cause of slavery. By holding the negroes until January, it would have been possible that the two Virginians would have realized that they could wait two more months before having a hearing on their arrest warrants. They might have lost interest and returned to Virginia and eventually the negroes would have been freed."

The older man paused in his account and retrieved a small pinch of tobacco from a pouch in his pocket and filled his pipe.

"That is what the judge should have done, but that is certainly not what happened. The Virginians left the court and returned in a minute with the negroes. They had taken care that they not be chained in front of the judge lest his sympathies be aroused. As they entered the courtroom, a strange look crossed the countenance of our judge. It was as if he recognized one of the negroes. It was a strange expression which I could not decipher. I was sitting at the bar, and I noticed that one of the negroes held his eyes low in a subservient manner and the other looked the judge square in the eye. It seemed to me that one negro knew our judge, though in truth I could not swear so. Neither negro said anything, but the one continued to look at the judge. The judge avoided eye contact with the negro and directed his attention to the Virginians. Within a few seconds, the judge endorsed the warrants and he told the Virginians that they could be on their way. Surprised that he did so without argument, the two Virginians hurried from the courtroom pushing the negroes before them. The one negro cast a glance over his left shoulder making eye contact with the judge. It was just an instant, but it was unmistakable. Outside the courtroom, we all heard the rattle of chains as the negroes were shackled. Their chains clanked as they were led down the marble stairs into the cold." Henry paused to light his pipe, then continued.

"We all were shocked by the judge's rash action and there was a muffled whisper of protest. The judge looked sternly at the spectators and us and retired to chambers. We waited in the courtroom for the judge to reappear, but he did not do so. Presently, the judge's secretary entered the courtroom and advised the attorneys that court was in recess until the following week. Widow Prough was quite upset that her case was not heard. She commented that she had practiced her testimony all night."

The younger man was lost in thought.

"James, it is no concern of yours. These matters — the negroes and the letter from Virginia — are no concern of yours. There is nothing that can be done and there is little cause for you to upset yourself. What happened to the negro Jones is unfortunate, but it makes no sense to upset yourself over it. Come, the traders have brought fresh ale from Philadelphia. We owe it to ourselves not to disappoint the tavernkeeper on the square."

4

"It's something new, dear," Sallie explained as she placed a steaming casserole on the table before me. "Now, try it and give me your honest opinion."

My mind flashed back to the first time she requested my honest opinion of her cooking, not three days after we were married. Unfortunately, I was not properly warned by either of my parents, and I have no older brother, so I rendered an honest opinion of her chili as requested. The scene that followed would not soon be forgotten. I made a mental note to warn my son, if I should ever have the good fortune to be a father, lest he make the same mistake.

"Tastes a little like hot chicken salad with Chinese noodles," I ventured.

"That's exactly what it's suppose to be, hot Chinese chicken delight with crispy noodles. Do you like it?"

I faced this dilemma at least once a month for the last five years. I knew Sallie had tried to create something special for me. She had made an emotional investment in the casserole believing that I would like it. If I were critical, she would be hurt and the evening would be ruined. On the other hand, if I raved about it, I would be forcing down hot Chinese chicken delight with crispy noodles once a month for the next forty years. I stalled for time by slowly chewing my second mouthful pretending to assess the flavor. My mind searched for an appropriate response.

"It's not bad, dear. Where did you get the recipe?"

My tactic was two-fold. First, to be non-committal, and second, to distract her by telling me where she obtained the recipe.

"*Country-Kitchen Cooking Cookbook* . . . but 'it's not bad' is no answer to my question, dear. Should I plan on serving this dish again? It's a difficult dish to make."

"Sallie should be a lawyer," I thought. "She is not easily dissuaded."

[9

I reminded myself that honesty is the best policy only for people who order their dinners in restaurants.

"Yes, dear," I lied. "It's very good."

She looked at me skeptically. I knew she expected a detailed explanation of my 'very good' response.

"Well, the sauce is creamy and rich. The chicken is soft and tender, and the celery has a slight crunch to it. Of course, there are the crispy noodles. I guess what makes the dish so good is the variety of textures."

To emphasize my complete satisfaction with the dish, I reached for another helping. When she saw me place another heaping spoonful on my plate she seemed convinced, relaxed, and smiled at me. I knew I was off the hook, but that I could expect to see hot Chinese chicken delight in the future — and that I would learn to like it.

"I hope it's an acquired taste," I thought.

"Dear, remember on Friday when you came up to bed and told me about that slave letter you got at the auction last summer?"

"Yes," I replied after finishing as little of the remaining food on my plate as I could without arousing suspicion.

"Well, I have an apology. I think that your imagination, much as I criticize it, is one of your best features. I certainly don't want to discourage you. What is that letter all about?"

When we cleared the table and did the dishes, I retrieved the transcription of the letter and showed it to her.

"What do you suppose happened?" she asked.

"Well, the letter is a plea for help on behalf of Eben Jones. Apparently there was a law in Virginia that free negroes were required to register — probably with the county clerk or the clerk of courts — and to have with them a certificate of registration attesting to their status as free persons. I would guess that Eben Jones was stopped and questioned, and when it was discovered that he had no certificate of registration, he was detained."

"But what does that have to do with the attorney in Centre County?"

"Well, if Eben Jones was a citizen of Pennsylvania, then he would not be under the jurisdiction of the laws of Virginia regarding registration."

"Why not?" she asked. "Obviously he was not in Pennsylvania at the time of his arrest. If I'm speeding in Virginia on Interstate 81, I can't get off by claiming I'm a citizen of Pennsylvania and I'm not subject to the laws of Virginia."

"Good point, Sallie. It has to do with the clause of the Federal Constitution noted in the letter. Article IV, Section 2, Clause 1 is the famous 'Privileges and Immunities Clause.' 'The citizens of each state shall be entitled to all privileges and immunities of the citizens of the several states.' It has to do with legal status as to citizenship, not the violation of a crime."

"I don't understand, dear."

"What that means is that if Eben Jones in 1827 — or you in the current year — are a citizen of Pennsylvania and you are not required to carry proof of your citizenship here in order to maintain your status, then in Virginia you cannot be compelled to do so. If you were to move to Virginia and become a citizen of that state, then of course you would have to comply. But if you are a citizen of Pennsylvania under the Constitution, Virginia could not impose a registration law upon you . . . or Eben Jones.

"I see . . . I think. But what about *habeas corpus*? Isn't that about a crime being committed?"

"I think you're confusing *habeas corpus* with *corpus delicti*. *Corpus delicti* is evidence of the commission of a crime. The existence of a dead body may indicate that a murder has been committed. The writ of *habeas corpus* has nothing to do with a dead body. It is a legal proceeding. A person being held in custody against his will has the right to have the legality of the denial of his freedom tested in court. A writ of *habeas corpus* is nothing more than a request for a court to determine the legality of the restraint. Basically, the people holding the person requesting the writ must justify the right to custody. In Eben Jones' case, if he were able to prove in court that he was a citizen of Pennsylvania, then the fact that he violated the registration laws would be immaterial, and the judge would issue a writ freeing him."

"That's why it was so important that evidence of his citizenship be sent down to Virginia."

"Exactly."

[11

We went about our routine for the remainder of the evening. I was hoping that the plight of Eben Jones and the *dramatis personae* of the affair would awaken Sallie's interest. If it did, that interest was well disguised. She seemed to tire of the matter. I was not sure whether her momentary interest was only to humor me and my imagination or whether she was genuinely interested in a slave who was dead and gone.

"Maybe we could drive down to Nelson County, Virginia, sometime and poke through the court records there."

"Where is that?" she asked as she climbed into bed.

"Southwest of Charlottesville. About a nine-hour drive from here."

"Let's think about it . . . maybe in the spring — and then we could go to Williamsburg. I have a big day at the bank tomorrow."

"Goodnight, dear," I murmured as I turned off the light.

5

I think many people have an incorrect perception of lawyers. It is my experience that there are so many lawyers that a stereotypical lawyer cannot be described with any precision. For this lawyer, earning a living and paying the bills are full-time worries. I rarely concern myself with a house on the lake, a ski condo, and a fifty-foot sail boat. I leave those to my high-powered colleagues.

In any case, keeping the wolf from the door meant immersing myself in domestic relations work during months after I began fantasizing about Eben Jones. I would much rather have been investigating Eben's past than a client's husband who had spent a weekend at the No-Tell Motel with a young woman named Bubbles. After meeting Bubbles and comparing her attributes to those of the estranged, I felt that I was representing the wrong party in the divorce. Escape from that wife was justified. However, I have long been a believer in the maxim of "judge not."

My interest in Eben was reawakened one evening at home. Sallie said I looked tired and I ought to take an evening off. I really did not feel much like going out or working so I turned on the television.

While flipping through the evening offerings, I found that the educational channel was running a special program on anthropology. The scene showed a group of older men and women inspecting an archaeological site somewhere in the African desert.

"Look at them," Sallie commented. "Grubbing around in the dirt with little toothbrushes brushing off fossilized bones."

"It's interesting work," I protested. "At least they're engaged in a noble pursuit."

"Like what?"

"Well, they're pushing back the frontiers of ignorance about the past. All I do all day is prepare a deed or mortgage, or file a divorce complaint."

"So? What's wrong with being a lawyer?" she defended. "It is a noble pursuit, too. I've always been proud of your standards and ethics."

"Thanks, but I'm not comparing. I was only defending the men and women on the screen from your comment about them grubbing around on the ground with toothpicks."

"Toothbrushes. They even claim that they can tell you what an entire mastodon looked like by one broken little toe bone fragment."

"I still think it's noble," I responded.

At this point I was not sure where the conversation was leading us. I had learned long ago that getting into an argument is easy, but getting out of one without hurt feelings and unpleasantness is difficult. I made a mental note to remind my son that the marital home is not the proper forum to practice debating skills.

I was content to drop the subject and stood up to change the channel to a mind-numbing sitcom that would put the matter of anthropology to rest. My self-preservation instinct was also alert to the necessity of remembering this conversation and filing it under "unproductive topics of conversation" in my brain's memory bank. I changed the channel, but I could not change the subject.

"You know," she continued, "your defending those anthropologists is very appropriate. After all, they can tell you all about the sex life of an extinct animal from one bone fragment. They learn everything from the smallest shred of evidence. They fantasize to the point where all the answers are obtainable from the slimmest known fact. You're the same. Not three months ago, you were all excited about that slave Elmer Jones."

"*Eben* Jones."

In the millisecond that my response took to reach Sallie's ears, I knew she had trapped me again. She had purposely misnamed Eben to prove that I had not forgotten Eben and that I was just like those men and women grubbing around the African desert with little brushes. I, too, could find all the answers to Eben's riddle in one short note from a lawyer who was dead and gone to another lawyer who was dead and gone about a black man who was dead and gone.

"Clever woman," I thought, "and a very wise one." She kept silent and did not press her advantage. We both knew that she proved her point. She did not have to rub it in. Deep down I wished that she had pointed at me and fallen to the floor in a side-splitting orgy of laughter. As if to reassure me that there was nothing important to the recent events, Sallie went to the refrigerator and retrieved a bottle of Yuengling Lager, my favorite beer, for me.

Later, as the sounds of the night rose and fell outside, I again lay awake. I was more like those anthropologists than I cared to admit. I should be making use of my training as a lawyer. By only daydreaming about Eben and the attorneys, I had completely failed as a lawyer. I had not approached the matter with my own training and skill.

Facts, facts, facts, and the interpretation of those facts is my stock in trade. I tried to clear my mind of all extraneous thoughts and concentrate on the matter as if a client had brought me the letter to discern the meaning.

I had difficulty concentrating on the facts. Somehow fantasies always work better than facts in bed. I congratulated myself on this profound insight.

"Where did you get this letter?" I fantasized being interviewed by an important and rich lawyer.

"At an estate auction in Boalsburg, Pennsylvania, late last year," I answered.

"Whose estate was it?"

"A retired banker from Bellefonte."

"What was the nature of the other items at the auction?"

"They were all memorabilia-type things — old deeds, coins, paper money. There was a journal of a local man who visited Gettysburg the day after the battle. The pages were even watermarked by the rain that fell that day. There were other things which seemed to be trivial."

"Were either of the attorneys famous?"

"Not that I know of."

"That eliminates any autograph or historical value in a monetary sense. Was the slave famous? Dred Scott's father? or Booker T. Washington's grandfather?"

"Probably not," I answered.

"One fact seems clear. The letter survived over 150 years. Another fact. At the time it was written, it had no monetary value and no historical value. It was just an ordinary, unremarkable letter on its face. However, it was kept . . . not thrown out or destroyed. Someone was either too lazy to throw it out, or it was kept for a reason."

"Very good point," I answered the fantasy lawyer. "The letter was saved for some reason. It couldn't be returned for a deposit like a Coke bottle, nor could it be recycled. Someone had to decide to keep the letter rather than destroy it. Perhaps Petrikin elected to keep it for his files. I too am a lawyer, and I would never throw out such a letter."

"Yes, but after Petrikin died, the letter was preserved even though it has no apparent use or value. It is over 150 years old. The decision on whether to preserve it may have been made on several occasions as it passed from owner to owner. Now it is in your hands, and you are keeping it because you paid money for it. However, money probably was not the reason why this letter was preserved by Petrikin and those who held it afterward, at least the monetary value of the letter as a letter. The information contained in the letter may once have had value . . . to someone."

"What you are telling me is that if I find the reason why the letter was preserved, it may begin to unravel the mystery of Eben Jones."

"And it may not," the fantasy lawyer uttered as I drifted off to sleep.

6

The lawyer's room adjacent to the courtroom where I had been waiting for over two hours was smoky and hot, and the clerk had yet to call my case. Along the walls, the afternoon shadows were cast upon the portraits of former judges and county officials dressed in black coats and high collars. I wondered how many other attorneys had waited in this room since 1801 when the courthouse had been built. Perhaps James Petrikin had waited in this very room for the clerk to call him to court. I made a half-hearted attempt to keep my mind on reviewing Associated Realty's landlord-tenant case that lay before me, but my resistance was low, and a vision appeared of James Petrikin pacing by the far wall.

"Why not?" he asked as he paced.

The older man tried to calm him. "James, your health. You must heed the surgeon's advice. I accompanied you not three month's ago to Philadelphia to see him. We resolved then that you should not be spendthrift with your efforts. You have many other duties . . . your family, your clients. Many people are depending upon you."

"I am mindful of your devotion to me, brother, but is it not true that man may have a higher calling? One owes something because one lives among others."

"Ecclesiastical law? James, I beseech you, be sensible."

"You are the third person who has attempted to divert my efforts from helping secure the freedom of Eben Jones."

"Please, speak plainly."

"I am not certain, but I sense that there are those in this community who would prefer that Eben Jones remain in Virginia to suffer the indignities of prison or slavery rather than be free to return here to the county."

The older man paused as if considering carefully his choice of words. "James, there are those who would not wish you to proceed upon this perilous course. Further inquiry into the matter would be ill advised. I may assure you that . . ." He was interrupted by an elderly gentlemen making his presence known in the room by clearing his throat. Both attorneys turned toward him.

"Mr. Petrikin, your case is now to be heard."

I looked toward the door where the clerk of court was calling me, a puzzled look upon his face.

"Your case . . . your case . . . Associated Realty? The judge is waiting."

Reality. I did the best I could to look dignified as I entered the courtroom with all eyes upon me. The judge seemed none too pleased that I had not heeded the first call to court.

"My apologies, your honor. I did not hear the clerk call the case." I smiled as sheepishly as I could.

Experience had taught me that if I were to admit my error, appear befuddled, and submit to his admonition, the judge would be satisfied. His authority would be secure.

"Proceed with your case," the judge said, his forced sternness passing. He assumed a bored, passive expression and the case started.

Within an hour the testimony had been heard and the case completed. The judge rendered a decision from the bench and the case was won. My clients were thrilled. They sang my praises as we left the courtroom. I smiled as sincerely as I could, acknowledging their thanks, remembering that a happy client is a paying client.

However, winning brought me no pleasure. A lawyer is supposed to win cases. I have never ceased to wonder why the thrill of victory is not as wonderful as the agony of defeat is terrible. For me, victories are hollow. On the other hand, defeats leave emotional scars. I have quite a collection of scars, some superficial, some cut to my very soul. I hide them from the prying eyes of my clients, colleagues, friends, everyone — even Sallie — with the lawyer's gift for disguising his true feelings and intent. Hidden from view, those old wounds ache when my moods become grey and stormy.

When I first noticed these feelings as a young lawyer, I did not believe that they were real. I thought the emptiness was my embarrassment at losing. However, I learned the pain is real, imbedded in my soul like shrapnel from an old war wound.

I cannot but wonder if other attorneys feel as I do. However, true to the profession, I know that I will never bare myself to another lawyer, lest my weakness be exploited and used as a weapon against me in some future professional or personal battle. Bitter experience has taught me that today's trusted ally is tomorrow's adversary. It is the way of all practicing lawyers. It has to be. Survival demands it. There is no other way.

In front of the courthouse I waved to my clients as they passed happily on their way to the pub on the other side of the town square to celebrate the victory. There was a chill in the air as the late afternoon sun disappeared. A mix of depression and resignation overwhelmed me. The briefcase in my hand seemed to weigh me down as I slowly descended the marble steps to the street.

7

The incident in the attorney's room at the courthouse taught me something about myself. I retreated to my imaginary characters when the frustrations of my professional life became too burdensome. The fantasy world I could create at the drop of a hat had the same effect upon me as a drug. The real world would recede and there would appear a bright new vision of characters who did exactly as I asked. Sallie is a banker and much more practical than I. Since early in our marriage, I've done the best I could to hide my fantasies from Sallie, lest she misinterpret and somehow feel a personal failure in her inability to fulfill my selfish need for things to be exciting, fresh, and interesting.

Marie, my paralegal-secretary, thinks my daydreaming is unproductive. I remember overhearing her complaining to another legal secretary that I was not aggressive enough and spent too much time on things that had no possibility of monetary return. To use her words, my future as a lawyer "has definite boundaries." Her words have little impact on me. In a way, I am proud of not being single-minded. However, it gnaws at me that she might perceive my law practice as a little rat surviving on the scraps and crumbs brushed from the judicial dinner table by big, aggressive, grey flannel–suited law firms. Worse still is the possibility that she might think of me as a caricature of a lawyer like those portrayed in old cowboy movies. It conjures up a vision of a cigar smoking, bespeckled, bald, overweight buffoon, a pompous fool with no apparent understanding of the world around him.

I resolved with new energy that if I could find one shred of evidence that Eben Jones had been in Centre County, I would continue the search — and the fantasies. Otherwise, I would try for the umpteenth time to stick to business and live up to Sallie's expectations of me. I vowed to return to the courthouse the next day.

Early the next morning, I told Marie that I had important business in Bellefonte. She gave me a look of feigned understanding. It was the type of look that the little league coach would give me when I returned to the dugout after striking out again. I always explained to him that I had tried my best. I remember that look well. We both knew I did not try and that I did not have the courage to stand in the batter's box and attack the ball. The limited shelter of the farthest corner of the dugout was a lonely place for me.

"No matter," I tried to reassure myself as I headed to Bellefonte.

The courthouse was built in the early 1800s. The clerk of court's office had become cramped over the years with the rows and rows of big heavy docket books lining the walls. Most of the older court records had therefore been saved on microfilm. I was relieved to find the first records of the county's court of common pleas still in book form. The letter from Attorney Perow had mentioned that Eben Jones had filed a case in county court. If he had, the record of that case would be in the docket books.

I took a deep breath. If I found nothing, the game would be over. The huge emotional investment I had made in Eben would be gone forever. The possibility of finding the truth gave me pause. What if I found nothing? I would be cast adrift with my fantasies shattered. I replayed in my mind the scene which resulted in my decision to have the matter settled one way or another. Marie and Sallie were depending upon me. Somehow I recaptured my resolve and pulled the first index book down from its perch at the farthest corner of the last shelf.

The book was thick with dust. I opened it and began my search of the period from 1801 through 1827. I was surprised to see how little the law had changed as I reviewed the index of cases. The listing of civil cases included action on contract, debt, writs of execution issued in favor of banks and mortgage foreclosures. Lawyers sued clients. Clients sued lawyers.

My research was interrupted by Oscar Brumbaugh, a senior member of the bar whose office was nearby. I had once overheard Marie telling one of her friends that I would probably end up like Brumbaugh. Since then I had tried from time to time to observe Counsellor Brumbaugh to see exactly which of his characteristics might be applied to me now or in my declining years. Personally, I always found him to be a gentleman. He knew a lot of history but precious little law for a man who had been in practice for fifty plus years. It was commonly said among the members of the bar that Brumbaugh was living proof that practice does not make perfect. The bar generally thought of him as a buffoon. At bar association meetings he regularly delivered a canned speech on the tragedy of the county commissioners' plan to transfer the road dockets from the active shelving in the clerk's office to the archives in the historical museum. When he began his tirade, many lawyers would groan and repair to the bar to have their drinks freshened. I remember being one of the few lawyers who supported him on the issue, and I always voted for the resolution condemning the county commissioners for their disregard of these important county records.

Other lawyers belittled him and the tired Harris tweed sportcoat he wore daily, winter and summer. The simple truth is that Oscar Brumbaugh was no threat to anyone. Their cruel comments behind his back only lay bare their pettiness and lack of kindness and understanding.

"What brings you into the deepest recesses of the county records?"

I could not tell by his tone whether he was genuinely interested in my presence. He had never seen me there before.

"Just checking the old indices." I tried to be as non-committal as I could. I did not want him to launch into one of his prepackaged speeches of the low standard of ethics among the younger lawyers or their lack of love of the law as the chief factor undermining the pillars supporting the nation. I had heard both on several occasions.

"Never seen one of you younger lawyers doing any such thing ... too much concern with billable hours. Anything I can help you with?"

I was concerned that he would impede my search so I thanked him but declined. Then it occured to me that his interest in history might prove beneficial. I climbed down from my perch on the step stool and explained that I had purchased an old letter at auction and was checking some facts.

"Your interest in history doesn't surprise me," he said settling as best he could into one of the straight-backed wooden chairs.

"Oh?"

"You're not like the rest of them — the lawyers, I mean. Oh, you're fit enough ... probably go to some health club like the rest. And you wear a charcoal grey suit like the others. But you're not like the others. I mean that as a compliment."

I must have looked at him suspiciously because he continued with his explanation.

"It's your tie that gives you away."

"My tie? What's wrong with my tie?"

"It has a grease spot at the knot. I'll bet that all of your ties do. I don't mean any disrespect by that. I only mean that it is very revealing, that's all."

I considered his observation and pondered momentarily whether to press him for an explanation.

"So you're interested in history, or at least some part of it. Of course, the past is better than the present or the future. It is more — to use modern parlance — user friendly. What has happened is done. Over. Gone. No need to worry about what is going to happen. It already happened. Only the interpretation of events is left, not the events themselves. And the subjective interpretation of history is particularly interesting. People view events differently; it's human nature. Name any lawyer in the county who has been dead and gone . . ."

"James Petrikin," I offered.

"Strange you should choose him," he said after a short pause carefully considering my choice.

Before I could ask what he knew of James Petrikin, we were interrupted by an older woman who I took to be his secretary.

"Oscar, I've been wondering where you were. This was the first place I looked. The widow Bell is waiting for you. I forgot to mention that you have a ten o'clock appointment with her."

There was only kindness in her voice, no reproach. I was sure that Brumbaugh had forgotten about the appointment, but his secretary had permitted him to save face by assuming responsibility herself. I hesitate to think what Marie might have said had I been late for a paying client.

Any insight from Brumbaugh would have to wait, and so would my search. I had to get back to my office. Deep down I was relieved. My possible disappointment was deferred until another day. On the way out of the courthouse, I stopped in the men's room. I caught myself looking involuntarily in the mirror at my tie. Sure enough, the knot was darker in color than the rest of the tie.

8

When I returned to the office, Marie greeted me in her usual fashion with a "you're-late-for-no-good-reason" expression.

"Your appointment has arrived early. I put her in the library. At least the library is cleaned up. I don't think you'd want this person to see your office in its present condition."

In response to my quizzical look, she continued.

"The young woman is exceptionally attractive."

"I'm old enough to know better, Marie."

"No man is old enough to know better when it comes to sex and women," she responded.

She was right. I remember going through several divorces with men in their sixties, even seventies. Each one had acted like a teenager when their fragile male egos were involved. It is easy for a man to say he knows better. But deep inside most men know that their behavior is controlled not by ethics or morals but by risk-assumption considerations, including the fear of the consequences of discovery.

Marie's indication that the client was attractive was an understatement. She was beautiful, but in a non-threatening way. I have always considered models beautiful in a threatening way. If you were with a model or a woman who looks like one, no matter how well adjusted your male ego might be, you would feel threatened. The threat might come from other men ogling at her. There is also the matter of other women wondering what kind of man you might be when you are with such a gorgeous woman. At any rate, for me beautiful women come in two varieties, threatening and non-threatening. My appointment was beautiful—and non-threatening.

She stood up when I entered the library.

"Please," I said, motioning to her to be seated. I was somewhat mystified by her apparent show of respect. I took a seat across the conference table from her. As a rule, I never take the head of the table unless other attorneys are present. Clients feel more comfortable sitting across the table from their attorney.

For a long time she said nothing. I sensed either a domestic or criminal matter because of her delay in explaining her situation.

"My name is Erika Williams. Have we met before?"

Her eyes narrowed slightly as she scrutinized my face, gauging the truthfulness of my answer. My mother used to look at me the same way when asking whether my homework was completed.

"Not that I recall."

"A lawyer's answer," she remarked.

I nodded.

"I believe that I am about to be charged with a crime, and I seek the advice of a lawyer. You have been recommended to me."

I nodded again. I expected her to ask the stock question posed by a person charged with a crime for the first time about whether everything she was going to say would be held in the strictest confidence. Experienced criminals never ask that question. They know the rules of the game.

"I don't know the exact name for the crime from the criminal code — theft of a large sum of money. In any case, I need to consult a lawyer. I am in a position to pay a small retainer for listening to me and a sizable retainer if you decide to take the case and we reach a mutual understanding."

I nodded again.

"Let me anticipate your concern," she ventured after I did not respond immediately. "You are no doubt concerned that if I stole or embezzled money, your fee could not be guaranteed. A constructive trust might be imposed on all my money depriving you of the fee you might rightfully deserve."

She was referring to the legal principle that stolen money may be traced from the criminal to whoever has received it. The court has the right to declare that the recipient holds the money "constructively" as a "trustee" for the injured party. Many lawyers learn of this legal principle the hard way.

When I looked at her inquiringly, she seemed a little defensive. "I saw it on 'Perry Mason' once."

"And the episode comes to mind in this instance?"

"Not really. I believe in preparation and I have tried to anticipate your questions and concerns about taking my case."

"Who is about to level these charges against you?"

"The university police."

She was referring to the police at the university in town. The department is euphemistically referred to as the Department of University Safety.

She went on to explain that she was employed in a position where she had to account for large sums of money and a large sum had come up missing. The trail of the money ended with her and there was no reasonable explanation of where the funds might be.

"I'm not sure that they actually will charge me with a crime, but I was working in my office in the administration building and the goon squad showed up with a search warrant. Then, quick as a wink, they were looking under a potted plant. They retrieved a baggie from under the potting soil — you know, one of those sandwich bags. Inside was a blue 3–1/2 inch diskette. The leader of the pack smiled knowingly, and they left, not even bothering to clean up all the dirt, explain, or say goodbye."

"What was on the diskette?"

"I don't know. But my fear is that the codes are on there."

"Codes?"

She paused. She deliberated for a moment. "Look, I may be paranoid. But all of a sudden everyone is treating me like I have a social disease. No one talks to me. Yesterday John Harley, the Vice President in charge, suggested quite strongly that I might consider taking administrative leave with pay until certain facts are sorted out. I feel like I'm in purgatory."

I expected desperation in her voice. A normal client might break into tears, but I sensed that this was no ordinary client. I heard no desperation and saw no tears. But I did expect an earnest plea for assistance. I was not disappointed.

"Perhaps you could see your way clear to hear me out if push comes to shove. Could you? . . . Please."

"I will agree to consider the matter with you if, as you put it, push comes to shove."

[25

"Thank you." In an instant she was on her feet. She gave me a sweet, socially correct smile, and I walked her from the library. My eyes followed her through the reception area and out the door.

"You men are all alike. Put your eyes back in their sockets," Marie remarked sarcastically as I passed her desk.

I stopped. An irrestible impulse passed through me like an electric current. Before I knew it I said, "Marie, you're starting to let your jealousy betray you. You women are all eager to belittle men for their attraction to a woman. But face it, you know she is beautiful and deep down, you're envious. Instead of accepting it as fact, you deny it and blame the man for his attraction. How frustrated you must be to have to do that."

The instant the words passed my lips, I regretted them. I did not know what to do. I had never spoken to Marie like that before. I felt terrible. I went into my office and closed the door, not knowing what else to do. I tried to work but I was too upset. A short while later, there was a soft knock at the door, and Marie entered.

I braced for the storm to follow. I expected the usual tirade followed by her resignation as my assistant. I deserved it for being so cruel.

She cleared her throat. "I'm sorry, for saying those sexist things. The fact is that I am jealous of her — her appearance, her poise, the effect she has on men. What woman wouldn't be jealous of her? And, you're right, I took my frustrations out on you. I have too much respect for you as a person to subject you to that. Please accept my apologies. And, as for your remark, I had it coming."

I sat in silence for a moment then stood up. I gently took her arm and walked her back to her desk. "I guess we've both learned something," I ventured.

"Yes," she chuckled, "that our new client will be the best thing — or worst thing — that has happened around here for a long time."

9

Late that evening I went to my closet and pulled out my tie hanger. I removed my favorite ties and inspected each one for grease spots. Sure enough, all of my favorite ties were discolored where the knot would be. When Sallie asked why my ties were laid across the bed, I related what Brumbaugh had said.

"What do you suppose he means?" I asked.

Sallie thought for a moment as she readied herself for bed. "I suppose it means that you don't have your ties cleaned, or don't purchase new ones often enough."

"But what does it reveal about my character?"

"Well . . . even though you look the part of a conservative lawyer, you don't really pay close attention to your appearance. Your shoes are not always polished; your belt is old and the leather is cracked; you let your hair get too long before getting it cut . . ." she paused, then added, "I wouldn't say that you are sloppy or anything like that . . . it's your level of concern. It means you're concerned about something other than looking like the perfect image of a lawyer. You're just less self-concerned, I guess."

As I pondered her answer, I replaced the ties and resolved to shop for new ones—and a new belt, too. I took out my shoe shine kit and worked on my shoes in the next room.

When I returned, Sallie was propped up in bed, reading a novel. I turned on the television and flipped to Top Ranked Boxing on ESPN. A cruiserweight fight was the main event; I settled on the floor in front of the bed to watch.

Sallie lowered her book. "You and your boxing matches . . . and you're such a gentle person. How can you stand to watch grown men trying to bash each other's brains in?"

"You don't understand what boxing is about, philosophically speaking," was my response.

I could see her girding for my discourse on why watching boxing could be justified. I did not want to disappoint her.

"Okay, let's hear it," she said as she marked her place in the book and laid it beside her on the bed.

"You have to understand that boxing, championship bouts in particular, is the highest form of courage and drama. The champion, fighting alone in the ring with only his fists and his training and experience risks everything during every second of every round. If he loses the bout, the championship belt is gone. He stands to lose it all—money, power, prestige. But he can only prove himself as champion—and have the benefits of being champion—by continuously fighting against opponents who are also intent upon being champion. The champ knows intellectually that his reign is limited though he believes in his heart that he'll always be champion. Eventually someone, a hungrier, more motivated boxer, will come along and, with one blow and a ten count, the championship is gone. After all, that's how he got to be champion—by beating a champion and taking it all away from him. All is risked and all eventually will be lost. No one can be champion forever. There will always be someone willing to fight to be champion."

I paused to see if my message was getting through. I was pleased that Sallie was paying close attention. "You see, with baseball and football, the best players do not assume the same risks—a strike out here or a fumble there. Even in crucial games such as the World Series or the Super Bowl these lapses are forgiven and forgotten over a long season and a long career. Barring a career-ending injury, these players come back to play again another day. Not so for a boxer. Oh, he might fight again, but it is never the same. There is a new champ, all in an instant. You see, it's the risk factor that makes boxing so intriguing. Think of it . . . a willingness to risk your power and prestige time and time again . . . until you lose. Few of us are ever put in that position."

Sallie thought for a moment. "Perhaps this partially explains your fascination with Eben Jones. You don't have to be a boxer to take risks. Do you think the attorney in Virginia might have risked his professional reputation or standing in the community by trying to get a runaway slave freed from jail? What did it cost him to defend Eben?"

I smiled at her. "You're right, Sallie.... I think you understand."

"Your principles are talking... that's one thing I like about you. Another is your fascination with my legs... wouldn't you like to..." Her voice trailed off as she turned off the light.

I switched off the boxing match and joined her in bed.

Later, I could feel her warmth as she snuggled gently against me. In a few moments I felt her breathing soften. She was asleep and I was alone. I recalled my new client and tried to picture her in my mind. She had light brown hair, fashionably pulled back revealing her ears and neck. Her piercing green eyes were the most noticeable feature of her strong yet soft face. Her pale skin had a healthy glow. Her hands were small, and she used no colored nail polish.

I noticed she stood about 5′ 7″. Her posture was good and she had an easy, graceful manner, but her demeanor was all business. I judged her age to be mid-thirties, though she could have been older or younger. I didn't recall whether she wore perfume. If she did, it was not remarkable. My overall impression was that of an attractive woman, not a jerk-your-head-to-look type. Rather, she was the type of woman who would be sitting in a public place, and your eyes would find her. Once your eyes settled upon her, you would turn your attention to her time and time again, voluntarily and involuntarily. She definitely made an impression.

I could not help thinking that I had seen her before. Perhaps it had been in a restaurant, at a basketball game, in the concert hall. As I drifted off to sleep, I wondered when I might expect to see her again.

10

My mind returned time and time again to Erika Williams over the next several days. I busied myself handling routine matters for routine clients. Some landlord-tenant cases prove to be interesting, but my practice is usually a boring mix of general practice matters. As a young lawyer I had a vision of making it big, a bright comet shooting across the legal sky. But I was properly cautioned by the senior partner on my first law job that it was unlikely during a fifty-year career that the inventor of a Xerox-type machine would call upon me for patent work, or that a multi-million-dollar personal injury case would find its way to my desk. I have found that many lawyers waste their entire careers dreaming of the "big case" that will make them famous. The vision of being the subject of a segment on "60 Minutes" or being interviewed on the "Today" show is alluring. After all, we lawyers have big egos that must be properly fed, and nothing satisfies the appetite better than having your name in the headlines and being on the eleven o'clock news. I realized long ago that waiting for the "big case" was a trap and not the salvation of a law practice. It is always better to stick to business. I learned that if I take care of the clients and the little cases, the practice will take care of itself.

My heart leaped when Marie buzzed the intercom to tell me that Erika Williams was on the line.

"Hello."

"This is Erika, Erika Williams. . . . Remember me?"

We both knew that I remembered her.

"Yes, of course. How can I help you?"

"I think push is about to come to shove. I've got to see you. They've placed me on leave, and now I think I'm being followed, and my phone is tapped. I'm calling from a pay phone at the gym."

"I could see you after lunch . . . say 2:00, or a little after."

"It won't do. I don't think I want them to know I'm going to an attorney, at least not yet."

I knew what she was leading up to. My instincts told me that I should not meet her anywhere but in my office with Marie present. I did not know her. My instinct for self-preservation told me I could fall prey to the inference of participation in whatever she might be doing . . . or worse.

"You decide, Erika, and let me know, but I cannot meet you any place but here. I know it's safe to talk here. Since you've been advised that you are on leave and there is a cloud over your head, it would only be natural that you consult an attorney. To do otherwise raises more suspicion. Think about it."

There was a pause as she considered my statement. "I suppose that's good advice, but I can't come at 2:00. That's when I'm scheduled to do my work-out at the health club. I think part of their plan is to put me under such pressure that I'll act without thinking. You're right, though — it would be unnatural of me to not seek the advice of a lawyer when I am clearly at risk. Thanks for the good advice. I'll be in touch."

I was about to hang up when she continued as an afterthought. "By the way, you'll be receiving a call from my brother's bank in Toledo. He's wiring you a retainer. I sent him my promissory note for it so that you can trace your fee to him."

She hung up.

A few moments later Marie buzzed me.

"I just got a call from a bank in Toledo requesting wiring instructions. I gave them the information. Is that okay?"

"Sure."

I had not discussed a fee with Erika. For initial consultation on the matter I had planned to ask for $500.00. I would consider a higher retainer if I agreed to take her case. Marie appeared at my door a few minutes later.

"I just got a call from our bank. $10,000.00 . . . how shall I book it?"

"Erika Williams . . . retainer for Erika Williams."

Marie looked at me skeptically. We had been together through good and bad times over the last several years. We had never received such a large retainer.

"I don't know what's going to happen, Marie."

Marie hesitated at the door for a moment. I usually told her what was happening on a case. She was my assistant and often her counsel and practical advice tipped the balance in a client's favor at trial. I did not want to exclude her from anything. I knew she expected an explanation of the huge retainer but was too polite to ask. She never asked about such things.

"I think it's a criminal case. Do you know anything about her?"

Marie came into the office and sat in one of the side chairs. I half expected her to know everything that happened and to advise me not to get involved.

"I've seen her. She works on campus, I think. Once or twice I remember seeing her at the deli across from the old dormitory... also at the frozen yogurt place. She is always with somebody—usually men. That accounts in part for my reaction the other day. As a woman, I think she gives other women the impression that she has power over men and knows how to use it. But I don't want to prejudice you... it's only an impression."

In the past Marie has told me to stay away from a client if her impression is totally negative. I usually heed her advice, and when I don't, I usually pay the price.

"Your assessment? Is it okay to get involved with her case?"

"Her case, yes. Her, no. I got no negative vibes, if that's what you mean. However, I would use caution."

"Forget the money, Marie. You know when we take a case for the money we end up earning it twice or three times over, and we regret it. There is no such thing as a free lunch. If the fee is $10,000, we'll earn it. You know that. Besides, at this point we don't have to take it for the money, we're doing just fine. You know that."

We both remembered days past when we celebrated any fee that made it possible to pay the bills. Now things were on a more solid footing, though we never ran much of a surplus.

"Well, my only advice is to keep all options open as long as possible. Don't let go of the eject button until absolutely necessary. After all, there is no harm in finding out what is expected of us."

"It's a deal."

We smiled at each other. I was pleased by the definite bond of trust between us.

Marie went back to her work. I shuffled a few papers but my mind just wasn't on the mundane matters that lay before me.

My mind returned to the discussion I'd had with Sallie about ultimate risk and ultimate reward. She had brought up Charles Perrow, the Virginia lawyer as a symbol of courage. A man willing to risk something for a cause. He was trying to free a man he was convinced was not a slave. There was probably no fee involved there. How could a runaway slave or even a "free man of colour" have accumulated any money to pay the legal costs for a writ of *habeus corpus*? Perrow must have been defending Eben Jones *gratis*, as a matter of conscience. His actions could not have been popular. Such an action would not be good for business. His references included the phrase "unfortunate Eben." Perhaps Christian charity or the immorality of human bondage played a part in his decision to help Eben Jones.

I realized that my return to Eben Jones fantasies was an escape from Erika Williams' case. I did not want to start thinking about her case until I knew we had one. I heard the door chime ring as someone entered.

Marie appeared at my door again. "She's here. Shall I take her to the library?"

11

This time Erika did not rise when I entered the library. I took the seat across the table from her and nodded to her as a signal that she could begin. Although she did not seem upset, the fact that she had to clear her throat twice betrayed a hint of nervousness.

"It's a long story. Basically, I am going to be charged with embezzlement of university funds, but it is kind of touchy . . ." her voice trailed off.

"We can do one of two things," I began. "I can let you tell the story; or I can ask questions so we get the story in a logical sequence — that is, from a lawyer's point of view."

"The second choice might be better," she responded.

In answer to my questions, she provided the basic client information. I learned that she was 35 years old, a graduate of Ohio University with a degree in finance and accounting. She had first worked for an accounting firm in Columbus, Ohio. She got involved with one of the partners and was married but divorced a year later. When the divorce became inevitable, she resigned and began a job in Akron as an accountant. She was very successful and was hired away at a much higher salary by an another firm that specialized in handling educational institutions' investments. Someone at the University had heard about her, and John Harley, one of the vice presidents for finance at the University went to Ohio to see her. After lengthy negotiations, she was hired and had worked in the investment branch of the finance office ever since.

I asked her about her personal life. She indicated that there was not much to tell. She had not remarried. I sensed that she was withholding information from me, not to obstruct me but on grounds of relevancy to the matter at hand. I did not pursue it.

After obtaining more background information, I let her tell me about the current problem.

"It all started about two months ago. You see, we handle the investments for the University. We don't do the selection or trading, but we do the accounting and are responsible for the funds. Apparently there are certain funds that are 'off-budget' and secret. That is, the University does not acknowledge that they exist and therefore has no duty to account for them. I stumbled upon these funds once when I was working on the computer analyzing some data for a report. I don't know how it happened, but I got a blank screen and a prompt for a password."

I am only minimally computer literate. "What password?"

She explained that the computer refused to reveal data unless a special word or set of numbers was entered.

"Well," she continued, "I was surprised. I thought I knew everything about the system and all the accounts. I sat there for the longest time not knowing what to do. I played around with a series of names and numbers trying to get into the screen, but it was hopeless to guess the password. There are millions of combinations of letters, words, and numbers. Then I tried to think about anything that might be unusual, or anything I felt was being kept from me. After a while, I remembered John talking on the phone in a hushed voice — you know, that telephone voice we use when we are trying to be very discreet. When he became aware of my presence, he said he would check with the old man and the call ended abruptly. I don't know who might have been on the other end of the line. I assumed it might be a higher up like the president of the university or maybe something clandestine like the C.I.A. Over the next several months I heard references to the old man, but I was never told who the old man was."

She paused in her story to verify that I was following. I nodded, and she continued. "As I sat there in front of the blank screen, I entered the words 'old.man.' Nothing happened. Then my secretary knocked at my door and handed me a phone message. It was from a salesman. He left an 800 number for me to call. You know — in place of the numbers for the exchange and phone number there were letters like B U Y S T O X. . . . you know, a name suggesting the product or service. On a hunch, I looked at my phone and matched the letters O L D M A N with their numbers of the phone. I entered 6 5 3 period 6 2 6. Voilà! The screen came up, revealing accounts I never heard of. Numbered accounts with bank numbers we don't usually deal with. Huge balances in the hundreds of thousands of dollars. I was afraid to reduce the screen to print, but I was suspicious, and my curiosity was aroused. I printed the screen and took the paper home to study.

"I looked up the bank numbers . . . you see, each bank is assigned a number — a routing number — like for wire transfers. The number of your bank is on your checks. No local banks. Banks in faraway places . . . mostly in small communities . . . the Midwest, the Rockies. No California banks. A few days later, I went into the computer again and compared the balances of the various accounts. They were basically the same. I forgot about this. I told myself that I was not high enough up in the organization to deal

[35

with these accounts, or they were assigned to someone else to monitor. Then John left for a business trip out west. The next day, I looked at the accounts again and one of the accounts in a Colorado bank had lost an even $250,000.00. Several days later, I was reviewing some routine requests for reimbursement. One was submitted by John."

"Let me guess," I interrupted. "He was in the same city as the bank on the day the balance changed."

"Yes, of course. Shall I continue?" she asked, with a hint of irritation at my interruption.

I nodded without defending my interruption.

"I printed the screen again after the withdrawal. Next to the change in the balance was a number ... four digits 4 1 3 0 which are John's extension number at the office. On a hunch, after the screen was revealed I entered the password ... actually the pass number ... then entered 4 1 3 0. That number and another appeared on the screen. I copied the other number and exited the program. I began my search for the identity of the holder of the other number. I got a list of all the extension numbers for our department. Nothing fit. Then I looked up the house numbers of all the higher ups in the department ... nothing. Then with the help of the computer I ran a search of all university employees' social security numbers. Only one match ... a secretary in the College of Sports Medicine."

She paused again, making sure I hadn't lost interest and was following her.

"About three weeks ago, I was in John's office. By his phone I saw a Rolodex. A card was up listing the name of an attorney. I noticed that the last four digits of his phone number were the numbers I was looking for. Too much of a coincidence."

Again she paused and looked at her watch.

"I came in here unannounced and without an appointment. It was kind of you to see me. Do you have another appointment?"

"It wasn't kind of me to see you. You've paid for my time.... No kindness is involved—you are a client. Out of respect for the time constraints of all my clients, I do my best to be on time for each appointment. You will be shown the same courtesy so long as you

36]

are my client. I'm not trying to be stuffy. You know how frustrating it is when you go to the doctor and are kept cooling your heels for an extra hour. I manage my law practice in order to provide the best service possible. I know you understand. Someone will be here . . ." I paused, looking at my watch, "in about five minutes."

"Let me continue quickly then. They installed a security program in the computer that can identify the workstation from which entry into any file has been made. In other words, if I call up the secret file, my work station can be identified as having been used to gain entry."

"Did you know about the security system at the time it was installed?"

"Not exactly, but I knew someone was putting something in. One evening about 5:30 someone from a software company came in as I was about to leave. He said they were checking the network, but I saw him enter data and make a check mark on a paper on his clip board. He said that everything was fine. He erased the screen and went to turn it off when I stopped him. I told him I was awaiting an e-mail message about where I was to meet my boyfriend for a drink. After he left I was able to restore the screen that he erased. I figured out that my work station number is 731. Someone was trying to get better control of the system. At this point I really got paranoid. I had sensed that I was being watched closely by John. The fact that the security system was installed and I wasn't told about it opened up a whole range of possibilities."

"Well, it seems that you have a story to tell, Erika. In the interest of time, can you tell me, are they going to arrest you? If so, will it be soon?"

"They have subpoenaed all of my bank records, including the records of an account I didn't know I had in a branch of the bank I never visit."

"It is an account you didn't know you had, at the branch you never visit, that had funds you cannot account for, and by coincidence, it is the same amount that is missing."

"Not exactly, but you have the general idea. I see our time is up. If anything breaks, I'll call you. I know you don't have enough facts yet to be able to help me sort all this out. We'll have to get

[37

together soon. Meanwhile is there anything else I should be thinking about?"

"Try to remember everything you can. The smallest detail may be very important. Experience has taught me that it is the small things that are most revealing. At this point, they may already have searched your place, although you don't know it. In fact, if they have gone after bank records, it is likely that they have gone over your place with a fine-tooth comb. How else would they know that you have not converted the money to cash and stashed it at home?"

"But they didn't come with a search warrant or anything. Nothing is missing."

"My guess is that they have already been there and searched your place. They know everything that's there including your brand of toothpaste. If there were documents there that in any way indicated that you knew about this matter, they have photographed or transcribed them. They may do another search with you present. This has two purposes. First, it will lead you to believe that they have not been there before. Second, they will be able to tell if you have destroyed or altered any evidence of wrongdoing. I trust that when you knew trouble was coming you took the appropriate measures."

"Nixon should have asked me what to do with the tapes."

She stood up and smiled another of her socially correct smiles. I was five minutes late for my next appointment.

12

Over the next several days while my curiosity was in high gear over the Erika Williams matter, I made a conscious effort to stick to the everyday business of my law practice and to try to think logically about my other important case — Eben Jones.

I had been directing my energies toward verifying the information in the letter from Eben's point of view as recounted in the letter from Perrow. The Erika Williams case had re-focused my attention on thinking like a lawyer. I should have been trying to track down the letter as if I were investigating a crime and the letter itself, not its contents, was an important piece of evidence.

My first step was to try to identify someone who might be in a position to explain why the letter had survived all these years. I knew the letter had been part of a collection of documents relating to the county's history. At the auction where the documents were sold, most of the pieces involved land titles, military commissions and Civil War memorabilia. These documents usually related to nineteenth-century county history. There were no laundry lists, meaningless receipts of account, handbills, and the like. All the documents were important from a historical perspective. This only reinforced my original belief that the letter was saved for a particular purpose. If I found that purpose, it might shed some light on the entire matter.

I started by calling the county's unofficial historian who had been editor of one of the newspapers for many years. Like Attorney Brumbaugh, this history buff was closely identified with the movement to improve the county's historical museum. Every week he had a column in the local newspaper about county history. I was busy with my law practice and Erika Williams, but I thought it might be profitable to schedule an appointment so that I could obtain the historian's opinion of the letter and where he thought it may have come from.

He kindly agreed to see me on short notice, and I visited him at his home. I took the letter and several other documents of historical interest. He welcomed me gladly and read the transcription of the letter. He had not seen the letter, nor did he know anything of Eben Jones. He referred me to *Linn's History of Centre and Clinton Counties*, a historical account of the county. He explained that John Blair Linn was credited with writing the history, although it was done by committee. Various individuals were assigned different topics and Linn served as coordinator of the project. The book was originally published in 1883 and reprinted by the Centre County

[39

Historical Society in 1981. I had a copy and made a mental note to re-check various references, including the early census reports.

I explained how I had come upon the letter. The historian remembered the auction and explained how the documents had found their way into the estate whose papers were auctioned that day in Boalsburg.

The deceased collector had worked as a trust officer for the bank. The bank was administrator of the estate of one of Linn's decendants who had occupied Linn's house. Apparently, the bank came into custody of a large box of documents, some of which had been collected by John Blair Linn and his committee when *Linn's History* was prepared. Originally, there were thousands of documents at the Linn House, but over the years, the vast majority had found their way to the trash heap. Only a small quantity survived and were kept at the Linn House. This box of documents was given to the bank for safekeeping. From the bank, the documents had found their way into the trust officer's private collection. Someone at the historical museum had inventoried the documents before the auction. The museum bid up and bought at auction most of the more notable collectibles including Linn's notebook written while viewing the battlefield at Gettysburg the day after the battle's end. I suspect that the rest of the documents were sold to the public either because of the museum's lack of funds or because the documents were of minimal importance to county history.

I wondered why my document, which on its face was not remarkable, was saved by Linn's decendants and not destroyed with the others. Why was a conscious decision made to give this letter to the bank for safekeeping? The historian speculated that it might have been because it had to do with slavery and the history of negroes in Centre County. But why would the decendants be interested in slavery or black history? His answer did not satisfy me.

I turned my questioning to the subject of James Petrikin. James Petrikin was the son of William Petrikin, an early settler and political figure. The letter makes reference to the case allegedly brought by Eben Jones against Peter Karthaus which was heard by William Petrikin, James' father. Perhaps the letter was saved by decendants of James Petrikin and found its way into the Linn Collection by that means.

James Petrikin died in 1838 leaving two children. His son Hardeman Petrikin was killed in the Civil War the day before the battle at Antietam. His daughter, known as Miss Mallie, ran a school for children for many years. When she died, she left money to the Women's Christian Temperance Union. The organization used the funds to build Petrikin Hall which still stands on the main street. Although it is likely that the Petrikin woman knew the Linns, the fact that the Linn's kept James Petrikin's letter was still a mystery.

The letter from Perrow thanked Petrikin for his response which was received on July 7, 1827. This meant that Petrikin had received at least one letter from Perrow, and Petrikin had responded to that inquiry. Whether Petrikin did the leg work and prepared the requested affidavits was not known. I made a mental note to find my copy of the auction list and verify that no other document either to or from James Petrikin was sold when I bought mine. I also made another mental note to include the historical museum on my investigation list. Perhaps the first letter from Perrow to James Petrikin was in the museum.

I left the historian, having thanked him for seeing me and providing what information he could. I felt satisfied that I was proceeding with my investigation in a logical and lawyer-like manner, even though my visit had not borne fruit.

Driving back to my office, I turned my attention to the Williams case. I had the sense that my powers of investigation might be called into play again. Like Petrikin, would I be asked to marshall evidence for a hearing on a writ of *habeus corpus* on behalf of an incarcerated client?

I was so excited by the prospect of action that I expected there to be a message from Erika that she was in jail and I was to come to her rescue. Marie brought me down to earth when she handed me a dozen routine phone messages from a variety of clients, none of whom was Erika Williams.

[41

13

James Petrikin sat at his desk. Henry, his portly friend, paced the floor.

"James, I know you feel you have made a pledge to aid that attorney from Virginia. You are much admired in our community, especially by our brethren at the bar, for your concern for the welfare of fellow human beings. Your commitment to a just cause is one of your best attributes. But you know well, that from our greatest strengths spring our greatest weaknesses. Your zeal for a client's cause taxes your strength. You have other commitments, too. I beg you to consider that slavery is a Southern matter. There is little you can do. You yourself said that Mr. Rankin's assistance also was solicited by the Virginian. He is less fettered by responsibilities than you are. Let him do the investigation and provide the requested evidence."

James listened thoughtfully. He had heard this entreaty before.

"Good friend, I know that you earnestly seek to serve only my personal welfare, and I am grateful for your concern. True, slavery is a Southern problem and there is little I can do here in Bellefonte that will change the course of political events."

Petrikin rose from his seat and paused as if gathering strength for a plea to the jury.

"I do not seek to change the laws of Virginia. I do not wish to campaign for the destruction of slavery. We are speaking of one man, Eben Jones, not slavery as an institution. If, through my meager efforts here in Pennsylvania, I can help secure the freedom of Eben Jones in Virginia, it is time and energy well invested. As men of property, education, and position in the community, we owe a debt to all causes which are just and moral. Though there be neither money, nor glory, it is the personal duty of each to do what we believe is right."

Henry was silent. James walked over and placed a hand on Henry's round shoulder.

"Henry, good fellow, I value your friendship and your advice. I know that you would not ask me to forsake my conscience. I intend to begin my search for the evidence that may establish that Eben lived here in the county. Personally, I do not remember him, nor have I heard his name mentioned, that I recall. The letter makes reference to persons who are known to me and I may be able to start my inquiries with them." James paused, then asked, "Have you ever heard of Eben Jones?"

"No. Never. Could your man have been one of the negroes that was captured in Penns Valley and brought before the judge last year?"

"The thought has occurred upon me, especially when I recall the events in court the day when the negroes were brought before the judge. I will check to see if the original arrest warrants are filed in court, but I fear that the names of the slaves will not be listed even if the warrants prove to be there. There was no reason to identify the negroes by name and no way for our judge to verify the names or identities either."

The two men stood silently for a few minutes.

"I promise you, Henry, that I will not let this case dominate my time or my energies. I know well that there are other important tasks at hand."

My imaginary conversation was interrupted by Sallie bringing me a Yuengling Lager. She settled herself in the chaise lounge beside me on our back deck. The evening was cool and pleasant, and there was a refreshing breeze. We sat thoughtfully for a few minutes. I expected the usual inquiry about when I might get around to mowing the grass.

"Have you made any progress with your letter — you know, the Eben Jones matter?"

I was pleased by her interest but a little suspicious. Sometimes she favors me with her attention to my avocations, only to soften me up for a request that she knows I would otherwise resist. My face must have disclosed my skepticism.

"Don't be so suspicious, dear. I am asking because I'm interested. I know how you are about those old documents. It's interesting to think about them, who may have used them, what they

[43

mean. I guess I'm just more practical. I don't see its relevance to the present. What happened is over — history."

I had no stomach for one of our "discussions" that left both of us frustrated and on edge. So I tried to explain my philosophy from a different perspective. "It is true that history is, to use a modern phrase, history. And most historical events and figures have no relevance to our daily lives. But you see there is no history for birds or dogs . . . it has no relevance to those creatures. What makes history so interesting is the human interpretation of it."

I was starting to sound like Oscar Brumbaugh, and I found that thought a little frightening.

"For example," I continued, "as a teenager, on a sunny Sunday in late November 1963, I was standing on Capitol Hill in Washington under a sycamore tree. President John Kennedy had been killed. I was in the crowd that watched as the President's cortege passed on its way from the White House to the Rotunda in the Capitol. I remember the feeling in the air as I heard the muffled drums and saw the riderless horse and flag-draped coffin pass. People all around me were sobbing. Though there were thousands there, there was no noise. No one spoke. Not even a whisper. There was an indescribable sadness; there was a sort of collective questioning of why this terrible event had happened. Anyone who was there at that precise moment in history was aware of its emotional impact."

Sallie seemed interested, so I continued. "Years later, I saw a film segment that showed the procession. In the background I saw the sycamore tree and the crowd beneath it. The film was historically accurate. It captured the event, but not the feelings. The emotion that had engulfed the crowd like a giant tidal wave could not be depicted on film or conveyed by written word. You had to have been there to have the full sense of what happened. When the last of us who stood under that tree is gone, history from a human perspective will have changed. The full range of the event, including its emotional impact, will be lost forever."

I half expected Sallie to brush aside my explanation, but she did not.

"I never thought about it like that before . . . I mean, the past.

You're right, of course. Personal history is like that, too. Our past and how we feel about it does color our thinking about the present. I guess, what you are saying about Eben Jones is that you have a letter, a shred of evidence about people dead and gone. Reading the letter one hundred and sixty plus years later cannot convey the anguish felt by Eben Jones or the feelings of the Bellefonte attorney either. But we know that those feelings were there, in human terms. . . . "

"And," I interrupted, "it doesn't mean that because we cannot share those feelings we should not think about the events or the people. It gives an added dimension to our own lives."

Sallie never likes to be interrupted in mid-sentence. I was afraid that by doing so, I may have broken the spell of the moment.

Sallie sat silently in the gathering darkness. "I guess I never looked at it that way before. You consider each of your documents a little slice of human history. I've always respected your attachment to your collection, but even after all this time, I could never understand why you treasured each piece of paper. There probably is a story — in human terms, as you put it — in each of the pieces in the collection. I've never thought of history in quite that way. We can read everything there is to read about the Battle of Gettysburg, but it's not the same as hearing the noise of battle and feeling the excitement, fear, and uncertainty. When the last veteran died, human history of the event died as well."

I had never before had enough confidence to talk to Sallie about my feelings and my fascination with my documents. I thought that she would think it unimportant because she is so practical. Living together and facing the day-to-day grind interfered with our talking about our thoughts and our feelings. In many ways we had come to know each other too well. We had negotiated a living routine and a level of comfort that neither of us dared disturb.

"Tell me about Eben Jones. . . . I want to know."

We spent the rest of the evening discussing the letter and its possible implications. From her practical perspective, she offered some ideas that I must admit I had never considered.

It was a wonderful evening. I felt happier and more contented than I had in a long time.

[45

14

As I drove to work the next morning, I still felt happy and contented. I knew intellectually that life's moods are cyclical, and that soon my euphoria would be replaced by despair. This thought took the edge off my sense of well-being. Although I consider myself a bit of an optimist and idealist, I guess my experience as an attorney has caused me to view the glass as half empty and not half full.

My thoughts turned toward Erika Williams' case. I could not dismiss the feeling that I had seen her before. I was also troubled by the fact that she did not camp out on my office doorstep. Experience had taught me that citizen-types who are in trouble with the law make excessive demands on their attorney's time. Yet Erika kept me off-stage, cooling my heels like a character in a well-scripted play. My sense of discomfort was increased by the fact that she never sought reassurance that our conversations were confidential. This failure to need assurance of confidentiality was unprecedented in my experience dealing with non-criminal types who are enduring their first brush with the law. Experienced criminals know without asking that their conversations with their attorney are sacred.

I chided myself for being so suspicious. I was skeptical by nature and by training as a lawyer. I dismissed my concerns as an overreaction and I was determined to wait in the wings until she called upon me.

Routine matters occupied my time the next few days. In my spare time I reviewed *Linn's* to verify that Eben Jones was not listed in any for the census information for 1819–20. He was not. I also learned a bit more about James Petrikin. On page 236 I found the transcription of a speech given by Professor Alfred Armstrong on November 10, 1874. The professor reminisced about Bellefonte in 1824, the year of his arrival. He described James Petrikin as a very handsome man "of brilliant talents" who excelled in music and painting, as well as being distinguished for his wit and humor. The speech also mentioned that Petrikin served in the State Legislature. Petrikin was "cut off in early life by consumption, leaving a widow, son and daughter." His son was killed in the Civil War, "a sacrifice to his country's safety and an honor to the place of his birth." I then made a startling revelation on page 269:

"The *Bellefonte Patriot* of Nov.16, 1826, records the fact that on Saturday previous a number of Virginians made their appearance in Bellefonte, having before the dawn of day, in the name of and by the authority of the Commonwealth of Virginia captured and made prisoner two negroes a little distance from the town. They were claimed as runaway slaves. They were paraded through the streets, bound hand and foot with ropes and taken to jail. There was many an eye to pity, but none to save.

During the day an investigation took place before Judge Burnside of the right of those claiming them to carry into bondage these miserable blacks, and resulted in their being awarded according to the evidence adduced, and, according to law, the property and slaves of those having them in custody."

I had imagined Petrikin and his friend Henry talking about this event. This reference in *Linn's* confirmed that it had taken place. Was Eben Jones one of the blacks?

If Eben had run away from bondage in Virginia and was seeking to return to the place of his citizenship in 1819, the letter from Perrow most certainly would have made reference to the events of the previous year. Eben Jones' return was evidence of his tie to Centre County. Perhaps he had friends or relatives that would shelter him. Perrow might have contacted a friend or relative, but it is also likely that the Virginia attorney would solicit the assistance of a local attorney more familiar with the legal process and evidentiary requirements for a writ of *habeus corpus*. There was, however, no reference in the letter to any friends or relatives or any events that happened after 1819. There were only references to what Eben said he did.

Cooking Christmas dinner or buying beef on a trip to Penns Valley were hardly acts that would substantiate Jones' claim of

[47

Pennsylvania citizenship. In fact, these events were more likely the recollections of a transient. The only reference that could reasonably substantiate citizenship was Jones' use of the Centre County civil court system. There was mention of a civil suit brought by Jones against Peter Karthaus. Transients do not use the civil court system, local citizens do. Visitors feel more comfortable using the civil courts where they live.

This track led full circle to the morning I was in the clerk of court's office to look up Eben Jones' case against Peter Karthaus. While the personal remembrances could not be verified, the existence of a court case could. I resolved to track down that case.

15

I sat at the kitchen table with a coffee cup in hand and unfolded the morning paper.

The headline read "POLICE DISCLOSE INVESTIGATION OF FINANCE OFFICE." The article indicated that criminal charges against certain highly placed officials were "imminent." If I still represented Erika Williams, I would be hearing from her that morning.

When I dressed for work I chose one of my new non-grease-spotted ties to wear with my charcoal grey suit, my new belt, and my freshly shined wingtips. Expecting to be on "Eye-witness News" at eleven o'clock, I wanted to resemble the lawyer I knew I was not.

Marie was waiting with a message from Erika that I should meet her at the county courthouse at 9:15 A.M. I arrived a few minutes before the appointed time.

Our courthouse is not a hotbed of media news coverage. The previous week the county commissioners had argued at great length about the merits of prohibiting the citizens from putting grass clippings in the trash to prevent overburdening the local landfill. One television station devoted a segment to the issue on the news, showing the county commissioners in session and a citizen raking grass, bagging it, and taking it to the curb. The reporter of that insightful piece needn't worry about where to spend the Pulitzer Prize money.

I was therefore surprised to find several television station news teams, a live remote hookup, and about a half dozen photographers waiting outside the courthouse.

I approached one of the photographers and asked the cause of the excitement, although I already knew. She explained that they had been tipped off by the police that a "big-wig" at the University was about to be arraigned.

An arraignment is held after charges are filed and the accused is taken into custody. The accused has an opportunity to hear the charges. After the arraignment, a district justice or magistrate sets a preliminary bail amount. A plea to the charge may be entered at that time.

Erika had come in the side door, thereby escaping the newspeople. I slipped into a seat next to her. Her case was called. We stood and approached the magistrate. The charges were read. She was released on her own recognizance. The whole process took only a few minutes.

We spoke briefly about her coming to my office that afternoon. Since cameras are not permitted in the courtroom, the reporters were waiting outside. Erika said she was going to make them wait. I excused myself and left the courtroom. The reporters said nothing to me, though they must have known I had been with her. No cameras were focused on my non-grease-spotted tie, my new belt, and my freshly shined wingtips. I tried to convince myself that I was happy not to be on camera.

When I returned to the office, I told Marie that we could expect Erika Williams that afternoon and that I would be in conference with her as long as it took. Marie seemed to brighten at the prospect of some action. Although she knows that the wills, divorce cases, and real estate settlements are the bread and butter of our

[49

practice, there is nothing like litigation to get the body juices flowing again. After all, the courtroom is the highest form of legal drama . . . the pit where combat among attorneys and litigants takes place.

I tried to prepare myself mentally for the battle ahead. Experience has taught me to measure carefully my actions on behalf of a client. Although it is essential to be an advocate for your client's cause, it is a disservice to clients to side with them as friend and confidant. Most clients expect you to believe their stories. They confuse the role of the attorney as advisor and advocate with "being on their side." When questioning a client closely about the facts of a case, they are often disappointed or outraged. "Don't you believe my story?" or "Don't you trust me?" are the most common responses.

I always carefully explain the distinction between being an advocate-attorney and being a friend. I sometimes lose clients whose anger is not assuaged by my explanation. Better that the hard questions come first from me at the conference table than from the opposing counsel on cross examination at trial. It is better to let go of those unwilling to accept my skepticism than to disappoint them with an adverse ruling in court. They feel let down, and worse still, they often do not pay the bill.

When I first began practicing law, I did not understand the concept of legal truth. At any early age, we accept certain facts as true and govern our lives accordingly. As we grow up, we are encouraged to tell the truth. Legal truth is different from the commonly accepted concept of truth. My first trial as a lawyer involved a traffic accident, and it clearly illustrates the difference.

The plaintiff and defendant crashed at an intersection controlled by a traffic light. I believed my earnest client's story that the light was green when she entered the intersection. I was sure that if a lie detector test were administered, my client, the plaintiff, would pass with flying colors . . . namely, green. At trial, I was surprised to hear the defendant testify that the light was also green when she entered the intersection. From the standpoint of absolute truth, the testimonies of plaintiff and defendant were irreconcilable. The light could not have been green in both directions simultaneously.

They both had sworn to tell the truth and nothing but the truth. I was certain someone was lying. Cross examination of each party proved fruitless. Both plaintiff and defendant gave highly credible testimony that the light was green in their direction.

The decision rendered by the jury was that the light was green in the direction traveled by the defendant, and the plaintiff's case was dismissed. I could not explain the jury's action. I believed my client and had convinced myself that we would win the case. We both were crushed. I was unprepared for an adverse decision.

In assessing the case later, I realized that legal truth is not ultimate truth. The reasoning of my client — and all clients — was colored by her own justification, mitigation, or excuse for her actions. Such rationalization occurs over a long period of time as a client mentally revisits the events surrounding the accident time and time again. It is only human. We do not easily accept our own failure to live up to certain standards. So we tell ourselves that we are not bad; that we would not do such a thing; or that the other person had it coming. We are all capable of making right in our own minds what we have done that might be wrong from an absolute truth standpoint. We come to the conclusion that we acted properly. To do otherwise flies in the face of the human nature.

It was therefore possible for both plaintiff and defendant to testify under oath — and tell nothing but the truth — that the light was green in both directions. Attorneys who do not understand or appreciate the concept of legal truth do themselves and their clients a great disservice. They do not prepare themselves or their clients for the possibility that the other party's truth is more believable than their own. For lawyers, there is no such thing as absolute truth. What really counts in all legal proceedings is the ability to produce the more believable truth for the judge or jury.

16

I asked Erika to repeat her story from the very beginning. I took copious notes on a legal pad and I reviewed them carefully, trying to organize the facts. I asked several questions to clarify the chronology of events that led up to her arrest.

Citizen-types charged with a crime find themselves unwillingly thrust into the legal system. They are cast adrift confused and frightened in uncharted waters. They have no idea what to expect, and they desperately want to win the attorney over to their side. An attorney's thoughts must remain independent, thereby improving the prospects for making clear, unbiased decisions regarding the defense. An attorney must still reassure the client that everything will be done in defense of the clients' interests. The best way to instill confidence in an attorney is not to side with clients, but to make them feel that they are in competent hands. It is essential that they understand that their honest and complete cooperation with a qualified attorney is their best hope of survival.

I sat there trying to decide whether I needed to sell Erika on my competence and the necessity of her cooperation. I briefly explained what was going to happen procedurally.

"I know that you will do everything you can for me," she said when I finished.

When I said nothing, she felt she had to continue. "I suppose you are wondering why I have chosen you to defend me. Please understand that I mean no disrespect to you, nor do I discount your abilities in any way. As you know, I am placing my freedom in your hands."

"That is confidence enough."

I thought that would end the matter, but she continued. "I had thought that out-of-town counsel would be better, but I need someone on the scene who can follow up with some thoughts I have. There are several respected local criminal attorneys. However, as you will see, my case will go beyond the typical case. Others may be involved. I trust no one who has a high profile. They all have interests spread throughout the community. I'm not certain they would hold in strict confidence what I tell them. You are unmatched for honesty, diligence, and thoughtfulness here. I have verified this. And you are a loner like me, not one of the herd like the others. I am willing to trust you, but you must do two things."

Usually I like to have a free hand. I distrust clients who think they know how best to proceed. Rather than overreact, I decided to hear her requests.

"First, you must let me make all the non-procedural decisions. My life, my career, and my freedom are at stake. I know you would do this anyway. Second, you must agree to personally investigate this matter. I trust no one outside this room to find out what actually happened."

Again I was silent. No client had ever made such requests. She had carefully considered and probably rehearsed in her own mind every detail of this meeting including how she would give me my marching orders.

"We understand each other?" she asked.

I smiled. "Let's put it this way, Erika. I understand the meaning of your requests, and I agree to honor them. Will I have a free hand in my investigation, or am I to honor any secrets . . . in other words, is it total war? You understand that total war means we let the chips fall where they may."

I considered in my own mind the fact that she might be guilty and that my investigation might reveal this. This is always a dilemma for me as an attorney.

"As you put it . . . total war."

I looked through my notes again. I studied her face carefully.

Before I could ask, she said, "Let me anticipate what your first investigation will uncover."

I nodded.

"John Harley and I were lovers."

I felt as if she had read my mind. I was thinking of asking her, but I had intended to doe-see-doe around the issue until a more appropriate time later in my investigation. I was very careful not to appear distracted or puzzled by her quick statement.

"Were or are?" I asked.

"Were . . . are . . . I don't know . . . but let me assure you that I was not intending to shock you with this. If I were investigating, I would wonder if there were any special relationship between me and my superior in the office, especially when it is likely that he is the one who blew the whistle."

"What can you tell me about him? Please try to be as dispassionate as possible."

She described Harley as a man in his early forties, married, with no children. It was his wife's second marriage; she had two daughters by a previous marriage. The two daughters lived with their father and not with Harley and his wife. I had not met Harley, but the picture she painted of him was puzzling. He did not fit the picture one might have of a comptroller. Based upon his education and corporate experience, I would not expect him to be in a university job earning a salary in the mid-fifties when in corporate life he could have made at least triple that amount.

"I think the thing that attracted me to him," she continued, "was the fact that he seemed to be a cut above the others. Witty, charming . . . not self-possessed or self-important. Concerned for others, courteous. Never threw his weight around. All please and thank you . . . a perfect gentleman. He always wore expensive suits, fresh bright ties . . ."

I wondered if I had remembered to put on a new tie, or if I had by habit chosen one of my greased-spotted ones.

"You know, his appearance made a statement that he was really together. The others think they are so big and important. They demonstrate their insecurities in their every action. . . . Some wear narrow dull ties. . . . They use those pocket protectors — you know, those plastic things for the shirt pocket that say Black & Decker or George's Plumbing Supplies."

I nodded.

"Well, over the months, he never came on to me, though I could tell he was interested. I really don't know how it happened, but it did — not in a burst of passion, but gradually over a long period of time. We often worked late together . . . it just happened. You see, if you are going to have an affair, it is usually in the office. It minimizes the logistical problems. There is the opportunity to be together . . . there is communication . . . being together is not only possible, it is necessary. While others might suspect, they can't be sure because the demands of the job make togetherness a fact . . . affair or no affair."

I nodded and thought of my own situation. I had never really looked at Marie as a potential lover. She is older and somehow did not seem attractive to me. I believed that she might be hurt though, if she thought I did not find her attractive. The fact is that she is attractive. I also understood what Erika meant about working closely. I recalled representing several dentists who fell hard for their dental assistants.

My domestic relations practice taught me that men — and women — generally don't have affairs unless they are having trouble at home. Most men and women who are happy with their domestic situations will not go astray.

"Erika, was Harley having trouble at home?"

"He didn't speak much about his home life. Men who are looking for something outside their marriage usually do complain about their spouses. You know — they aren't happy; they aren't understood; they aren't respected; they are taken for granted; they aren't loved . . . whatever . . . there always is a reason."

I noticed that she had omitted lack of sex. I attributed the omission to the fact that she was a woman. I was convinced that men view their sexual relationships differently from women.

"For a single woman . . . affairs are dangerous, and I carefully avoided any such thing. But John never complained about his home life . . . it was as if he loved me for me, not as an escape from his wife. I never felt used."

"And you recently began to suspect that he had another lover?"

For the first time in all of my conversations with Erika, I caught her off guard. She blushed and seemed to be confused. I could sense that she felt she was no longer in control of the interview. It was as if I had departed from her prepared script. She lowered her eyes and nodded.

[55

In the silence that followed, I reviewed my notes again. I considered saying something comforting but rejected the thought. We had agreed that it was better that the chips fall where they may.

"I now have enough information to start working on the case. Go about your regular routine. We have time before the preliminary hearing to gather information and make decisions. I'll call you in the next few days. Chin up."

She managed a weak smile.

17

One of my touchstones in life is the belief that I should view everyone and every situation as a skeptic would. Think the worst of everyone and everything and — while I will not always be right — I will never be disappointed. Sallie and I go around and around on the subject. She sees the glass as half full, and I view it as half empty. I cannot really account for the difference in perspective. I imagine that genetics, childhood experience, environment, education, and professional training all contribute to this difference in our views of life.

I mulled over the fact that Erika had not asked me if I wanted to know if she were guilty. Criminal types do not raise the issue. They look to me for an escape from their detection and capture. It is my job to uncover the loophole or technicality; exploit and destroy the weak witness; ferret out the police's procedural error; confuse and hang the jury; create the reasonable doubt; or plead leniency and raise the sympathy of the sentencing judge. To the criminal, it is not necessary that their attorney be convinced of their innocence. It is a business transaction only — do your job, get them off, and earn your fee.

Citizen types are different. I am often asked by such clients if I wanted to know if they were guilty. Since I learned about legal truth early in my career, I have found that the client's statements about guilt and innocence have little bearing on the course of events. Clients have told me they were innocent and were found guilty by the jury beyond a reasonable doubt. I have even had a client who admitted guilt only to discover later that the crime was committed by another. If a client committed the crime and admits it without my having to ask about guilt or innocence, it changes the game plan considerably. I immediately think about a plea bargain rather than a trial. I then search for all the bargaining chips I can find.

The fact that Erika did not behave like a normal citizen-type client was disturbing. I allayed my concern by focusing on her personality. She appeared to be organized to a fault. I was certain she had carefully planned each of our interviews and her story was set forth in a logical sequence with attention to detail. After all, she was an accountant by trade. Such meticulousness would aide my investigation. However, my nagging skepticism kept creeping back. I had the feeling that she was a very complex person carrying a lot of emotional baggage for a woman her age; and she wasn't particularly forthcoming. I tried to dismiss this last concern by recalling other cases. Even when clients are innocent, they do not tell me everything, sometimes because they are not convinced of its importance or are too embarrassed to share the information. This thought provided me some comfort.

I finally sought the psychological escape hatch that permits criminal defense lawyers to live with their consciences or to permit their consciences to atrophy beyond recovery. It was not my job to prove that Erika was innocent. The Commonwealth of Pennsylvania must prove her guilt to a jury beyond a reasonable doubt. Those are the rules of the game; thankfully, I do not make them. I only follow them. It is not morally wrong for me to represent a client who may be guilty. Under the rules, it is permitted and even demanded of a defense attorney.

I was off the hook psychologically; I felt better. I could not help wondering if Charles Perrow used that same logic in 1827 when he was seeking the freedom of Eben Jones. It must have been an unpopular act in Nelson County. Perhaps Attorney Perrow was a man of principles, or at least believed that every person, black or white, must have his or her day in court—even if it was a hearing before a judge to return a runaway slave to bondage.

Convinced I could now proceed, I began work on the case. I reviewed what I knew of the events that led to Erika's arrest. She was charged with embezzlement. Fifty thousand dollars had been traced from a university account to an account in her name. It was part of her job to move money from one university account to another. However, for her to "spend" the money, that is, transfer it to a non-university account, required either prior written authority or access to special codes. The codes controlled the release of money from a university account to a non-university account. Although it was general knowledge that she knew of the existence of the codes and may occasionally have been given access to certain codes, she did not have authority or permission to use any codes to "spend" money outside the university. On April 15th, fifty thousand dollars was transferred out of a university account. A corresponding entry was made indicating that the funds were disbursed to satisfy a debt to a performing arts group that did work for the "Great Performances" program.

An audit of the Performing Arts Department revealed that the group had been paid an amount in excess of the contracted amount. An inquiry was made and the agent for the group denied the overpayment. An extensive search was made for the missing money. The trail led to several banks and finally to Erika's account in an out-of-town branch of a local bank. Outside auditors were brought in to investigate and document everything. The police received an anonymous tip that Erika had a copy of the codes buried in a potted plant in her office. Another tip was received that Erika had the money stashed in her townhouse, but the police discovered no money during a complete search. They did find an account number written on the back cover of her phone book. They traced the account number and found the money. The account address was a post office box in a nearby town. Postal authorities confirmed that the application for the box had been signed by Erika; there were several bank statements in the box. The bank records also showed Erika's social security number and signature on the account card. The account had been opened in January, the same day that the post office box was rented. No disbursements from the bank account had been made. A small amount of interest had accrued.

On April 15th, Erika was in her office working with her computer. One secretary recalled the day because Erika had worked through lunch and asked the secretary to bring her some frozen yogurt. She also worked past the normal quitting time of 5:00 P.M. Another secretary who worked in the main part of the office until midnight remembered the evening because she was working on her personal taxes. She sought Erika out because she was an accountant and asked her some questions about filling out the tax forms. The secretary's husband came by at 11:00 P.M. to sign the forms and take them to the post office for mailing. Although the secretary only remembered seeing Erika once or twice during the evening, there was no doubt about the date and the fact that Erika worked late.

When the transaction was traced, it was determined that the order "spending" university money was made from Erika's workstation computer. The computer's security system listed her workstation as the origin of the disbursement of the funds. After the funds were traced, Erika was suspended from work. Outside auditors were called in to investigate and issue a report. When the report was tendered, charges were filed. These facts, as presented by the police, were damning. But there was no "smoking gun." No one saw Erika transfer the funds, nor had anyone seen her withdraw any money from the account. Smoking gun or no smoking gun, there was a mountain of evidence linking her to the disappearance of the money.

As a general rule, I try not to take work home with me. I do this for myself as well as Sallie. After all, she has to contend with the moods I bring from the office as well as moods induced by my avocations. This is not an easy task for a practical woman like Sallie. It is easy to leave my briefcase at the office, but the day's events are often lodged in my memory and they follow me home. Erika's case came home with me that evening.

I thought and re-thought about Erika's description of the events. I had to keep reminding myself that I did not yet have enough facts. Clients are not the only source of facts, and they are not always the most reliable. I resolved to talk with the police the following morning.

18

I was ushered into the Department of University Safety in the basement of a building on campus and was told by the receptionist that the investigating officer would be with me shortly. In a few minutes a young woman appeared, and I rose to meet her.

"We've met," she said. "You handled my house closing two years ago. You have so many clients that you've probably forgotten."

My mind raced to recall her. I have tried to develop the skill of remembering something about every client, even those I see only for a short time at a real estate settlement. Remembering something about a client is an important public relations tool. Most people are flattered when I recall personal details about them. It makes them feel special, and a client with good feelings means referrals and repeat business.

"I remember you. At the settlement table you were hoping that you might find a suitable substitute here for the Skyline Chili you were leaving behind in Cincinnati. Have you found it?"

She smiled, pleased that I remembered her. "No, I guess there is no substitute. I've adjusted though; now I'm addicted to Philly cheese steaks."

We were off to a good start. I didn't expect my remembering her would somehow ingratiate me, but it was something positive. Experience has taught me that by being positive at the beginning of a relationship, good things may happen. I am always amazed by attorneys who badger and bully people in an attempt to obtain something. It probably stems from insecurity or a mistaken belief in the general population's respect for lawyers.

People do not respect attorneys as they do doctors, ministers, uniformed bus drivers, or mail carriers. Most people would not object if their child became an attorney or if their son or daughter married one. Still, they generally do not like lawyers, nor do they feel comfortable dealing with them on any level. The one possible exception to this rule is a person's own attorney who is perceived as somehow different, more friendly and non-threatening, and competent. Unfortunately, not enough lawyers understand this phenomenon, and many go on throwing their weight around to the detriment of all lawyers.

People usually choose whether or not they will cooperate. By being friendly and forthright, the odds of success are improved. Putting people on the defensive or pressuring them often achieves the opposite. On many occasions I have avoided potential problems by smiling and asking: "Gee, I can't seem to figure this out. I'm sorry to impose, but could you please help me with this? I don't know what to do."

Although I knew that the investigator would not disclose anything that was to be kept from me, I did not want her to think I was a personal adversary. I was only doing my job as was she.

"I'm representing Erika Williams. I wanted to talk to you about the police reports."

"I can show you the report we used to base our charges, but you'll have to talk to the D.A.'s office about anything else. By the way, I think the D.A. is handling this himself."

"Don't often catch this big a fish?" I asked.

"We get our share, but you'll have to discuss this with him . . . unless he's out campaigning."

I understood the reference clearly. The D.A was preserving his option of making political hay at Erika's expense. He could prosecute it himself if it looked like an open and shut case. Or, if the going got tricky, he could assign it to an assistant who would take the fall in a losing situation. This was my payoff for remembering her; now it was back to an adversarial professional relationship.

[61

She knew I would do everything in my power to uncover and exploit the slightest procedural error that she or any of the police might make.

I read the affidavits and the report. Erika had known most of it. In fact, her story was so close to the substance of the report, I was suspicious.

"Has Erika Williams read these?" I asked.

"Why don't you ask her?" she responded quickly and a little too harshly. Then she added with a sheepish smile, "I'm sorry. I'm starting to sound like one of those hardboiled television policewomen. Yes, Erika Williams asked to see the court file after the arraignment. I guess you must have left the courtroom. I showed them to her there."

I tried to conceal my surprise. No client of mine has ever asked the magistrate or the arresting officer to see the court file.

"It's all business," she began. "I know you know that. But . . . off the record . . ."

I nodded my assent.

"Let me tell you . . . we're pretty well together on this one. Normally when we catch someone like Williams we get restitution and a resignation and some promises that the person never be seen in these parts again. We're not unreasonable if we can solve a problem so it won't come back to bite us in the future. We can't do that in this case . . . orders — and I mean orders — from on high."

I thanked her for her cooperation. She gave me a genuinely friendly smile, and I left with a lot less to be happy about than when I arrived.

My next stop was Erika's office. I had called and asked for John Harley. He was not there but the next in command gave me permission to speak with some of the office staff. The young woman who had been working the night of April 15th had been transferred to the regular day shift, and I received permission to interview her.

Polly Morrat was a small woman in her early thirties. Her supervisor offered me the use of a small, unused office. Without appearing to distrust the facilities, I suggested that we talk outside. I made the excuse that it was her chance to get fresh air on a nice day. She seemed grateful, so we walked outside to a shady spot a distance from the building.

When we were seated on a park bench, I began the interview. "Ms. Morrat..."

"Polly," she interrupted with a smile.

"Polly, you understand that I am one of the attorneys for Erika Williams and that I am conducting an investigation. I know you've talked to the police. It was your duty to do so, and neither Erika Williams nor I hold anything against you for that. Each of us is responsible for cooperating with the authorities if there is a possibility that a crime has been committed."

I did not want to appear as if I were doing anything more than background on the case. Although she appeared to be at ease, I did not want her to feel that I was cross-examining her.

"I did not see any crime being done," she noted quickly.

"We know you didn't. I just want to follow up on the details of the interview you gave the police. You said you were sure of the date because you were doing your taxes at the last minute." I tried not to sound accusatory regarding personal business on her employer's time.

"Yeah, I know I shouldn't have been doing personal business at the office like that, but everyone does it.... It was an emergency." She seemed a little defensive. She knew it was not right, but her legal truth was one of self-justification. Everyone else did it, so it was acceptable conduct.

I nodded. Reassured, she continued. "Yes, because I did my taxes I am sure of the date and time."

"Now, you said in your interview with the police that you saw Erika Williams a couple of times. The report did not indicate when you may have seen her after you came on duty at 5:00 P.M."

"The police asked me that, too. I only remember going into her office about 6:00 to ask her how to figure the taxes and fill out a part of the form. Once she came out to my desk, though."

"Oh? What happened?"

"She came out about 7:30 and saw me working on my taxes. She made some comment about how complex the tax forms were. She said she was having trouble with her computer and asked me to go

[63

over to the computer substation to check out a diagnostic program. You know, one of those computer programs that can tell what, if anything, is wrong with the hardware and software."

I know nothing about diagnostics but I did not want to interrupt her, so I nodded and she continued. I wondered later whether I simply did not want to reveal my ignorance about computers.

"I went over — it's just down the hall — I checked it out and in thirty seconds I was back with the diskette. She was waiting by my desk when I got back."

"Why didn't she go get the diskette?"

"I never thought about that. . . . She is a supervisor, I am a secretary. I guess she felt that it was my place to go get it. I don't know. It was a little unlike her though. She would never send a secretary out to get coffee or run a paper here or there. She almost always ran errands herself unless we happened to be on our way someplace."

I added her comments about Erika's character to my growing list of facts.

"Was there any other time you saw her?"

"Other than when I went in to get the advice about the taxes?"

I nodded.

"No. I can't see her office from where I work. I knew she was there because the light in the hallway to her office was on, and the secretary who left at 5:00 said she was still there. I went in to her office at 6:00. I didn't see her again until she came out to ask me to get the diskette. When I got back from dinner at about 9:00, I found the diskette in my 'in' basket by the secretarial pool. I don't know how long it had been there. I really didn't look in my basket until I finished the first set of taxes and ate dinner."

"Did you leave your office to return it to the computer substation?"

"Yes, right after that I dropped some papers on my desk and went down the hall and came back."

"And you didn't see Erika again after she came out to get the diskette?"

"Well, yes and no. I went by her office once and the light was still on. The door was cracked a little and I could hear music playing — she sometimes kept the radio on when she worked late. I don't remember seeing her, she was obviously there."

"Did she often work late?"

"Many times."

"How often — once or twice a week, more often?"

"At least twice a week. Please understand . . . I didn't know her well, but she was always so nice to me. When my husband was injured and in the hospital, she used to ask about him and once she even covered for me so I could go see him and take him his favorite ice cream."

"On the nights when she was working late, did Mr. Harley also work late?"

"I think I know what you're driving at. The police asked the same thing. I mind my own business. I may be young, but I know never to get involved in office gossip. I may not be one of the girls, so to speak, but I keep away from that sort of talk so I can keep my job and get regular raises."

I thought about asking her if she had heard others speak of a relationship between Harley and Erika, but the tone of her answer was confirmation enough.

"That night, April 15th, was Erika still here when you left?"

"Yes, though I can't swear to it. I heard the music, and I think she was on the phone talking to someone when I began securing the place. You see, I'm the last staff to leave at night."

"What time was that?"

"I told the police it was midnight, but I think it was a little before that."

This was information that the police did not have. When I obtain information that is at odds with the police report or that the police do not know, I usually pass over it casually. To do otherwise alerts the person to the inconsistency. Often the police will re-interview people and discover the information if my reaction indicates that the information is important. People do not want to be misleading or inconsistent. It could lead to trouble if they are called as a witness at trial.

"When do you go for your lunch, uh, dinner break?"

"Normally, I leave about 9:00. I get to pick my own time as long

[65

as the other night secretary is here to cover. But I was doing my taxes, so I'm not really sure. Let me think... I probably went out about 8:00 or a little after; I know because it was between doing the local and state forms and the federal form. The federal one is the hardest and took the longest. I was done by 11:00. My guess is I went about 8:15."

"You mentioned that there is another night-time secretary?"

"Terri Parsons. But she couldn't have seen Erika from where she sits. She is at the reception station in the outer office. The only time I remember seeing Terri was when I went to check about going out for a bite to eat. I remember she was working on her taxes, too."

"If Erika left her office, would you or Terri Parsons have been sure to see her?"

"No. You see, there is a staircase that comes up from the back of the office. All the supervisors use those back stairs. That way they can escape if they don't want to see someone waiting for them in the outer office. I shouldn't say this, but they don't have to pass the president's office going out or coming in that way. No one can see them come in late or leave early. We're not allowed—that is, the staff—to use those stairs. They may even be locked at the bottom. You'd have to have a key to come up, but going down and outside... no problem. There is one of those panic bars that opens the door to the outside but you can't get in without a key."

"Did Erika have a key?"

"Of course she had one. She was administrative, we're staff. I guess you don't appreciate the difference. Erika—Ms. Williams—knows the difference, but she never let it interfere. She never threw her weight around. As I said, she was respectful toward everyone—administrative, staff, even maintenance. She was well respected, but she was distant. She never let anyone get friendly, or perhaps personal would be a better word. As I say, everyone liked to work with her, or for her, but she was all business. She never talked about her personal life. No men came to see her. No flowers ever came. You know, even if a person is all business, from time to time there is some indication of a personal life—pictures on the desk, personal phone calls. When I went on night shift in January,

I expected her to loosen up a little since it was after hours. I thought she'd send me out to get supper . . . whatever. All business, but exceptionally respectful of the feelings of others."

I added this information to mental file on Erika. "I've imposed on you enough. You've been very honest and helpful. Erika and I appreciate it. One last question . . ."

She smiled and nodded.

"Who was it that assigned you to the night shift in January?"

"Mr. Harley."

"And when you were transferred to day shift again . . . was it Mr. Harley?"

"Yes, it was the day Erika cleaned out her desk. Why?"

"Just wondering."

19

I was confused by the day's revelations. Why hadn't Erika told me she had read the police reports? She certainly knew more than she was telling me. I felt uneasy. I am accustomed to clients who depend on me, eager for me to craft a defense to rescue them from the storm, grateful for whatever attention I bestow upon them. Being able to play the role of knight is one of the chief benefits of doing criminal defense for citizen types. I enjoy the hero role. With Erika, I felt like an actor playing a supporting role in a script over which I had no control.

To regain control of my own emotions, I felt it was time for a change of pace. Instead of returning to the office, I called Marie and told her I had an important mission at the courthouse. As usual, she did not believe me and mumbled something to the effect that she would be sure to bill the courthouse time to our elusive client, Eben Jones.

[67

"Am I that transparent?" I asked myself. I knew the answer to my rhetorical question.

Erika's case had taken the edge off my quest for fulfillment of my fantasies. Still, I wanted to continue to try to unravel the mystery of Eben Jones. I went to the docket books containing the cases from 1801 though 1828. The cases were indexed alphabetically by surname in order of date filed. There were indexes for both plaintiffs and defendants. I knew that Perrow had reported to Petrikin that Eben Jones was supposed to have filed a case against a man named Peter Karthaus. Karthaus is a familiar name in the county. The small town of Karthaus in an adjacent county is named for him. The name was misspelled in Perrow's letter as Carthouse. Looking for the name "Jones, Eben" or some corruption of it, I carefully read down the list of names in the "J" section of the plaintiffs' index. There was no case listed as having been filed by Eben Jones or anyone with a similar name. Next, I ran through the index for defendants under both "C" and "K" looking for either Peter Karthaus or Peter Carthouse. Again my efforts went unrewarded. Evidence of the lawsuit was my main hope in proving the existence of Eben Jones. Without verifying the existence of the lawsuit, there was no practical way to confirm that Eben Jones was ever in the county.

Obviously, I could not interview any of the people mentioned in the letter. They, their children, grandchildren and great-grandchildren were all dead. The memory of events in the day-to-day life of these people was gone. Oh, I might find their dates of birth and death. Through diligent research I might find a report of the role some may have played in certain historical events such as the Civil War. But their thoughts about the world around them and the people they knew are gone forever. In terms of ultimate truth, this loss is unimportant. Their thoughts are of no consequence or relevance to anyone now alive except to satisfy the curiosity of a frustrated attorney living more than a century and a half later.

Disappointment began to overwhelm me as I sat there in the straight-back chair in the furthest corner of the clerk's office. In 1827, this very index book would have been on the shelf in the main part of the clerk's office. James Petrikin no doubt held this very book in his hands as he too searched the index of cases for the year 1819. I wondered what his reaction was when he did not find the name of Eben Jones. It was quiet in the depths of the clerk's office. I called upon my God-given gift of a hyperactive imagination, and as I sat there a vision of James Petrikin appeared.

"There are no other entries for the year 1819?" Petrikin asked the clerk.

"No, Squire Petrikin. Those are the only ones. Most all of those cases have gone to judgment or have had a *non pros* entered by the judge. You know how his honor is about keeping the civil docket moving. No civil case makes it to the October term a second time."

"Unless it is filed by one of the Judge's friends," thought Petrikin. It was a thought he did not share with the clerk, who owed his job to Judge Burnside.

"Sir," asked Petrikin, "Do you recall seeing any case filed by a negro called Eben Jones? Or have you ever heard that name before? No one knows more people in the county than you, good fellow."

"Ah, it is true that I know many souls in and about this county. Souls living and souls entered into eternal rest, what with having charge of the voter role, the assessments, jury lists, and the like. This is not a large county in population. I recall no one white or negro with that name, though I must admit that my circle of friends does not include men of color. They are not encouraged to join in the political life here, or anywhere that I know. They have no property, they are tenant farmers and laborers, they do not serve as jurymen. They are not even named in the census reports I send to the Secretary of the Commonwealth. They are listed not by name as you or I might be named in the reports issued by the township supervisors. They are only numbered — 'seven men of color' — that includes negroes and mulattos."

"Dear clerk, I am seeking information about the negro Eben Jones so as to provide affidavits to be used by an attorney in Nelson County, Virginia, as evidence supporting a writ of *habeas corpus*. It seems that the unfortunate Jones was arrested without proper papers and remanded to jail where he awaits his day in court. His defense to a return to slavery is his claim to be a citizen of Pennsylvania, a free man not subject to the registration laws of Virginia. By letter, I am asked to assist in obtaining such information as may support his claim. What more noble cause than that of helping in the establishment of his claim to citizenship of our Commonwealth and thereby gaining the freedom of Eben Jones?"

The clerk gave Petrikin a suspicious look.

"Ah, Squire, the noblest and purest pursuit of all, that of seeking justice in an unjust world. The problem, good fellow, is that justice is a worldly concept which people define differently. Oh, the Scriptures speak of divine justice and divine law. It is in the human interpretation of justice that trouble arises. Much earthly evil is borne of a belief that justice demands that people obey this or that person — or this or that belief — or this or that law. I do not belittle your concern, sir, but establishing the freedom of this Eben Jones will have little consequence."

"Except to Eben Jones," interjected Petrikin.

"Ah, but sir, you see, the Virginians — even this attorney from Virginia — have the belief that slavery is just and right because it attends the needs of negroes who are incapable of caring for and governing themselves. I have been there and have observed the institution of slavery first hand. That is the Southern belief, and I dare say, the belief of that attorney who has written earnestly soliciting your assistance."

"That might be so. I am the first to admit that I may not know the full consequences of this. But what does it matter? If I forward affidavits, I will have satisfied myself that I have done right by my self-sworn duty to my fellow man."

"Mr. Petrikin, I have no quarrel with your duty or sense of honor. It is known by all you serve those causes well here in the county. I say only that your belief in serving justice and the belief of the Virginian may not be one in the same."

"The letter mentions a civil case filed by Eben Jones against Peter Karthaus. An attorney from Mifflin County and a man named Getts were Jones' counsel. The matter was heard by William Petrikin and Jones was represented by counsel, so I assumed a record of the case would be found among your dockets. However, perhaps the case was heard in the Squire's court."

"Then, Mr. Petrikin, there would be no written record of it. The Squire's court is not a court of record. None is demanded by the laws of the Commonwealth. A written record of the case would exist only if either party appealed the Squire's decision. It would then appear as a civil matter on the dockets and be set for trial during the next court of common pleas quarter session. If there is no entry, either the case was not appealed or did not exist at all."

My journey back to 1827 was interrupted by one of the assistant clerks tapping me lightly on the shoulder. She told me that Marie had called requesting that someone in the clerk's office return me to reality as soon as possible and favor her with a return phone call.

"That is the chief problem with reality . . . lack of control over events," I thought as I dialed the office number.

20

Erika's preliminary hearing was scheduled for the end of the following week. This left little time to complete my investigation and prepare a tentative defense. Normally, at the preliminary hearing, it is determined whether there is probable cause to believe that the defendant committed the crime. The preliminary hearing is the point in a criminal proceeding when Perry Mason always managed to destroy Hamilton Burger's case, find the guilty culprit, and spring his client. In real life, most defense attorneys do not attempt to defeat the state's case at the preliminary hearing. At trial, the state must prove the defendant guilty beyond a reasonable doubt. That is the standard of proof for the trial. At the preliminary hearing, the state has the burden of proving only that there is enough evidence, direct or circumstantial, to warrant continuation of the prosecution. Although the defense has an opportunity to present evidence, most defense attorneys do not wish to reveal their cases at the preliminary hearing stage unless their evidence clearly demonstrates that the defendant did not commit the crime. Tactically, this is the correct way to proceed. However, less scrupulous attorneys in possession of evidence that exonerates their client may not wish to present a case at the preliminary hearing. These unconscionable attorneys know that at a full-blown trial there is always more career-enhancing publicity, the client is more grateful, and the fee is much larger.

The next major step in my investigation was to learn more about John Harley. After a number of requests, he finally granted me an interview. He suggested that it might be more appropriate if he were to visit me. It is out of character for a high-level administrator who exercises so much power to come to another's office. High-powered executives prefer to meet on their own turf. Visitors are then at a psychological disadvantage. They must conduct their interview sitting in an uncomfortable side chair, taking notes on a pad balanced precariously upon a knee. The lights are carefully arranged to make it difficult for the visitor to view the eyes of the person behind the desk.

I was not sure why Harley might relinquish his home field advantage. I believed that every move he made was calculated to gain him the greatest possible leverage. I could only assume that he was not afraid of me and he wanted me to know it up front. In any case, he arrived at the appointed hour. A lesser person would make a statement by being late, thus making the other person wait for the appointment. People who intend to make a statement that they are in control know to be on time for every appointment.

I took him to the conference room and let him choose his position at the table. As I expected, he chose the seat at the head of table which provided a view of the French doors opening into the hallway. I took a seat at the other end of the table.

We instinctively took the measure of one another. I could feel him taking me in and analyzing the information. He appeared just as I had imagined him, very businesslike. There was no grease spot on his Liberty of London tie. He wore a freshly cleaned and pressed white shirt with a crisply starched collar. He was fit and trim, and nothing about his clothing, grooming, or manner was overstated; rather, it bespoke of a man in complete control. It was easy to see that he was used to dominating those around him.

I expected him to open the meeting with a statement about how distressed he was with the turn of events and how concerned he was that Erika have the best possible representation. I did not expect him to launch into a self-justifying monologue about how Erika betrayed the trust he had placed in her at the office. He would know that any such remark would kindle the fires of suspicion about his own involvement in the matter. Nor did I expect him to manifest outrage at Erika's arrest. Outrage was not part of his arsenal of behavior-influencing weapons. His force of personality, well-reasoned verbal presentation, and commanding appearance were the weapons upon which he relied.

He began by expressing his concern for Erika and his confidence in the resources that I could muster for her defense. He carefully gauged my reaction to his opening remarks. I sensed that he was weighing my reaction about his concern. When I remained impassive, he continued with background information, giving special emphasis to Erika's competence and loyalty to the University. When still I made no comment, he assured me that I could have free reign in my investigation in his department. I could have access to any people I might like to interview, and subject to university security requirements, I was free to examine any system or file.

I could see that my silence was having an effect. He was used to receiving verbal information, analyzing it, and making his next move. He did not appear to be frustrated, but I could sense that he was unsure about me. By not responding, he had no way of knowing how much I knew about him, the case, or his relationship with Erika. It was then that he decided to gamble.

"Erika and I have had a special relationship. By now you know that... or you have suspected it. Let me confirm it for you. I know better than to ask for your discretion when you are pledged to the defense of your client."

At this point I think he was hoping for an assurance that I would use the information about his affair with Erika if, and only if, all other possibilities had been exhausted. I could give him no such assurance. Even if I were in a position to do so, I certainly would not have given any such assurance without a cost to him.

[73]

He knew what I was thinking. "I really did not expect your assurance. You must represent your client. And, I cannot appeal to you for her sake. The possibility of disclosure of an illicit relationship is not so threatening for Erika as the possibility of a term in the state prison. And, I can tell by your silence that this request is not negotiable."

At this point, his objectives in coming to my office had not been achieved. It was clear to me that he was there to present himself favorably, size up Erika's attorney, and if possible, obtain an assurance of non-disclosure of his relationship with Erika. It was also possible that he had assured Erika that he would help in her defense. What better way to prove his loyalty to Erika than coming to see her attorney upon request?

"Mr. Harley..."

"John," he interrupted.

He had shifted ground. He had hoped to appear as a crisply efficient administrator. Now he sought to ingratiate himself by appearing friendly, cooperative, and less formal by inviting me to use his first name. I decided that I would not offend him by continuing to call him Mr. Harley, but I would not fall into his trap. I would not address him by name.

"You understand that I am bound to investigate the matter fully. It is merely routine for me to ask you where you were on April 15th, the day when the money was transferred from the University's account."

He thought about it for a moment.

"Well, the theft of money is not like a murder when there is a specific time of death. With murder, suspects are asked to pinpoint their whereabouts at a given time. 'April 15th' covers 24 hours. Can you be more specific?"

His reference to the word 'suspect' might have been casual, or he could have been fishing for information about whether I considered him a possible suspect. I decided not to rise to the bait.

"Were you in the office that day?"

"Yes, I arrived at about 9:00 and had a series of meetings. At noon I left for a luncheon appointment and returned at 1:30. In the afternoon, I had a staff meeting — Erika attended — that lasted until about 3:15. An investment service representative came in at 3:30 and we met till a few minutes before 5:00. I then prepared the calendar for the following day and made some assignments. I always stay in the office until the day-shift staff leaves . . . it's good business. Then I met my wife downtown at the Tavern restaurant at about 5:45. We ate dinner, visited at the table of some friends — do you want their names?" Even when he appeared to make matter-of-fact statements, Harley's words were carefully chosen. His reference to friends was a test. If I did not consider him a suspect, I would not need to verify his whereabouts that day and I would not require the names of the friends for corroboration.

I nodded and said, "If you please." I could sense that he was weighing my request. Was I merely being thorough or did I consider him to be a suspect? I did not intend to relinquish any advantage I enjoyed by satisfying his curiosity. He paused to give me their names and business telephone numbers which I dutifully took down on my legal pad.

"At 8:10 we left the restaurant. At about 8:15, I parked the car behind the administration building and went back to the office to get my briefcase. I didn't want to take my briefcase downtown to the restaurant, and my wife had taken the car after dropping me off for work that morning. My wife waited in the car. At about 8:30, I returned to the car and drove to Bill's Video to rent a movie — my wife wanted to see one — I was planning to work late at home . . . I did not need access to my office computer. We left Bill's Video at about 8:50 and arrived home about ten minutes later."

The first thing I noticed about the narrative was that he was not very precise about the timing of events during the day, but after 5:00 he detailed his report with more precision. He reported his location at smaller time intervals. During the day, he must have left his office on several occasions, if only to go to the men's room. After 5:00 he was careful to supply precise times and locations. This meant that the money disappeared after 5:00 P.M. and that Harley knew it. I made a note to see if it was possible to determine the exact minute when the transfer of university funds was made.

"When you went back to the office at 8:15 to get your briefcase, did you use the back stairs?"

[75

He was unprepared for my question, but as a seasoned business-type veteran, he did not betray his surprise. "Yes. My wife was listening to the radio in the car so I left the keys in the ignition. I had to return to the car to get the keys to gain access to the back stairs."

"Do you remember speaking to either Polly Morrat or Terri Parsons that evening?"

"I passed Polly Morrat's desk, but she was not there. I asked Terri Parsons where Polly was and she reported that she had taken an early dinner."

"Did you see Erika?"

"My office is down the hall from hers. Her light was on and her radio was playing, I assumed she was there, but I did not go into her office."

"Given the nature of your relationship, was it not unusual for you not to have stopped at least to say hello or goodbye?"

"That was not our practice. We knew when we were to speak to each other and when we were not. Perhaps she could explain more clearly."

I could sense that he wanted the interview to end. Normally, if he were with subordinates, Harley would have looked at his watch at this point. The subordinates would have understood the cue and excused themselves. Harley knew I would think ill of him if he were to look at his watch as a signal that he wanted to leave. He needed my continued respect. Therefore, he waited for me to end the interview. Having obtained all the information he was going to provide, there was no point in continuing. I also wanted his respect.

"I certainly appreciate your taking time from your busy schedule to come to my office for this interview and I appreciate your candor. May I call you if I have further questions?"

We both knew it was a request he could not refuse.

21

The movies and television have given the general public an inaccurate picture of an attorney's professional life. It is true that both media have time constraints, so cases which normally take months or even years to evolve are presented as if the daily life of the attorney is dominated by a rapid series of exciting events surrounding one case. While attorneys argue among themselves about every topic imaginable, contention being the nature of the beast, they almost unanimously agree that daily professional life is boring. An attorney's life is filled with a series of routine and uninspiring tasks, punctuated here and there with a few unique and challenging experiences. Almost all attorneys have some memorable cases and unforgetable clients. But if one were to divide the hours of excitement generated by memorable cases and unforgetable clients by the number of hours in a forty-year law career, it would be determined that the average bus driver has a more exciting life.

Even though I found myself immersed in the Erika Williams case, the vast majority of my time was still spent on routine legal and administrative matters. There were clients to counsel, wills to write, real estate settlements to attend, community projects to do, and of course, there was my life with Sallie.

I have handled hundreds of lawsuits in my two decades of practice and on an intellectual level I understand the emotional swings involved. There are highs and there are lows. I know to expect these vicissitudes, but when I am caught up in the maelstrom of litigation, I still get swept away.

I was in the courthouse, reviewing the court file and cross-checking the dates and times from my notes with the affidavits filed. Some young attorneys from the county's largest law firm were in the clerk's office on the other side of one of those electronic files. I overheard them talking about Erika's case and her attorney.

"He's a solo. How good can he be? I hear he is a real character — no one can really work with him. Why would someone like that Williams woman choose him? Why not Lenker over at the Campbell firm? Why not that heavy hitter from Hollidaysburg?"

"She must have decided to retire to prison. I wouldn't let him defend me for a parking violation.... but remember two years ago he got that guy Stephens off when everyone thought he was going to be making license plates at Huntingdon for ten to twenty. I was there. His final argument to the jury was very good."

"He was lucky. Booker, the former assistant D.A. handled the prosecution, if handled is the appropriate description. It was mishandled from jury selection on."

A female voice entered the conversation. "Have any of you ever had a case against him? I don't like him one bit ... professionally, that is. He exploited my inexperience. I was furious. Then I used the same trick on that new redhead over at the McNair firm — the one who thinks she's God's gift. He didn't seem so bad after that. He's not just another lawyer, believe me."

"That's crap. If he were anybody he'd be somebody — you know, in a firm. He'd have his own firm or be a senior partner."

My defender remained silent.

They all laughed and went back to their work. In a few minutes they finished and wandered out of the clerk's office passing the desk where I was working. It was clear to all of them that I had been privy to their conversation. The young woman who had risen to my defense lagged behind the others. She turned as if to make an apology. I winked at her and gave her a knowing smile. She smiled back, relieved that she did not have to defend her associates.

My worst fears were realized. I was considered an eccentric by the younger set, a sort of Oscar Brumbaugh in the making. To these young lawyers my being a sole practitioner was a sign of professional weakness. Their identity as lawyers was very tightly interwoven with the firm for which they worked. For them little mattered except the name of the firm. Honesty, ethics, perserverence, and legal skills counted little. Employing this logic, my twenty years of law practice, mostly as a sole practitioner, placed me near the bottom on the lawyers' pecking order. I tried to dismiss the thought, telling myself that I did not live my life to impress these young bucks.

"Let them think what they please," I told myself in an attempt to save a psychological sinking ship.

These words, logical and sound as they were, did little to restore order. It was no use. The fact is, I was just like everyone else. I did care what people thought of me and it hurt deeply to realize that other attorneys viewed me in a less than favorable light.

I told myself that I had tried hard to do my job as best I could, to be honest and fair in my dealings with everyone, including other attorneys. But I was alone. I had no firm meetings to preside over; no Friday afternoon post-work happy hours, gathering around the piano bar, ties loosened, laughing in camaraderie with associates after a tough week; no firm Christmas party to arrange. Sole practitioners are like dinosaurs, obsolete lawyers perceived by members of firms as eccentrics or underachievers. I began reliving my vision of my law practice as a little mangy rat scurrying about the floor, foraging for crumbs tossed from the legal dinner table by the lawyers who were members of powerful and prestigeous law firms. Reality was certainly more threatening to my ego than my musings over Eben Jones, James Petrikin, and Charles Perrow. That is why I kept retreating to them.

The young lawyers did raise a point I had deferred considering. Why had Erika chosen me to represent her? I felt qualified and competent. She said she distrusted high profile members of the bar. I had accepted her reasons and her $10,000 without questioning them. I had been swept up in the moment of excitement at the prospect of handling a difficult and challenging case for a beautiful woman. Her case fit neatly into the "white-knight" vision I had of myself. I would be a latter-day Charles Perrow taking an unpopular case with the deck heavily stacked against me, coming to the rescue of a client in distress. But as my mood had darkened, I feared that I might be a Don Quixote, tilting at windmills, obsessed by my belief in a noble cause in an unnoble world.

I always have moments of self-doubt when working on an important case, but these concerns somehow loomed larger in Erika's case. Why would a beautiful young woman, clearly caught in the tight grip of the law choose me to represent her? My overriding impression of her was that of a woman who tried to be in complete control of her world. All the information I had gleaned from personal contact with her and interviews with others indicated that she was very meticulous in everything she did. She did everything properly but lacked a human touch in her relationships. She could be kind and thoughtful toward others, but it was questionable whether her conduct was motivated by a genuinely caring heart or by a self-imposed duty to be the ideal person. One thing was certain. There was nothing spontaneous about her. She would first identify her goal, then devise the means to achieve it. Her choice to have me defend her was a well-reasoned decision, arrived at after careful consideration. When she first approached me, my ego chose to believe that it was my personal and professional competence that had brought her to my door. In all honesty, I now knew that if I were Erika, I would not have chosen myself for the defense. I was now convinced that there was more to the matter than I was being told or was able to discover thus far.

22

All the dates and times taken from my interviews matched those in the court file. I returned to the office for a meeting with a private investigator I had hired to help with the case. Rick Place bore no resemblance to any television detective except perhaps Colombo. His appearance was unkempt, but his powers of observation were astounding.

"The signatures on the post office box rental agreement and the bank account card are definitely Erika Williams.' . . . But there is something intriguing about them."

"How so?" I asked.

"Well, they are exactly alike," He sounded pleased with himself.
"So?"

"Don't you see? When I say exactly alike, I mean exactly alike. One is a duplicate copy of the other. No one signs their name exactly the same way twice. The only time you get an exact copy of your signature is when you use one of those autopen machines like those politicians use for letters. It is physically impossible for a person to sign his name exactly the same way twice. There are minute variations in the signature each time. Both of the signatures on the cards are exactly the same. But I am sure the signature belongs to your client."

"What about pressure on the paper?" I was proud that I remembered a Nero Wolfe mystery which discussed the differences in pressure applied by a person writing his signature.

Place disregarded my allusion to Nero Wolfe. "I checked that. The signatures were done with what appears to be a felt-tipped pen—very smooth black ink. The pressure is the same on both pieces. I don't think that the signatures were traced—they're both too smooth. When signatures are traced, under a magnifying glass it is usually very apparent—minute corrections in direction are detectable. Of course, computer technology—laser printers and scanners—makes anything possible. You could sign with a felt-tipped pen on white paper, scan it into the computer, and print it with a laser printer. It wouldn't take a computer genius to do it."

"Have you told anyone about this?"

"Please . . ." He took offense at my question.

"No offense intended. What I meant to ask was whether you did your customary investigation." I was referring to Place's uncanny ability to draw the police investigators into unwittingly divulging information.

"Well, I had coffee with the guy up there who is the handwriting specialist. He seemed quite sure that the two signatures were unquestionably Williams'. He showed me a loop here and line there, telltale things that indicate a signature is genuine; but I noticed on the evidence tags that he had examined one at 4:44 P.M. one day and the other at 9:17 A.M. the next. They are in separate evidence packets. I don't think he checked them side by side. If he had, I think he would have noticed that they are identical. He showed me a specimen of her signature taken from another account card at the same bank. He was so smug about his findings that I doubt he'll check them again unless specifically ordered to do so. He didn't show it to me, but I know he'd already finished his written report."

"What do you think this means for our case?"

"The signatures are those of Williams. We don't know if she signed either of them. We do know that she didn't sign both. Here, they let me make photocopies." He handed me the copies. "Oh yeah, the chief investigator—a woman—said something to me about trying to talk some sense into your head about making a deal with the D.A."

I asked Place to verify the whereabouts on April 15th of everyone I had interviewed. I called John Harley to get permission for Place to visit the offices and talk to the employees.

Next I called Jacki Snow, my friend who works with the university computers. She gave me some background on the university's networks. I tried to guide the conversation to the security systems. She was hesitant to supply me with any information about it, but when I explained that I was defending Erika Williams and there was intrigue, she opened up.

Each network has its own security system. Most of the systems were not designed to hide data, but to prevent someone from implanting a virus in the data storage. Most of the systems were backed-up. That is, duplicates of the information were constantly being made and kept separate from the main system so that if the memory becomes infected, the data would not be lost. Or if there were a loss such as a fire, duplicate and even triplicate records were kept of the most important data. Duplicates of student and employment records are kept. The most closely protected information backed up at the university is the list of names and seat locations of the football season-ticket holders.

Jacki was not familiar with the university's financial systems. She had heard that about six months ago, an intricate security system was installed. She explained that normally, there was front-door security. That is, there is a log-on entry into the system. In order to gain entry into the data bank, the operator has to identify himself or herself with a password or pass number. Also, in order to prevent loss, it was not possible to move money without the proper code number or code word. Even then, for certain accounts, a second password or number was required. This was typical of all financial systems in order to comply with certain audit standards. To further secure the system, a backdoor could be installed which would identify by operator and workstation any movement of funds. This is not a loss prevention measure, but a loss detection one. If funds were moved, the security system could identify the operator number and location of the computer which had made the transfer.

"Would the backdoor system give the date and time when a transfer was made?" I asked.

She explained that without that information, it did little good to identify the operator number and workstation. Then, she made some comment questioning my investigative abilities. Would I not want to know when any transfer of funds was made? Someone could enter another operator's number and the other operator might be blamed for a loss. The date and time of the transfer was essential for identification purposes.

I wanted to find out the exact time when the transfer of funds was made on Erika's workstation. Also, I needed to know whether it was possible to fool the computer into believing that an order originated from a workstation other than the one actually entering the order. Could a computer disguise itself? After promising to write her mother's will, Jacki agreed to do some snooping for me. Jacki Snow never gives anything away.

That evening at 5:00 I went to see Terri Parsons. Like Polly Morrat, Terri Parsons was supporting herself and her graduate student husband on her salary as a secretary. I sensed immediately that she was more reluctant to talk to me than Polly had been. She had more to lose. She was at the bottom of the ladder in the office.

She had already given a statement to the police. Although she did not see her, Parsons was sure Erika Williams had been working that night. Erika had called on the intercom line once to inquire whether Harley had left a file for her. She remembered noting that it was the intercom line, not an outside line. She remembered the

[83

night because Polly Morrat usually left for dinner at about nine. That evening, she took an early dinner a little after eight.

In my experience, when a person has not clearly thought out something, there are pauses and corrections. Items are mentioned out of sequence. Events come to mind after the memory is triggered by one statement or another. Chronological order is arranged and then re-arranged. I could tell that Parsons had been over the story several times before, probably with the police or Harley.

"Did Erika Williams have her own phone line, or do all calls come through the telephone console on your desk?" I asked.

"Miss Williams has ... er, had her own line."

"Does the line to her office come through the console?"

"Yes, it's right up in the second row ... there." She pointed to the telephone and a row of lights indicating the existence of a line.

"That evening, other than the call to you on the intercom line, do you remember ever seeing the light for her line go on?"

She paused and thought carefully. I could tell that the question was a new one.

"I remember it was quiet. We don't get many calls. I do overflow typing of letters, memos, you know, general office stuff that the regular secretaries don't get to during the day. Now that you mention it, I do remember that her line was used that evening. Let me see. When an incoming call is received, it rings in the office or at my desk. The little light blinks until someone picks up the line. After a few rings, the light is solid if it is answered, or it blinks until the person making the call hangs up and ends the call. Sometimes the blinking light catches my eye or if the phone is in an office nearby, I can hear a ring and I instinctively look at the phone. If the person is in the office, but away from their desk, I might pick it up, but mostly I don't. Usually I am facing the computer and I can't see the phone so I don't notice. But that night, Polly was expecting a call from her husband about picking up their taxes to take to the post office ... it was April 15th. Polly was working on her personal taxes, you see, she mentioned that if her husband called, to ask ... actually, I think her exact words were 'tell him to get his ass down here by 11:00 ... and I was kind of keeping an eye on the phone ...

you see Polly is one of the higher up secretaries with her own line . . . all the rest don't have lines and they have to come through here. When she went out I kind of kept a watch on the phone. I saw a blink, when Polly was out and started to pick it up, then I saw it was Erika Williams' line. It blinked, but she must have answered it because it stopped blinking and stayed lit. Polly's husband never did call while she was out. He came in about 11:00, just as ordered."

I asked whether Erika worked late often. She indicated that it was not uncommon for Erika to work late.

"I suppose because she did not have a man in her life," she ventured, "or at lease a regular man."

"Oh?"

"By regular man, I mean a man-man. In all the time I've worked here, no man ever called for her either personally or on the phone that came through my console here at the office. Though, I must say that from time to time I would see her walking with a man . . . and from time to time I would see her eating with a man at one of the restaurants . . . but they weren't men-men . . . just acquaintances or something. You can always tell when a woman is with a man-man . . . you know . . . someone she is interested in . . . it shows in the way she walks with him or sits at the table with him . . . you can tell . . ."

"And?" I prodded, without trying to seem too interested.

"Now mind you, I try to mind my own business, but there was an awful lot of talk that the reason she did not have a man-man was either that she preferred another gender . . . or she was otherwise occupied . . ."

She looked at me to see if I was responding to her innuendo. Again, I tried to maintain an open, but non-commital expression. She paused not knowing whether to continue. However, I could sense that she was no great admirer of Erika, so I expected her to explain herself.

"Well, there was a lot of gossip around the administration that Miss Williams was . . . to put it politely . . . engaged in an illicit relationship with one of the senior vice presidents. But, personally I never paid that close attention to her. I treasure my job here and the surest way to end up answering the phone during the graveyard shift at the surplus warehouse is open your mouth about something like that."

She paused.

"Now, don't get me wrong. I like Miss Williams. For a supervisor she was very good . . . never had me run any errands or she never sent me for coffee or anything like that. Sometimes when she was working late she would bring me a snack or a coke. She just wasn't friendly . . . and invariably when she was working late, the senior vice president would leave, then about ten minutes later she would leave . . . the others were suspicious about this . . . personally I did not care one way or the other. But certain higher up secretaries would always make jokes about forwarding all calls to the 'No-tell Motel.'"

As she continued with the story there was an increased edge of bitterness in her voice. When there was nothing more to tell, she relaxed visibly, and asked that I consider her remarks as confidential and for background purposes only.

I assured her that nothing she said was anything other than background for my investigation. In order to keep the line of communication open for the future I explained that I might have a technical question or two at a later time. She seemed reassured, probably because I did not probe further for more information about Erika and Harley and my manner, which was casual and relaxed. Also, I did not take notes in her presence, but wrote down the important points of the conversation later in my office. Often I did this to indicate to a potential witness that I was gathering background information only. People seemed to exercise more caution about disclosing information when their words were being transcribed.

After the interview with Terri Parsons, I tried to absorb the information I had been able to discover during the initial stages of the investigation. I sat in my office lost in thought when I realized that it was late and I had not called Sallie. We had plans for the evening and my arrival at home was long overdue.

23

Sallie was in no mood. I must admit that the combination of Eben Jones and Erika Williams had soaked up most of my attention. And I was not as attentive as I should have been to all the signs of a neglected spouse. True, I had said that I was too tired to take in a movie on three recent occasions. And, though I agreed to accompany her to a concert featuring Mozart's String Quartet No. 1 in A major KV 212, I dozed off during the *tema con variazioni*. When I began to snore, she elbowed me in the ribs. As I awakened suddenly, I glanced at her and she gave me THE LOOK.

All husbands who have been married more than a week are familiar with, and have been on the receiving end of, THE LOOK. Some husbands have argued that THE LOOK is an even more effective weapon than sexual neglect. This probably stems from the fact that sexual neglect must be employed over a long period of time in order to achieve maximum effect. Another possible disadvantage of sexual neglect is that it involves denial for both husband and wife. On the other hand, the effects of THE LOOK are instantaneous and there is no self-denial for the woman.

Having been on the receiving end of more than my share, I have tried to analyze THE LOOK. It might be argued that THE LOOK is unique to each woman. However, I am convinced that THE LOOK is standard issue to all women, though each woman customizes THE LOOK to suit her own personality and her own needs. I believe that I could effectively recognize THE LOOK if sent my way by a woman who was not my wife. Of course, THE LOOK would have no direct effect upon me. Women effectively employ THE LOOK only against their own men.

Chemical composition is always broken into parts, like water, two parts hydrogen and one part oxygen. As I see it, THE LOOK consists of two parts "I don't believe you did [or said] that"; one part "You're making an ass out of yourself"; one part "Stop now before you dig yourself a deeper hole"; and one part either "who do you think you are" or "what kind of fool do you take me for." In any case, when the concert was over I received THE LOOK again in the lobby, followed by a moderate dose of the silent treatment, also a favorite female weapon. I knew that Erika Williams was responsible for my receipt of THE LOOK.

Early in my career, I was in partnership with three other attorneys practicing law in an old rundown house which had been converted into an old rundown office. Everyone knew we were a marginal operation. We looked, acted, and did business as if we were marginal. In fact, everything about us was marginal. As a form of escape, we would gather monthly with our spouses and employees for a party. Once, after the second round of drinks, the wife of one of my partners began joking about our clients, who, not surprisingly, were also marginal. She went on and on about this or that "wacko" client. It was clear to me that she knew more about our clients than I did. The partnership did not last long, and I vowed that I never would burden Sallie with details about my clients.

At first, Sallie felt excluded from that part of my life. She felt I didn't trust her not do the same thing my former partner's wife had done. Then one day one of her friends told her that I represented a man known to them in a divorce. The friends asked whether it was true that he had been making love to a dental supply saleswoman. Sallie was off the hook. She could honestly say that I never discussed my professional cases with her. Thereafter, Sallie was much less concerned about the details of my practice. But I was not perceptive enough to realize that since she is not part of my professional life, I need to make an extra effort to include her elsewhere.

Sallie had seen pictures of Erika in the paper and had read that I represented her. She was concerned by the lack of attentiveness at home which coincided with my representation of Erika. Instead of expressing that concern to me, she told herself that it was nothing to worry about. She felt that if she said something to me, it would reveal her insecurity or that I might view any inquiry as a lack of trust on her part. Erika might be beautiful, but Sallie knew it was she I loved. Still, she reasoned, if I loved her, I would be more attentive to her needs. She decided to test me by making suggestions that we do this or that together. She gave me ample opportunity to demonstrate my affection and re-affirm my love. When I did not respond favorably to a series of carefully planned opportunities, her concern deepened to the point where she dispatched THE LOOK and employed the silent treatment.

We drove in silence to our favorite night spot. After ordering our drinks, I decided to attack the problem head-on. For me, it was a matter of self-preservation rather than wisdom. In my domestic practice, it never failed to amaze me how problems between spouses could have been resolved, if they only had communicated their concerns and inner fears with each other. Of course, wisdom comes easy when one's own insecurities are not at issue.

"It's Erika Williams, isn't it?"

"No," she paused. "Well . . . yes."

"Let's talk about it. I love you, and it hurts to think something is getting in the way of that."

"Well, I know you. I know how you can get carried away with things. Eben Jones is one example. You get so emotionally involved. It siphons off your energy . . . admit it." Sallie was on the attack.

"I know it and I admit it." I hoped that might end the matter, but it did not.

"I know you've handled cases for women — younger, pretty women — before and you've come through them all right. This Erika is different. You have this cynical attitude that you show the world but that's just your facade. You can't convince yourself that you are the cold passionless lawyer you think you are. That's why you love the Eben Jones thing. You're a romantic, and that's why Erika Williams is a threat to you, to me, and to us."

I was not prepared for this onslaught. I decided not to defend myself. Sallie knows me better than I know myself.

"Why do you think that?"

"She fits so neatly into the vision you have created for yourself. You know, white knight charging off to defend the damsel. I know . . . I was one of those damsels." She was referring to our past. She was so earnest. I could see how upset she had become.

"But Sallie, I wasn't married when we met, and I am older now."

"No man is older than fifteen emotionally when it comes to women. Any woman who thinks otherwise is a fool."

This behavior was out of character for Sallie. I had never heard her express her feelings quite so vehemently and I certainly did not want to argue the point. But my male instincts were aroused. At this point, the man usually says something like "I know what I'm doing." The opposite is true. Or the man attempts to shift responsibility to the woman with a statement like "Fine, if you don't trust me, I'll fire Erika as a client."

Most women know intuitively that if they express distrust, the man will stray. A woman's trust and the guilt associated with breach of that trust are two of the major reasons why men stay under control. Once trust is lost, there is no guilt nor any reason to toe the line. Despite the fact that my male senses were ready for combat, good sense prevailed. Believing that it was better to weather the storm, I said nothing.

I think Sallie knew that she had taken us to the brink. She smiled at me, reached across the table, and took my hand. "How come you snore in the concert hall and not in bed?"

We both laughed, relieved that the moment had passed. But the point she made was not soon forgotten.

24

Motive and opportunity are the criminologist's most basic considerations. Applying these to the Williams case was my next goal. I found it difficult to believe that Erika would risk her career for $50,000. She was educated as an accountant and financial planner and had made a substantial commitment to her career. I calculated her salary at approximately $40,000 and had it verified by my friend Jacki Snow. Why would a person earning $40,000 a year assume the risks associated with embezzlement for such a small sum?

Financial necessity is a compelling motive for embezzlement. In Erika's case, that need would have to be extreme for her to assume the risks of discovery, prosecution, loss of freedom, and termination of her career as a C.P.A. I had the investigator run a credit check on her. Her finances revealed that she was not in debt. Her Mastercard and American Express charges were always paid in full within the billing period. She had no other outstanding lines of credit and her automobile loan was paid down to a few hundred dollars. There was no financial pattern that indicated habits such as drugs, gambling, or conspicuous consumption. All of the financial information available indicated that she did not need money.

Some people need money just for the psychic gratification of having it. Often people who are reared in a deprived environment feel that they must have excess money to insulate themselves from financial hardship. Of course, they never feel they have enough. I have seen this behavior pattern in people who grew up during the Depression or who were desperately poor as children. They pay cash for everything. A background check of Erika's past revealed nothing abnormal regarding her family's financial situation. It was possible that she needed money to support a relative, or that she was being blackmailed. However, people will generally use their own money and credit for these purposes until the well runs dry before they resort to other means.

I simply could not bring myself to believe that Erika needed $50,000 so badly that she would risk everything that seemed to be important to her. But I know that with embezzlement, only the tip of the iceberg is visible. Most of my experience with embezzlement has been with businesses where employees or partners dipped into the till. In each case, a modest loss was discovered first. Financial inconsistencies were discovered when a partner or owner noticed a disbursement to an unknown creditor, a cash shortage, or a shortfall in the checking account. Further investigation by an internal or outside auditor uncovered additional inconsistencies, and the loss multiplied tenfold.

Although it was unlikely Erika would assume the risks of a $50,000 embezzlement, if that figure were multiplied by ten, the issue might no longer be clear cut. During our first meeting, Erika had mentioned "off-budget" funds that were not subject to the regular accounting system. If she had taken funds from those accounts, the University could not bring charges through the regular justice system.

Unless the stakes were a lot higher than $50,000, I could not convince myself that money could be a motive for Erika. While money is usually the motive for embezzlement, other reasons may motivate criminal behavior. The motives that seemed to fit in Erika's case were love, hate, revenge, power, and punishment. I wondered whether her involvement with John Harley could have any bearing on a motive to commit the crime.

I next turned my attention to the factor of opportunity. Harley was correct when he pointed out that embezzlement was not like murder. With murder, a time of death is established to limit the field of suspects who had the opportunity to be present at the scene of the crime. With embezzlement, normally it is not necessary to establish a precise time when the crime was committed. Embezzlement takes place over a longer period of time and usually involves a sequence of events. However, when the instrument of the crime is a computer, establishing the exact time of the crime is essential. If Erika was not physically present with the offending computer at the precise moment the crime was committed, then she might have an alibi. This still left open the possibilities of committing the crime using another computer and fooling the security program into believing that Erika's computer was giving the instruction to move the funds.

I decided to find the exact time when the funds were removed from the university account. Then I would try to pinpoint the locations of Erika and everyone who might have benefited from the theft—or Erika's removal from the University.

None of the information I had gleaned from the police reports mentioned the exact time of the transfer of funds, yet I was sure this information was available. The police had gone to great lengths to establish Erika's whereabouts during the evening in question. I therefore assumed that the transfer took place between 5:00 and the time Polly Morrat closed the office around midnight on April 15th.

It was time to see if Jacki Snow had been able to get the requested information. After eliciting a promise to write her sister's will, she revealed that she had attended a meeting about the security system. She explained something about a reference diskette, an internal clock, and a clock driver program, most of which was lost on me. She probably got technical with me to impress me and justify the "fee" she was extracting. After her lengthy explanation, I asked for the exact time the transfer took place.

"It can't be pinpointed exactly. The bottom line is that someone was messing with the time. They called me in to verify their findings independently. It was really exciting. They were able to reconstruct what happened. Now they are more convinced than ever that your girl committed the crime."

"How can you mess with time?" I asked.

"Are you sure you're a lawyer? You don't mess with time; you mess with the instrument that measures time. You know like when the legislature has to pass a budget or something by midnight on a certain date. Midnight approaches, they just sent the sergeant-at-arms up to the balcony to pull the plug on the electric clock before midnight. Time doesn't stop. The instrument measuring time stops. The same thing with the computer. According to the security records, the transfer took place at exactly 7:30 P.M. plus a few seconds."

"When did the actual transfer take place?"

"They think between 8:30 and 8:50, more likely 8:30. You see, they think Erika stopped the clock. The original print-out of the security information had 7:30, but the transfer took place at about 8:30 because the clock was stopped for about an hour. The way it was found was at 8:31 according to the computer's clock electronic data came in from Minneapolis. The transmission report returned to Minneapolis had 7:31 on it. It could not have been 7:31 in both the Eastern and Central time zones. The sender in Minnesota called to verify that the transmission had been properly received. The internal clock was re-set at 8:50. This was after the person

[93

who was supposed to be on duty at the computer center was located and had a chance to correct the time."

I tried to digest this new information. It was time to have a long talk with Erika.

25

"I violated your instructions. There was much ground to cover so I hired Rick Place to do some of the investigation."

I was not sure how Erika Williams might take this since she had indicated that she wanted me to do the investigation myself. She nodded her assent. I reviewed all I had learned from the various people I interviewed.

"Did John Harley make a commitment to help you with your defense?" I asked nonchalantly.

She thought for a moment. "John made no such commitment. In fact, since I was asked to leave the University, we have not been together . . . if you know what I mean."

"Do you believe there may be a problem?"

"I know married men run for cover at the first sign of trouble. Still, I am a little disappointed. I thought I knew him. I can understand his not wanting to be seen with me, what with my leaving work under a cloud, but he's shut himself off completely. When I think back over the months preceding the present unpleasantness. . ."

I found her choice of words very revealing. She characterized the matter as the "present unpleasantness." It was the first indication that she was just like other citizen-type criminal defendants who refuse to admit that they have been charged with a crime.

"There were signs that he was no longer interested. He communicated with me less often. On a number of occasions he cancelled our meetings at the last minute. Once he said he had to take his wife to visit her children for the weekend. That Thursday night I saw his wife at the grocery store buying a whole shopping cart of food, including lots of fresh vegetables."

"Fresh vegetables?"

"Yes—fresh vegetables. You don't buy lots of fresh vegetables on Thursday and leave them in the refrigerator over the weekend for use on Monday night. You might take some snacks—a can of soda, a bag of chips, or a box of cookies—in the car, but you wouldn't take fresh vegetables on a trip, would you? He was either staying home with her or going away alone."

Erika's powers of observation and deduction were obviously well developed. I would never have thought of the implications of a lover's spouse purchasing fresh vegetables. But I was not having an affair and would therefore not look for such signs.

"Anyway, I began to be suspicious. Suspicion leads to distrust. You start looking at every action for signs that the relationship is over. You start reading things into the most common words and phrases. It becomes an obsession. You begin a neat little laundry list of reasons why you were not in as deep as you may have thought. Reasons like 'oh, down deep I don't really love him' ... 'it would never work anyway' ... 'he is not that special' ... 'I can live just fine without him' and 'I'm too good to be wasting my time waiting for him.' Your suspicion that it is over becomes a self-fulfilling prophecy. You get so suspicious, and you build such a strong wall around your heart that the relationship is bound to crumble. Suspicion is a terrible thing."

It was the first time that Erika had talked with me about anything personal. I found her use of the word "heart" especially interesting. The overriding impression I had received from others' descriptions of her was that she was all business and had no heart.

"Well, did Harley make a commitment to help you? He seemed concerned about you when he was here."

"Don't be fooled. John came here to test you. He likes to go into the lion's den to let you know he is not afraid of you. He wants to see how you react. He weighs your words carefully. He measures you. He decides how to break down your defenses, then, he attacks, sometimes with threats, but most often with well chosen words." There was an uncharacteristic bitterness in her voice.

"And, in your case, Erika?"

"Kind words and poetry..." Erika's voice had a faraway sound. She seemed sad for an instant. Then she made a very obvious decision to change the subject.

"What can I do now to help with the defense?" She was all business again.

I explained the importance of establishing her location during the evening of April 15th. She told me that she had left the office after she asked Polly Morrat to obtain the diagnostic diskette.

"When did you return the diskette to Polly?"

"I didn't return it directly to her. I left it in her 'in' basket by the secretarial pool when I went to the dinner."

"What dinner?" This was the first I had any indication that she had left the office that evening.

"The Distinguished Donor Award Dinner for Judge Herbert Wibbleton held that night at the Inn on campus. I went because I was invited by the judge. His daughter, Jessica, and I have been friends since I don't know when. When she heard I worked here on campus she called and asked if I'd go. Then I received a formal invitation. I had not seen her for a couple of years. I sat at their table that evening. Of course, the judge sat at the head table, but I was with Jessica, her brother, his wife, Jessica's sister and the judge's brother from Rochester at the table right up front. You know Judge Wibbleton. A famous lawyer, made a lot of money. Gave the money for the new wing on the liberal arts building."

I vaguely remembered reading something about it in the paper when they had the ground breaking ceremony. I also remember the article about the judge in the paper after he was chosen to receive this year's award. The University certainly knows how to reward its benefactors.

"Well," she continued, "I attended the dinner. I was there the whole time. It was over at about 10:00 when one of the important guests had to leave — a former governor had to catch a late plane — also a friend of the judge."

"What did you do then?"

"I had left my computer and lights on in the office, so I went back to turn them off, but that might have been as late as midnight. You see, after the dinner the official party was invited for a drink with the president of the University. I tagged along with Jessica and we caught up on each other's lives over the next two hours. We went first to the special reception room in the Inn, but the president didn't show up. The official host was embarrassed and he made some phone calls. It seemed that the president was still in Harrisburg. The official host made a few more calls and a senior vice-president was trotted out to do the honors. I know that Jessica, her brother — the whole family could verify my whereabouts the entire evening. I never left Jessica. She even went back to my office with me. I wanted to show her where I worked, although it's not very impressive."

I thought about this turn of events for a moment. I was puzzled that the university police had nothing in their reports about Erika's attendance at the dinner. If it was crucial to their case that Erika be placed at her computer at 8:30 P.M., then they would have made more of an effort. Hundreds of people would have seen her at the dinner.

"Erika, when you went back to your office with Jessica, did you use the back stairs to the office?"

"Yes. Why?"

"Did you see anyone either in the stairs or in the office?"

She hesitated. "Did someone see us?"

I did not respond immediately.

"Were the lights on in the main part of the office?"

"Yes, I think so — or I would have had to feel my way in the hallway for the light switch. The only light would have been from the 'Exit' sign. I don't remember doing that, though I could have."

"Was Polly Morrat still in the offices when you were there with Jessica?"

"I did not see her."

"Did you leave the dinner table at any time?"

"No, I didn't, although I wanted to go to the ladies room. It was right down the hall."

"Why didn't you go?"

[97

"I asked Jessica if she had to go. She did, but they were going to show a video of the ground breaking ceremony, artist's renderings of the new wing and a brief statement of gratitude taped earlier by the president. They had television monitors all around so the people all could see. When the lights went out, I asked Jessica if she wanted to join me, but she thought it would not be appropriate for her to leave. It might have been misconstrued. You see, Judge Wibbleton is very sensitive to appearances. At that point I decided that it probably would be better if I didn't go either. Jessica and I went to the ladies room on the way to the reception room after the dinner."

I did not pursue it further. I asked Erika to supply the names and telephone numbers of the people at her table that evening. I also asked whether it was all right to disclose Erika's trouble to Jessica. She hesitated, but when she saw me raising my index finger, poised to lecture her, she nodded.

"Erika, have we met before? I can't help thinking that we have. It's been nagging me since the first time you came into the office."

She looked at me suspiciously. I decided not to defend or explain the question.

"I don't think we have ever met face to face. I do remember seeing you once at a presentation you gave a couple of years ago... on campus. I'm embarrassed to say that I can't recall a thing you said, though I remember I thought at the time it made perfect sense."

I paused for a moment then dismissed the thought. It probably was not important. I carefully reviewed my notes of the interview and the list of questions I had composed. I toyed with the idea of asking her whether she committed the crime, but I decided against it for the time being.

"Erika, is there anyone at the University who might have benefited from your being dismissed from your job or from the fact that criminal charges are being pressed against you?" The question surprised her a little. "Is there a person who wants your job? Did you know too much about those secret accounts you mentioned? Was John Harley trying to close out the relationship by setting you up to take the fall?"

She sat thinking for a minute. "I don't think there is anyone waiting in the wings to take my job. As for the secret accounts, I don't know any more about them than I did when I left the offices after I was suspended. As for John, he certainly has it within him to do something like that. When pushed to the limit, men are capable of anything—extreme brutality and cruelty, even murder—it's biological."

A horrible incident from my early days as a lawyer suddenly resurfaced. I had lost a wonderful client to an estranged husband's insane notion that his wife loved another man. I was inexperienced with law and life. I never saw the bullet coming. It has been a heavy burden, and I have never been able to put the shock and horror of her death behind me.

My distress must have been visible. Erika paused and looked deeply into my eyes. For the first time she displayed some sensitivity. "It happened to you? A client?" she asked tenderly.

"Fifteen years ago."

Rather than pursue it, she continued with her description of her relationship with Harley. "All he had to say was that he wanted the relationship behind him. I would have been crushed, but I wouldn't want to hang onto something that isn't right. Surely he knew I'd never make trouble for him."

"No man knows that—it's biological," I commented.

"But don't you think framing me for embezzlement is going a little far?"

"No, not if it forces you to resign and leave town in disgrace. If you tried to make trouble for him, you'd be a charged or convicted felon. The public and his wife would then expect you to make up lies, cause trouble and blame everything and everyone but yourself for what happened."

"I never looked at it like that. Maybe you're right."

After the interview ended, I felt better. Erika was acting more like a citizen-type criminal defendant.

26

Having had many of my earlier concerns about Erika resolved, I approached the case with renewed vigor. The major source of my optimism was her alibi. If Erika was not in her office at 8:30 P.M. on April 15th, then she could not have committed the crime. Of course, it was still possible that she could have programmed her computer to execute the transaction. According to Jacki Snow, the police were satisfied that Erika was in her office and that she had reset the computer's clock after she established her alibi by being with Polly Morrat at 7:30. I worried that the police might discover that Erika was not in the offices at the time they supposed the crime to have been committed.

I didn't entirely trust Jacki Snow. She had little to gain from cooperating with me. True, I had agreed to write wills for her mother and sister, but she owed her job to the University. If the powers-that-be discovered that she was helping the defense, she ran the risk of being transferred to the university hog farm at Skunk Hollow where she would spend the next ten years entering pig propogation records into the computer.

Over the years I have made a conscious effort to fully develop my sense of skepticism. Although I have also tried to seem positive and easy going, my skeptical attitude somehow always shows. This has been detrimental to my career. I have observed other attorneys successfully balance a very aggressive attitude with a smooth, ingratiating desk-side manner. From a marketing standpoint, the ability to portray aggressiveness and friendliness simultaneously is a definite asset. Clients want their attorneys to be hard as nails to their opponents, but soft and friendly to them. Unfortunately, my skepticism usually prevails. I try to console myself with the belief that being critical of everyone and every situation has never let me down when pursuing evidence and measuring the people involved in a case.

I strongly suspected that the district attorney was holding back information about Erika. I could not believe that the police hadn't pinpointed Erika's whereabouts for the entire evening. I reconstructed the scene, placing each of the *dramatis personae*.

Polly Morrat was in the office that evening working on her personal taxes, from 5:00 until a little before midnight. She left the offices about 8:15 and returned about 9:00. Terri Parsons was in the office at the same approximate times except for her dinner hour. John Harley was careful to place himself with his wife and friends at 7:30, but had no alibi for the time the crime actually was committed at 8:30. By his own admission he was in the offices at approximately 8:30 and he admitted being near Erika's office at about that time. Someone else, not presently known to me, with a key to the back stairs could have entered the offices without the knowledge of either Polly Morrat or Terri Parsons. Once inside the inner offices, the crime could have been committed by this mysterious suspect "X".

I turned my attention to John Harley. He had both motive and opportunity to commit the crime. He had access to all the codes including Erika's personal password and knew how to retrieve information and make transfers. Did he have the ability to change the clock in the computer? Of course, if he had changed the clock in the computer, he would have arranged an alibi for 8:30 P.M. when the crime actually took place.

I called Polly Morrat. She answered politely, and I identified myself. She said she was not sitting at the number she had given me. A warning bell sounded in my brain. Terri Parsons had told me that Polly had a separate line that rang at her desk. Someone else planned to listen to our conversation. Rather than ask my original question, I decided to use another tack.

"Polly, thanks for taking my call. I have just a couple of questions. Was anyone besides John Harley, Terri Parsons, and Erika Williams present in the office the night of April 15th?"

She paused for a moment. "Yes, my husband came by to pick up some things I had for him, and the maintenance people were in to clean up, empty waste baskets . . . that's all I remember."

Her reference to her husband's picking up "some things" meant that someone was on the line listening. In our previous conversation, she had clearly stated that her husband was picking up their tax returns to take to the post office. Apparently she had not disclosed that to the police or her superiors in fear that she might be criticized for doing her personal taxes on university time. I concluded that the police, or John Harley, or both were on the line listening.

"Polly, it seems that the records at the university indicate that the embezzlement took place exactly at 7:30 P.M. According to your affidavit and what you told me, Erika was with you at exactly 7:30. I just want to verify that."

"Yes. The punchcard at the computer substation has 7:29.54 on it. I was only out of the office a minute . . . not enough time for Miss Williams to leave my desk, go to her office, enter the proper commands in the proper sequence and return to my desk. I am absolutely positive of that."

"Thanks very much for your cooperation. Goodbye, Polly."

I decided to test Erika's alibi. I called Jessica Wibbleton and identified myself. I asked if she had heard from Erika in the last several months. She reported that she had not spoken to her, but both she and her father each received a nicely written "bread and butter" note from her. Her proper rememberance of their hospitality certainly fit into the emerging picture of Erika Williams. I explained that I was Erika's counsel and I had some questions to ask her, though I did not expect her to answer them without verifying my authority with Erika. I suggested she call Erika at home to confirm I had permission to make certain inquiries concerning the evening and night of April 15th. I heard concern in Jessica's voice.

"Erika is fine. However, she needs your help and understanding." I was certain that would ensure Jessica's compliance.

A few minutes later Marie buzzed me saying that a Miss Wibbleton was on the line.

"Erika told me what happened. She gave me your office number. However, I have a question for you. When did Erika first see you?"

"At a program I gave on campus. She doesn't remember the topic and neither do I."

She was satisfied that my authority and identity were authenticated. "How can I help?"

I asked about her recollection of the events of April 15th. According to Jessica, Erika came to the dinner just as the cocktail hour was completed. Judge Wibbleton had arranged for Erika to be seated with Jessica and the rest of the family near the head table of dignitaries. Jessica thought that the people were seated and the program started at about 7:45. Since one of the dignitaries had to catch a plane to Washington, some of the program was presented while people were still eating. Jessica recalled that Erika was at the table during the entire dinner. After dinner they all went to the reception room at the Inn. On the way, they made a detour to the ladies room and joined everyone waiting for the president. The party broke up about 11:00 P.M. Erika took Jessica back to her office in the administration building. They went up the back stairs gaining entry with Erika's key. Erika went directly into her office. Jessica recalled that Erika played with her computer for a minute or two, turned it off, turned off the radio and lights and they left. Erika did not show Jessica the other offices. They went back to the Inn for a drink and parted company at about 1:15 A.M. Except for the "thank you" note she had not heard from Erika since that night but that did not strike Jessica as unusual.

Jessica explained that they often did not see each other or call between Christmases. They became fast friends at a ski party over the Christmas holidays when they were in college. On that occasion they made a solemn pledge to call each other on Christmas Day for the rest of their lives. So far, the pledge had been honored even when Jessica was aboard a ship in the Caribbean the Christmas before last.

"Would your father remember Erika being present?"

"Yes, I am sure that he would. You see, he always remembers those in attendance at programs doing him honor. He would be a good witness. But, I must tell you there is a better witness than either my father or me."

"And who might that be?"

"It's not a who, it's a what. A video was made of the entire program. I am sure that Erika is visible the entire time. My father has the video. I can make a copy of it and send it to you — Federal Express, if you like."

I thanked Jessica for her offer.

27

It was nearly 5:00 when I finished my conversation with Jessica. I went into the conference room, sat in one of the chairs, and propped my feet up on the table. Marie hates it when I do that. The church across the street started chiming the hour. It is part of Marie's daily routine to time her departure so that the door closes behind her as the fifth chime sounds. I instinctively took my feet off the table. Marie appeared at the door, keys in hand.

"It's okay, Marie, you can take off. I'll keep my feet off the table until you reach the elevator, and the door is closed. After that, who knows?" I smiled.

She came into the conference room, placed her keys on the table, sank into one of the chairs, took of her shoes, and put her feet on the table in a rather unladylike fashion. "Okay," she said, "let's have it."

I brought her up to date on my investigation. It was almost 5:45 when I finished.

"It's too pat. We're missing something."

I noticed how she said "we" rather than "you." It is a real comfort knowing that even though I am a sole practitioner, I am not alone. I trust Marie's judgment.

"Like what?"

"Well, for one thing, even though the cops are not the mental giants they think they are, they would not be content to rely on Morrat's statement as definite proof that Erika was at her computer at 8:30. They must have something else. And they couldn't possibly be dumb enough to believe that we still think that the crime was committed at 7:30 even though you tried to slick Polly Morrat and whoever else was listening."

"Could someone be trying to frame Erika for this crime?" I asked.

"It sure looks that way. The signature cards are evidence of a frame-job, not to mention the diskette with the codes which were literally planted in her office in that pot. And, of course, there was the search which conveniently revealed an account number where the missing money was located. All the evidence points to a frame-up."

"Marie, remember that coin shop case we had about five years ago?"

"Cappy's Coins. Yes, of course. Embezzlement. By the time we were through, Cappy's partner didn't have two nickels to rub together. Pardon the allusion, I couldn't resist. Cappy cleaned him out. So?"

"Well, Marie, if you think back, the partner came to us after a friend of his bought a coin from Cappy . . . a silver dollar . . . and the receipt was not recorded in the company books and the deposit book did not include the money from the transaction. It was a small loss, but the partner became suspicious and he began to investigate. As the investigation continued, the losses mounted from a few hundred dollars to tens of thousands. Remember?"

"Yes . . . now that you mention it, there was that insurance agent, what's-his-name. You know, the missing premium check — the house that got struck by lightning and the owner had paid for the policy, but the insurance company had no record. It turned out that the agent had been stealing from the insurance company for years."

We both sat there thinking for a few moments.

"Looking at it logically," Marie ventured, "embezzlement seems to fit into a pattern. The person takes a small amount and gets away with it. No one is the wiser. Then, encouraged by past success, the person goes back again and again, and the bites get larger and larger . . . until the person's luck runs out or they get so greedy that the crime cannot help but be uncovered."

"You're right, Marie. That's one type of embezzlement. It starts out small . . . as a sort of cottage industry perpetrated by a person who is not a professional. The criminal is not intent on stealing a lot of money at first. It just gets out of hand and the stakes get higher as the thefts continue. It's usually an employee or partner. But what if the embezzlement is a business? If it's a business enterprise, the thieves know that they can't get away with stealing money indefinitely. They would go for the big hit — a home run, cover their tracks, and move on to the next victim. The professional thief knows that you cannot return to the chicken house a second time — the farmer will be waiting."

Marie was skeptical. "Yes, but at the University, there are so many controls."

"But Marie, that's why the University is perfect . . . especially for the big hit. You see, it is a muscle-bound giant. It is so complex that a person with the right tools could do the crime, set up someone to take the fall, and be gone before they even knew that the money was missing."

"But they didn't get the money."

"Marie, they didn't get the $50,000, but they got someone to take the fall. What if it was intended to be a big hit — say three million dollars? One thing we know about embezzlement is that only the tip of the iceberg is visible. Isn't $50,000 a good insurance policy? Even if we can prove that it was a frame-job, and get Erika off the hook, the real thief is long gone."

Marie thought about it for a moment. A strange look crossed her face. It was as if she'd had a revelation.

"The same could apply to Erika. Suppose she's the professional. Suppose she took millions and then arranged for herself to be framed. She hired us to discover the frame, defend her in court, get her off. Our role in her artfully conceived plan is to prove in court that she was framed. We do so. She is acquitted. We earn our ten grand. She tearfully thanks us. Everyone — the University, the police, the public — feels guilty about what 'we the people' did to poor little Erika. She resigns quietly. Everyone would understand why she couldn't stay after what happened. In fact, everyone is relieved she is leaving so that the unpleasantness of trying an innocent young woman can be forgotten. She leaves with the money. Her investment: ten thousand to us, fifty thousand that she gave back, and ten weeks of risk while we unravel the frame-job. She walks away scott-free with however many millions. She uses the money to go to law school and gets admitted to the bar. As a lawyer she can steal money from people legally. The perfect crime."

Marie was certainly more suspicious than I. I would never have thought of the case in that light. As I was pondering the possibility, Marie got up to leave.

"And please. . ." Marie reminded me, "take your feet off the table."

As was the custom, I did as ordered, until I heard the elevator door close.

28

On the way home that evening I wondered why my musings over the lives of James Petrikin, Charles Perrow, and Eben Jones seemed to involve only the Bellefonte attorney. My fantasies rarely included Perrow or Jones. After giving it some thought, I decided that I identified myself more closely with James Petrikin than with Attorney Perrow or Eben Jones. As for Eben Jones, I had not a shred of belief that I could relate to his life as a runaway slave. Although all practicing attorneys are basically alike in their perspectives, factors such as time, age, and social and political differences arise which make it difficult for them to relate to one another. I could not imagine what it might have been like to be a lawyer in the South during the early part of the nineteenth century.

James Petrikin was different. Although we lived more than a century and a half apart, I walked the same streets he had and tried cases in the same courtroom he had. I may even have used the same chair in the attorneys' room at court. These were tangible links between us. Petrikin was a logical choice for the fantasies spawned by my frustrations with practicing law.

James Petrikin lived and worked at a time when most lawyers were sole practitioners. Fathers, sons, and brothers may have practiced law at the same location, but each lawyer had his own clients and performed all manner of legal services in the community. Women did not yet practice law. In the early part of the nineteenth century, there were no estate planners, merger and acquisition specialists, bond counselors, or malpractice lawyers. And there were no gigantic highly specialized law firms. I knew Petrikin to be a sole practitioner and a generalist from reading the indexes in the courthouse. His name was listed as counsel for both criminal and civil cases, he wrote deeds, probated estates, filed partnership papers, served on many specially appointed boards and was named as trustee for charitable associations. I envied him. I wished that I too could have enjoyed the status that came with being a lawyer in those days.

The law is different now — Sally was right. I love the law but dislike lawyers. I declined so many after-work drink invitations from other lawyers that they stopped inviting me years ago. I do not play golf or tennis, and I do not drive a Mercedes with a clever little vanity license plate that says "ESQ" or "L A LAW." Instead of gaining the respect of my colleagues as a competent independent like Petrikin, I am considered an eccentric. Knowing lawyers as I do, I know I am the butt of many jokes around the poker table at the country club.

I first started practicing law in a firm as an associate, and I was unprepared for all the office politics involved. Young associates who fished in Montana, played golf at well-known courses, and knew which wine to order were the ones noticed by the senior partners. I would be assigned research at the Supreme Court Library while they had the privilege of carrying the senior partner's briefcase to court or attending meetings with important clients. I sat in the office and drafted reams of boring pleadings while they were assigned to investigate interesting cases involving sex and violence.

I convinced myself that mastering the trade was more important. I kept my shoulder to the wheel, working long hours for the firm, studying the law, and learning as much as I could. I did not understand that when the other young associates took the partners to lunch, played golf, and stroked clients' egos, they also were polishing their skills. I learned too late that mastering the law is only part of being a successful lawyer. Self-marketing is as important to monetary success as legal knowledge. For the savvy young associate, playing tennis once with a client at the tennis club was worth more to the firm than two artfully worded, carefully reasoned legal briefs. Those young associates knew that clients do not read or understand legal briefs. Clients do understand the ambiance and comraderie of the tennis club. Knowing when to order an Amstel light beer or an Absolut vodka martini on the rocks with a twist was more important than knowing when to file a writ of *mandamus* or a writ of *prohibition*. When it came to advancement in the firm, the lawyers with good backhand strokes and winning smiles rose faster.

At the end of my first year, there was a party in honor of the most senior partner who was retiring after 30 years of active practice with the firm. This happened before I met Sallie, and being limited in my social acumen, I attended alone. The other unmarried male associates were accompanied by attractive, charming young women, each dressed in appropriate attire designed to reveal her best physical attributes. Long shapely legs and full upright breasts made important impressions on the male senior partners.

At dinner, the next most senior partner toasted the retiring partner, elloquently paying homage to his years of devoted service. He thanked him on behalf of all of us for his steady, guiding hand over the years. He was to be "of counsel" to the firm. He was assured that he could retain his office, which happened to be the biggest, with the largest most impressive desk and a spectacular view of the city square below.

The celebration lasted well into the night. On the way back to my apartment, I stopped at my office. The retiring partner's office light was on and I peeked in. He was sitting at his desk, head down, crying softly. I took care not to make my presence known and quickly left the offices. I did not understand such a powerful man with an illustrious career reacting like that.

Over the next several weeks, the retired partner came by the offices regularly. All the associates were respectful toward him but less quick to please. They did not invite him for drinks after work nor did they seek his advice. His former secretary did his bidding only if it fit into her schedule. Each of us — associates, employees, and partners — intuitively knew that he no longer held power over us. Our futures were not in his hands. There was respect toward him, but it was respect without fear.

Before he retired, the firm's copy of the *Wall Street Journal* was on his desk first thing every day. One morning he came into my office searching for a copy. He looked as if he had aged ten years. His collar was not crisply pressed and he needed a haircut. The old self-confidence had left his eyes.

"I'm taking the wife on a month long trip to Maui. We always wanted to spend time there. Now, I guess we have our chance," he told me half-apologetically.

During his absence, the new most senior partner took over the retired partner's office with the large desk and the spectacular view of the square below. Everyone moved up a notch on the firm's letterhead.

I knew then that I would never be a senior partner in a law firm. I had no desire to claw my way to the top, only to be tossed out onto the trash-heap of retirement with its resulting loss of power and status. I opted instead for a sole practice without power and, in the eyes of other modern-day attorneys, without status.

James Petrikin and the mystery surrounding Eben Jones was a refuge from the loneliness of sole practice. I wondered how Petrikin might have dealt with the issues of the Erika Williams case. I thought I knew how he would have dealt with the Eben Jones matter. I was sure that he would have honored his commitment to assist in securing the freedom of Eben Jones by marshalling what evidence he could in support of Perrow's writ of *habeus corpus*.

Petrikin probably did with the Jones case just as I did with the Williams case. He was given certain facts, and based upon those facts, he conducted his investigation.

Petrikin was much younger than Judge Burnside. Still, he was a lawyer and although he was not Burnside's equal in age or status, he would not have hesitated to discover what light Burnside could shed on the matter. Petrikin would have approached the judge at the most opportune moment to question him about whether he remembered Eben Jones. Perhaps it would have been at a lodge meeting or a public celebration; or perhaps on a hot summer day in the cool shade of the elm trees in front of the courthouse in Bellefonte.

"Ah, Judge, it is a most uncomfortable day. These trees cast a shadow that hardly provides much respite. In my younger days, I would have repaired to the banks of the Bald Eagle to frolic at the rapids."

"Mr. Petrikin, I remember well my early days and how that stream's cool water provided so much youthful pleasure. I assure you that it is hotter than the devil's own lair in chambers. On days such as these I fear that my judicial sense is difficult to harness, and I can render no decisions that will be fair. The heat here on the Square is not so oppressive as that in chambers." The judge fanned himself slowly with his hat.

"Judge, do you recall a negro by the name of Eben Jones?" Petrikin asked the question without having made the proper preparation and without explaining the reason for the inquiry. No sooner had the words escaped his lips than he recognized his error. Now he would have to explain the matter and try to enlist the assistance of the judge.

"This is a strange question, especially on such a hot day. Pray, Mr. Petrikin, explain yourself."

"Judge Burnside, I have received an inquiry from an attorney in Nelson County, Virginia, asking me to obtain evidence about a man, Eben Jones — a negro — who claims to have been a resident of this county in 1819. One of this man Jones' recollections is that he assisted in the raising of your house on the Bald Eagle. I thought that perhaps you might remember him."

"And, Mr. Petrikin, if I do?"

"Then, sir, it would be evidence that he was in fact here in Centre County. It could be construed as evidence of his residence."

[111]

The judge thought for a moment, carefully weighing his words.

"It would seem, sir, that if I had a recollection of his working at my house on the Bald Eagle, that would hardly be probative evidence of his residency. You know well that the Bald Eagle is used by many boatmen and the road nearby by horsemen and those on foot as a main line of transportation. Many idle persons—those down on their luck—follow that trail and stream to the Susquehanna. They stop at nearby towns and settlements searching for a few pence. They say they are here to stay the season and they will do honest labor for food and shelter and a few pence. We hired dozens of these laborers every season. Negroes, Indians, immigrants... most work for a few weeks until their first pay. They drift back to the stream and river or the trails to continue their wanderings. They could hardly be considered residents. If they attempt to stay and do not work then the Overseers of the Poor prosecute them and send them on to the next county. After all, that is how many come to this county; they are banished by a neighboring counties.

"But in answer to your question, I know of no negro named Eben Jones. I know few people of color. The only one I know by name is Dalila who cooked for us around that time."

The judge's tone was abrupt. It was clear to Petrikin that further inquiry would be fruitless. The best he could hope to achieve was to beat a hasty retreat and continue the investigation elsewhere. Before he could escape, the Judge continued, lecturing him.

"Take care, Mr. Petrikin, that your sense of Christian charity is not abused. There are those in slaveholding states who use unsuspecting people like yourself to track down runaway slaves. They make inquiries and claim to be helping secure the freedom of family members. Information is provided as an act of charity and conscience. Then these people use the information for the purpose of capturing runaways. Sir, this is a kind and gentle valley. Beyond those mountains to the south and west, there is a world that does not hold the same values as we do here. Take care that your crusade to help in the establishment of the freedom of Eben Jones does not result in the enslavement of your ethics and ideals, or your soul."

Petrikin bowed slightly, tipped his hat and, begging the pardon of his honor, Judge Burnside, left the judge standing in the shade of the tall elm trees in front of the courthouse.

29

By the time I reached home that evening, both Marie and Judge Burnside had given me plenty of food for thought. When I opened the door, I was greeted with a less than enthusiastic welcome. Sallie had expected me at 6:00. I was more than an hour late, and dinner was ruined.

Before I married Sallie, several of my more experienced friends had cautioned me about my habit of being on time for every appointment and honoring every commitment. I considered this trait a virtue. My friends viewed it as a character flaw. They warned me that keeping to a schedule and being on time for every meal or appointment would lead to serious trouble. If I established a pattern of being late, when I honored a deadline for dinner, people would be complimented and I would be thanked. And more importantly, if I happened to be late, I would only be meeting their expectations. Try as I might, I could never wrap my mind around their logic.

I approached the matter differently. By being predictably prompt I believed I would build a huge reservoir of goodwill. Then if I occasionally disappointed, it would be forgiven based on past exemplary conduct and punctuality.

Nothing could be further from the truth. My predictability haunts me at every turn. When I am late for a social engagement with Sallie's garden club, instead of being thankful that I am there at all, Sallie chastizes me for being insensitive to her friends. If I am late for dinner, or forget an appointment, it is so uncharacteristic it arouses all sorts of suspicions. Before I realized the wisdom of my friends' purposeful unpredictability, it was too late. My behavior patterns had already been established to Sallie's satisfaction. I sentenced myself to a lifetime of predictability and punctuality.

Though being so predictable is difficult, it can have its advantages. Once I was trapped in the elevator at the office building. When I did not appear at a restaurant at the appointed hour, within five minutes, Sallie had tracked me down, called maintenance, and had me released. On balance though, punctuality and predictability have proven to be serious disadvantages for me.

Since Sallie is so accustomed to my arrival at the appointed hour, she was doubly disappointed and upset when I was late that evening. I had been so involved with my discussion of the Williams case with Marie and my fantasies of James Petrikin, that I had lost track of the time. It was a perfectly innocent lapse, but Sallie seemed to overreact. I should have said something like "I'm sorry I'm late, dear" and given her a short sweet kiss. That would have been sufficient. Instead I made an unpardonable blunder that only a novice husband would make. I told her that she need not worry, I was not with my client Erika Williams.

Women view that kind of statement differently than men. I should not have said what I did, but I meant nothing by it. It immediately raised the issues of "the other woman," guilty conscience, marital trust, and suspicion of the worst kind. I exposed a raw nerve for Sallie. "And why would you make a statement like that? Do you have something to hide? Is THAT woman dominating your thoughts?"

Having said that, Sallie may have wished to retract it. Now self-esteem and honor were at issue. Once the gauntlet was tossed, it was not so easy to retreat. I was caught on the horns of a dilemma. I could deny that I was doing anything wrong, or I could evade further confrontation by mobilizing my legal skills of obfuscation. I tried to weigh the consequences of each course of action. Denial would make a clear statement of innocence, but I would sound defensive. On the other hand, if I changed the subject, I could avoid an argument that neither of us could win. I opted for the latter because if offered the best chance of defusing a dangerous situation.

"Dear, I'm sorry I'm late. Let's go out . . . or better yet, let's call for a pizza and stay here."

She eyed me suspiciously, realizing that I was changing the subject. However, Sallie is an immensely practical woman. "Let's go out. Dinner is ruined. If we order in, I'd have to clean up the ruined dinner and the one we got. This way, I only clean up once."

Over dinner, I was not certain that the unpleasantness had actually passed. After her second glass of wine, I told Sallie that the reason I was late was that Marie and I went over all the details of my case. I explained that I valued Marie's advice and that during office hours the crush of everyday business did not permit us to discuss cases.

My stars protected me that evening. At the restaurant, Marie and her husband passed our table as they were leaving. Marie commented that she had stayed late to discuss a case and since she did not have time to prepare dinner, her husband took her out. She joked about remembering to stay late at least once a month so her husband would take her out more often.

Sallie was a little embarrassed. She smiled, reached across the table, and took my hand. "I'm sorry for jumping down your throat like that. . ." Then she paused. "but why did you say you weren't with Erika Williams?"

This time it was only an inquiry.

"It's a male thing. There was nothing to it. I didn't mean to be defensive or to question your confidence in me. I was just a male defending himself. That's all."

Sallie seemed satisfied. Unlike many women I have known, she is more accepting of an explanation couched in male-female terms. She understands quite clearly that men and women view their worlds through biologically focused eyes and that trouble can arise when differences in perspective are involved. Although peace was restored, I imbedded the event in my memory, hoping not to make the same mistake again.

[115

30

True to her word, Jessica Wibbleton sent me a copy of the video of the awards dinner held on April 15th. Attached to the cassette was a note saying "Please do everything you can for my friend Erika."

I took the cassette home to watch it on my video cassette recorder in the comfort of my own den. I told Sallie that I had important legal research to do.

"Are you sure you're not going to watch something X-rated?" she asked. "If you are, I demand my right to stay and watch."

"No such luck, Sallie."

I did not think I would be violating any confidences by permitting her to watch, so I invited her to join me. After all, it was a public event. I figured that she would be bored within a few minutes and leave me alone.

From the beginning of the tape it was clear that the video camera was recording from the back of the banquet room, some distance from the head table. It was difficult to capture the features on the faces of those in attendance, but some people were still recognizable. The main object of the tape seemed to be to document the overall event. No attempt was made by the operator to change the lense for close-ups of the participants.

The program opened with the master of ceremonies looking at his watch and calling the assemblage to be seated. "Ladies and Gentlemen, we have all enjoyed the cocktail hour. There will be more time for us to renew acquaintances and make new friends after dinner. It is now almost 7:45. Since the Governor, one of our honored guests, must catch a plane to Washington this evening, please be seated so that we can begin the program."

I wanted to time the program so I set a spare watch to 7:45.

"That's Erika," Sallie commented, "up at that front table with her back to the camera."

I had some difficulty locating her even though Sallie had pointed her out.

"When did this take place?" Sallie asked.

"April 15th. Why?"

"Just curious. You see, Erika has a bright blue dress with white trim."

"So?"

"Well, at this latitude on the Earth's surface, that dress is inappropriate so early in the season. See how the other women are wearing more subdued colors — greys, dark browns, purples? You know . . . late winter colors. Even the young woman at the table with Erika is wearing a dark green dress. Erika is the only one wearing a bright color . . . except, of course, the waitresses in white."

I had not noticed, but Erika was clearly visible in the crowd.

"Well, Sallie, what does that tell you?"

She thought about it for a moment. I could tell that she was concerned that she not sound derogatory. Erika might not be "the other woman," but Sallie still had certain territorial rights that needed to be asserted from time to time.

"She wore that dress so that she would be clearly visible in the crowd. You know, so that she would be noticed. She kind of sticks out like a sore thumb . . . and of course she is very attractive — to men, not women."

"So?"

"Well, if I were in a crowd and wanted to be remembered, I would wear something like that or drop a plate of food . . . something to call attention to myself. You know, like in the gangster movies when the big boss wants to establish an alibi — he takes his moll to a nightclub, tips the maitre d', buys drinks for everyone, gets into a fracas, insults patrons, all so that a hundred people can testify where he was on the night the rival mobster was shot."

"Why would Erika need to establish an alibi? She is there as the guest of Judge Wibbleton. She is sitting there with his daughter — her friend. . ."

"But, dear, that's just it. Jessica is a friend . . . a friend would be the worst kind of witness . . . friendship would place a cloud over her testimony . . . better to have others notice and be able to remember her and testify." Sallie was certainly suspicious, and she had a point.

The tape continued to run as dinner was served. The master of ceremonies interrupted dinner to announce that the program would have to start in order shortly. As people continued with dessert and coffee, various guests were introduced. A few came to the podium and made laudatory remarks about Judge Wibbleton's character and generosity.

Then three large screen television monitors were wheeled into the room and placed strategically so that all the guests would have a good view. The master of ceremonies then announced that although the president of the University regrettably could not be in attendance, the occasion was so auspicious that he had taped a few remarks. The lights went out while the president's message was played on the monitors.

I looked at my spare watch. It was 8:22. No one in the banquet hall was visible in the darkness, only the light from the three television monitors appeared on the tape. The president's words of gratitude were followed by a film segment showing an artist's rendering of the new wing of the liberal arts building and a news clip of the ground breaking ceremony. The guests politely applauded as the lights went on. Erika was still seated in her chair, her back to the camera. My watch read 8:31.

The evening continued with a series of speeches from various dignitaries. Finally, Judge Wibbleton had his chance to address the gathering. Nothing memorable was said, but I am prejudiced when it comes to evaluating statements from members of the judiciary.

At 9:19, the master of ceremonies declared that the proceedings had concluded and entreated the guests to travel safely to their destinations. The tape continued to run as wellwishers made their way to the podium to pay their repects to the judge. Erika was among those who approached the judge, shook his hand, and said a few words. She turned toward the camera and waved to Jessica who joined her on the podium. Jessica kissed her father on the cheek and walked with Erika to a side entrance. When the tape went blank it was 9:35.

Sallie dutifully sat through the entire tape. "Well, dear, you certainly bring home exciting entertainment for our evening's enjoyment."

"It's wonderful," I said, "that you take such an interest in my work."

We both laughed.

Later, in bed after Sallie had drifted off to sleep, I reviewed the tape in my mind. I was haunted by the fact that Erika was visible at 8:22 when the lights went off and at 8:31 when the lights went on again. It was during this interval that the crime was committed. I dragged myself from the comfort of our bed and went back to replay that segment of the tape. The light from the television monitors illuminated those at the head table, but Erika was not visible. I replayed that part a half dozen times. Something was not right, but I could not figure what it might have been.

I rejoined Sallie in bed, taking care not to disturb her, but she was awake.

"Can I help?" she whispered.

"The tape is Erika's alibi, Sallie."

"And—let me guess—the rival mobster was shot while Erika was at the dinner."

"It gets more interesting. The mobster was shot during the time when the lights were out and they were showing that stupid message from the president. Erika is not visible for nine minutes."

"Sounds to me like you have a lot of case and a lot of woman to deal with."

The next morning I was able to locate the office responsible for the video taping. The operator was a pleasant young woman named Joelle. She told me that someone from the Office of Special Events had inquired about taping the program. This was not an unusual request since many awards dinners and programs are taped. The honorees are presented with the tapes as "living histories" of the event. Joelle explained that the recipients were always grateful, that was one of the best features of her job.

Joelle kept a log of everything she did that evening, including timing the event. She offered to testify in court authenticating the tape as the one she made April 15th. She checked her log; she began taping at 7:46 and ended at 9:35. She had begun setting up the camera at about 5:30. At the request of the special events coordinator, she helped with the cables for the three television monitors. At the appropriate time, she left the camera taping the event and went forward to start the president's video-taped message. She explained that normally when there was nothing to see when the lights were out, she would suspend the taping of the event. Later she would get a copy of the message tape and splice a copy of it into the events tape. This time, because she was pressed into duty, she did not turn off the camera recording the event. When she reviewed the events tape, the message tape was visible and the audio was clear so she did not feel compelled to search for the message tape and splice it into the events tape.

Joelle was one of the first people I had encountered in my investigation who seemed to be happy with her job at the University. She was willing to cooperate by offering to testify at trial. As a precaution, I asked her for a photocopy of her log of the events of April 15th so that I study it. At first, she expressed reluctance, but I assured her that her personal notes were not really university property and there was nothing in them that indicated anything other than the faithful performance of her duty. Reassured, Joelle gave me copies. Later, when I prepared for the trial I was forbidden access to the university's copies of the events tape and Joelle's log.

31

I now turned my investigation to Erika; I needed more information from her. She complied with my request for an interview.

She sat at my conference table looking every bit as attractive as when I first saw her several weeks before. I pushed a legal pad and pen across the table to her without comment and sat looking at her for a moment.

"How have you been bearing up, Erika?"

"I'm a little apprehensive as the time approaches for the trial. I hope that you can tell me how your investigation has progressed."

I sat for another moment. Erika broke the silence. "I think I can anticipate your question. At this stage you want to know whether you should begin discussions with the district attorney about a possible plea bargain. What do you think our chances at trial might be, keeping in mind that the district attorney must prove me guilty beyond a reasonable doubt?"

She again by-passed the entire subject of guilt or innocence in favor of a more practical approach.

"Erika, it is true that the Commonwealth must prove your guilt beyond a reasonable doubt — that is the standard of proof — but from a practical point of view, we must introduce evidence of that reasonable doubt. Reasonable doubt does not exist out in the air somewhere for the jury to see. We have to show it to them."

"Am I not presumed innocent? Do I have to testify?"

"Yes, there is a presumption that you are innocent, but the jury will want to hear you say that you are innocent. You will have to swear to tell the truth, the whole truth, and nothing but the truth. Without your clear statement of innocence under oath, the jury will not have a basis of determining the reasonable doubt. Can you say that?"

I thought I had placed the issue of guilt or innocence clearly before her. The gauntlet was tossed to the ground at her feet.

"When my freedom is at stake, I can do anything."

Her assertion that she could do anything had a chilling effect upon me. I had not expected her to be different from other criminal defendants I had defended, but in one sentence she had reduced to rubble my idyllic vision of her as a damsel in distress. At long last she was acting like a criminal-type defendant. For citizen-types, the thought of lying under oath about their criminal activities was anathema; only after a painstaking inner battle might they consider perjury as an alternative to conviction. My face betrayed my disappointment. Erika reacted quickly, backtracking from her statement.

[121]

"I can see that you are disappointed in me for my willingness to lie to escape the consequences of my actions. I would only do so to assist you in raising reasonable doubt. I am simply reiterating my trust in your abilities to destroy the Commonwealth's case. If you were to tell me to assert my innocence, guilty or not, I would do so. You haven't asked me if I am guilty. You only asked me if I would be willing to say that I am innocent, whether I am innocent or not." She paused to make sure that I understood her. Then she continued. "If you want to know whether I have committed embezzlement, you'll have to ask me directly. You'll have to ask, 'Erika, are you guilty or not guilty?' It will do no good to ask whether I am willing to lie. Of course I am willing to lie, just like everyone else. It is a law of the jungle that people will sacrifice principles when they come face-to-face with their most dreaded fears. I hate to be cynical when it comes to things like honor and truth, but you will have to admit that what I say is true."

I paused, not wishing to discuss my views about honor and truth, but Erika had a point. Her admission mattered little to the preparation of our case. I had been hired to defend her with all the vigor I could muster, and she knew it. What I thought of her with regard to honor and truth was not relevant to our relationship. Nor should what I thought of her as a person have been important to me, but somehow it was.

This fact exposed my Achilles' heel as an attorney. As suspicious as I think I am, I am too sensitive. For deeply personal reasons, I have to feel that my client's cause is just and right. As a matter of honor, I must believe that the defense of a person is a humane undertaking, not a business deal. I desperately want to believe I am like Charles Perrow trying to establish the freedom of Eben Jones. It is this self-image that sets me apart in my own mind from other attorneys whom I consider to be money-grubbing and without principles. It is my ego-saving lie. But this was no time for self-examination.

"Erika, let us go over some of the details. I viewed the tape of the dinner for Judge Wibbleton. Did you leave the table at any time during the dinner?"

"No. As I explained, I wanted to go to the ladies' room, but

Jessica did not want to go. She was afraid that her absence would be misconstrued by her father."

"I find that hard to believe. Certainly her father knew that she had bodily functions."

"Of course. If she had gone alone, it might have been all right. But if she had left the dinner with me, the judge might have perceived that gossiping with her friend was more important that watching the honors being bestowed upon him."

"I think I understand Jessica's concern. But you could have gone alone."

"I decided I could wait. Don't you ever decide to wait? You assess the discomfort level and decide accordingly." She had me there.

I asked a series of questions about the signature cards at the bank and the post office. She did not remember signing either of them. She acknowledged that the signature was hers, but that everyone in the office had access to copies of her signature. I decided not to disclose to her that I had learned from Rick Place that they were identical.

I turned my attention to the buried diskette containing the codes. She had never seen the diskette before and did not know how it had been buried beneath her potted plant.

Each line of inquiry yielded nothing new.

"Erika, when the police found the account number written on your phone book, was the account number written in your own hand?"

"Gee, I hadn't thought about it. No. The numbers were blocked. You know, they were written as if someone was doodling. The numbers were written in block form and retraced with a ballpoint pen a number of times so they stood out clearly on the back cover of the phone book. Really, anyone could have written it. And, now that you mention it, it was kind of strange that it was written on the cover like that."

I asked about who might have had access to the book. She provided a list of people who had been in her townhouse. Included on the list were John Harley and his wife.

"His wife?" I asked.

[123

"Yes, once at the time push-came-to-shove John showed up at my door. He told me that his wife was waiting in the car. It really bothered me. He had brought over some papers for me to interpret—I was suspended from the job by this time—I remember sitting at the table making some notes when the doorbell rang. It was Mrs. Harley. John answered the door. She said she was sorry to intrude. I could sense that she was just checking up on us, but as an excuse she asked to use the telephone. I told her it was in the kitchen and that she could help herself to the phone directory in the drawer below the phone. I heard her retrieve the book, flip through the pages. She made a local call—I counted the buttons being pushed. She spoke to someone for about three or four minutes. She must have replaced the phone book. I offered them a drink, but I knew they wouldn't accept. I finished the papers and they left."

"Were the papers important enough for John to come over to your place to get your explanation or was it an excuse?"

"It may have been an excuse, but the papers were important and only I could interpret them . . . there was a trustees' meeting the next day."

I thought about this development for a moment.

"Was that the only time you spoke to Mrs. Harley?"

"The only time after I began having an affair with her husband. It was not a pleasant moment. Later, I thought John did it purposely to make a statement to me. I really resented it. Now I'm not so sure he did it for anything other than business reasons."

"Did you write that account number on your phone book, Erika?"

She looked at me suspiciously. I smiled at her.

"Look, Erika, we've already played our little psychological game of guilty-not guilty for today."

She smiled back. It was the first genuine smile I ever received from her and I was momentarily reminded of her beauty. All previous smiles had been polite responses appropriate for the situation.

"I don't remember writing that number on my phone book. But I was always taking account numbers down. We had so many accounts to monitor at the office. It is possible that I wrote that number on the phone book cover . . . if a piece of paper wasn't handy. . . but it's unlikely. It could have been John, or his wife, or Polly Morrat—she was also there about that time with papers for me to review."

She thought about it for another moment.

"Or the phone book could be a plant someone brought into my townhouse. The new phone books come out in late January or early February. I don't ever clip the coupons in the book and I don't ever use the spaces inside the back cover to put numbers on. Come to think of it, there really is nothing to distinguish my phone book from any other. Mrs. Harley had a coat on . . . she could have switched phone books. John also used the phone in the kitchen a couple of times when he visited. Really . . . it could have been anyone."

Erika and I went over other details, but nothing caught my attention as fertile ground for further inquiry. After she left, I felt that I had adequately investigated the chief suspect—Erika. Now it was time to return my attention to the others. I called Rick Place and ordered background checks on John Harley, Harley's wife, and Polly Morrat. I also asked him to check whether Erika had a brother in Toledo, Ohio.

32

That night I was awake tossing and turning. I just could not shake the disappointment I felt that afternoon. I knew that my discomfort lay not with Erika but with my vision of myself. I thought there was something more noble about the way I practiced than other attorneys who engaged in law solely as a business. As it turned out, my defense of Erika was just business, and it did not feel right.

Sallie stirred. In the darkness, I felt her gaze.

"Can I help, dear?" she whispered.

I really needed a friend and I did not have one. According to the women's magazines, a successful wife is her husband's best friend. It is true that women have friends with whom they can share their innermost feelings. Men have buddies. They can tell their buddies off-color jokes and discuss sports or their lack of sex with their wives. But they do not tell their buddies anything meaningful. It is too risky. Like most men, I have many buddies but no friends. I shared my feelings with Sallie, half expecting her to doze off in mid-catharsis, but she lay there patiently listening as I explained what had happened.

"Sounds to me like you've come face-to-face with yourself and you're not sure you like what you see."

I did not respond; she continued. "I think it is very revealing that you didn't ask Erika directly whether or not she was guilty. You see, deep down inside you have to maintain the reasonable doubt that she is innocent. You feel it is more honorable to defend an innocent person than a guilty one. It fits right in . . . you have to believe that Perrow and Petrikin got Eben Jones his freedom."

As usual, Sallie was right. I wanted to preserve the belief about Erika's innocence. That is why I did not ask her point-blank whether she was guilty. After all, anything she told me was protected by the attorney-client privilege and I would have to defend her, guilty or not. In fact, if I knew for sure that she was guilty, I could set up a defensive scheme to deflect the district attorney's attack. From a strategic point of view, it made sense for me to abandon my need to believe that she was innocent.

"I know how upset you are, dear. Please try to get some sleep. Order will be restored in the morning."

Her words provided some comfort and she snuggled closer to me, placing her hand on my shoulder. It felt good. In a few moments I drifted off to sleep.

By late the next afternoon, Rick Place was able to make a preliminary report. I was especially interested in his background check of Mrs. Harley. He reported that Mrs. Harley should have been cast in one of those movies where the woman is capable of anything. In the realm of judicial history before equal rights, the mother was almost always awarded custody of minor children. Place uncovered court records detailing a long series of abusive events that resulted in a court order awarding custody of Mrs. Harley's two minor children to her former husband. I remarked to Place that even years ago this might have been possible. He indicated that the children's natural father had been killed and that Mrs. Harley's husband was only the stepfather. That was unusual, since natural parents rather than stepparents are granted custody except in the most extreme circumstances. She apparently had a very violent temper and had been institutionalized as recently as three years ago. The most interesting revelation discovered by Place was that Mrs. Harley had changed identities about the time she was released from the hospital. She had also changed her appearance as best she could and, with recently inherited money, had moved to Philadelphia where she met Harley. After a short courtship, they were married in Norristown, Pennsylvania. Shortly thereafter, Harley accepted his position at the University. Based upon these revelations, I asked Place to try to determine if it was possible that Harley himself was unaware of his wife's past. I already knew through Erika that Harley had spoken of his wife's children by a previous marriage. I wondered whether he knew all about his wife.

I was suspicious about the source of funds that Erika had used to pay our retainer. Place confirmed that Erika had a younger brother living near Toledo, Ohio, who was a rising star in an engineering firm. This report provided me some assurance about Erika, but I found myself wondering whether I was still groping for that reasonable doubt.

Inquiries about Polly Morrat provided no indication that she was involved. She gained little by Erika's departure from the University. Her husband was completing his graduate degree and she would be leaving the next summer. Her area of responsibility did not include transferring funds. She had no access to codes and was specifically prohibited from going into the database. There was some talk that she was attracted to Harley, but according to Place, many women were. Further inquiry into Polly Morrat's part would be fruitless.

I asked Place to use his best efforts to check Harley's office. I emphasized "best efforts," hoping he would take me literally. As an attorney I could not encourage or support breaches of the peace and commissions of crime.

The next morning I arrived at my office to find Rick Place waiting for me. He could hardly contain his excitement in his attempt to be professional.

"The smoking gun?" I asked jokingly as I ushered him into my office.

"I took your hint literally. With my pocket radio tuned to the security channel, I did my thing in Harley's office. If there was a pubic hair, I saw it — there were some — red in color. . ."

I looked at him skeptically.

He nodded and continued. "Well, I found what you were after."

He produced an envelope and laid the contents on the desk before me. I sorted through the offering. There was a specimen signature of Erika Williams. Upon closer examination, I recognized it to be the signature that was on the postal rental card and the bank signature card. There was an account card for the account opened in Erika's name. Next, I examined a list which I took to be the codes with a date of April 15th and a torn scratch pad paper listing a series of computer commands.

"Prints?" I asked.

"I thought you'd never ask. I ran them by the lab. The only prints I found were Harley's on the back of the specimen signature. No discernable prints or material on any of the other papers. But, that is not unusual for this type of collection. I'm surprised we lifted anything."

He reached into his pocket, produced a packet of letters, and spread them on the desk before me.

"What are these?"

"Just what you would not expect from a cold fish like Erika . . . love letters to Harley."

"Bull!" was my response.

"For true, for true. Look for yourself. Harley's prints are on the envelopes . . . the envelopes are generic — business-type, but cheap paper. There are no prints on the paper — the texture is all wrong for prints. But . . . in one of the folds there was a hair—the same hair as on Harley's brush in his bottom desk drawer."

"Contents? Did you read them?" I naively asked.

"I won't even respond. Choice words—you know, 'until death do us part'. . ."

I tried not to look too interested, but my eagerness was apparent and Place laughed.

"You'll be disappointed. All love . . . only a few references to places they made love."

The letters revealed a side of Erika I had not dreamed existed. They could only be described as soft and bright, full of poetry and wonderful allusions to flowers and music. She used words and language that conjured up visions of the happiness and contentment of fulfilled love. I knew that the love was now over.

I set the letters on the table and looked at Place. He sat pensively for a moment.

"Is it enough that you know that these papers and letters were hidden in Harley's office in a location that was so obscure that it took me five hours to uncover them?" he asked.

I nodded.

"I photographed them and ran them through the lab. Do you want me to put them back?"

I thought about it for a moment. If Harley had hidden them, he might check to see if they were there. I tried to calculate the impact of his discovering that they were missing. Then a thought occurred to me.

"Rick, if these were not planted so that the police would find them, why would Harley have kept the specimen signature, the paper with the codes and computer commands? It seems to me that any criminal attempting to frame someone would destroy the evidence. My God, that's how Nixon got caught. Everyone knows that."

He thought about it for a moment. "Well, there are those people who think they have to retain this type of evidence. If they destroy it, they may have nightmares trying to remember if they completely destroyed the evidence. It could be that Harley wanted to retain the keys to Erika's freedom. Hmm. . . . Or it could be that

[129]

Harley doesn't know these items exist. Maybe Erika planted them so that the police would find them and nab Harley. Although, on second thought, they were so well hidden that no one could assume that they would ever be found. I don't know why a man like Harley would risk keeping these things if he framed Erika for embezzlement."

"Put 'em back, Rick. If we need copies we have them. If we need the originals, we know where they are. If Harley had some reason for keeping them instead of burning them, that reason still exists. Nothing has changed. Can you lay a trap so that if they are removed, we can get some fingerprints?"

"Hmm... now you're starting to think like a detective. There is hope for you. I'll see what I can do. Oh yeah, in case something happens to me, you'll want to know that they will be behind the baseboard in his office, just below the doorstop."

33

In my mind the reasonable doubt that Erika had committed the crime was now replaced by probable doubt. The newly discovered evidence relieved me more than I cared to admit; I approached the case with renewed zeal.

I could not help thinking about James Petrikin's disappointment at not finding Eben Jones' name in the plaintiff's index at the clerk's office. For me, not finding Eben's name was an inconvenience. If the case against Peter Karthaus had been there, I would have been excited because I had discovered tangible documentary evidence that Eben had lived in the county. Even though I did not find Eben's name or the case in the index, I knew my fantasies would manage to bridge the gap left by the absence of concrete evidence of Eben's existence, and the story of the freedom of Eben Jones could continue.

But for Petrikin, the lack of documentary evidence meant he would have to obtain oral testimony of witnesses to events that had happened long ago. The memory of witnesses becomes clouded and confused over time beginning one millisecond after the event. What chance had Petrikin in 1827 of obtaining affidavits from citizens about an unremarkable black man who passed briefly through their lives years before?

Since the services performed by Petrikin were *gratis*, it was unlikely that he would have hired someone to interview witnesses who may have had contact with Eben. It is outside the scope of a private attorney's thought processes to spend money on behalf of a client in situations when there is likely to be no fee. Even today, an attorney who may do *pro bono* work and spend time counselling or representing clients, will draw the line at adding to personal or office overhead expenses for non-profit cases.

Since transportation was time consuming in those days, I doubted Petrikin would saddle up his horse and ride twenty miles into Penns Valley looking for a obscure unnamed Dutchman who sold a cow to Judge Burnside. Instead, Petrikin would bide his time at the social and commercial center of activity of the time, the county seat. As he came upon potential witnesses who may have known Eben, he would make appropriate inquiries.

Perhaps Petrikin could interview people at the annual harvest get-together. All the farmers and people involved in the iron trade in the surrounding valleys would bring their families to town to trade, swap stories, and drill with the local militia that was still active even though the last threat of Indian attack had been in 1778.

As a respected man before the bar, people would make time for Petrikin. It was not like today, when people are threatened or irritated by attorneys' questions. Then, people would have enjoyed assisting him and they would hear him out. Life was slower-paced and people cooperated with one another. It would not have been necessary for Petrikin to disclose the purpose of his inquiries. He would not have to appeal to an abolitionist spirit. Those feelings were decades away in this remote location. People would readily supply what information they could about Eben Jones.

The air carried the first hint of autumn. The sun shone brightly, but in the shade there was an unmistakable chill. The leaves showed the first tinges of yellow. Farmers' wagons carried no sweet corn. Their cargo consisted mainly of winter squash, potatoes, and cabbage.

Petrikin strolled down the dusty street nodding here and there as he passed acquaintances on his way to the picnic grounds along the creek. When he reached the picnic grounds he circulated among the farmers, tradesmen, and iron workers. Here and there he stopped to talk to a group of men discussing the politics of the day. Over to one side of the park, children waded and splashed noisily in the cool waters of the spring-fed creek.

His patience was rewarded. Petrikin came upon a familiar farmer, a long-time resident of the upper Bald Eagle Creek.

"Say, my good fellow," Petrikin began, "how was the harvest on the upper Bald Eagle?"

The question was more rhetorical than desirous of hearing about the crops. Even so, the farmer went through the growing season crop by crop for Petrikin who listened politely, nodding from time to time to demonstrate his interest. Perhaps as a gift for hearing him out, the farmer excused himself and from his wagon retrieved a small pot of honey which he presented to Petrikin. Petrikin thanked him, promising to put it on his bread the next morning.

"Isaac, do you recall any black men who worked for the judge at the time he built his house on the Bald Eagle, in the year 1819 or thereabouts?"

The farmer thought for a moment. He was puzzled by the inquiry but knew that it was impolite to ask the purpose of a lawyer's question.

"No, Squire, cannot say that I have any such recollection of any black men working for Judge Burnside. Oh, I have had occasion to see negroes walking along the old Indian trail on their way east or west. Sometimes they would come by the house looking for work in exchange for a meal or to bed down in the barn, but I cannot recall any staying more than a day. Once fed, they left. Coloreds are rare in these parts and my children would stare and stare at them. Once, when an old colored man and a younger woman were staying in the barn, the children approached them asking whether the color would wash off when they took a bath or went swimming. The coloreds laughed, but I could see that they felt different and distant from the life that we know as white people. Sometimes our lives are hard, but I would not trade my life for theirs, Squire."

"Isaac, do you recall if any of them had the name of Eben Jones?"

"Mr. Petrikin, I know no names of any coloreds. Years ago, I worked shoulder to shoulder with a negro man on the canal by where the Juniata meets the Susquehanna. We worked a month together and I never knew his name . . . he never spoke his name and nor did I ask it. We were paid our wages. He went east. I went west."

Petrikin nodded. He thanked the farmer for the honey and continued his quest for evidence that Eben Jones had lived in the county.

At times like these when my fantasies took over, I felt like Don Quixote, wishing for life in the past where an attorney's place in society was respected and secure. I had to remind myself that life for Petrikin also included small pox, polio, malaria, a myriad of life-threatening childhood diseases, and the tuberculosis which took his life. For him there was no pizza or baseball. I properly cautioned my imagination that the idyllic life was one thing, but life without pizza and baseball was quite another.

Fortunately, I succeeded in putting my fantasies on hold before they overcame my new sense of resolve. Taking the copy of the note of computer commands, I paid a visit to my friend Jacki Snow for interpretation. After extracting a promise from me to review a lease for her friend, Mary Jo, she put her computer through its paces, making knowing sounds such as "hmm" and "uh-huh" as she pressed keys and it changed screens. I awaited her verdict. When she continued for more than two minutes, I had the sense that she stringing me along to demonstrate the value of her services. I often do the same thing to impress a client of the intensity of my concentration as I review a contract or some other document. Nothing pleases a customer more than believing that you are giving your all for their cause.

[133

When she was finished I expected her to tell me that the commands probably had something to do with altering the clock in a computer database. However, I knew that Harley was present in the offices at the exact time that the embezzlement actually was committed. The command sequence to change the clock would not have fit with the other evidence recovered from Harley's office and with his story about the evening's events.

She smiled as she looked up from her computer.

"It's Greek to me," was her assessment.

I looked at her inquiringly. I had assumed that she knew everything there was to know about computers.

"I thought it might be the sequence of commands to change the clock. There are a series of commands that would do that. However, I think it is designed to fool the computer into believing that the time is to be changed, but there is no execute command. Or, it could be a series of commands to override the clock rather than change it. Or, it could mean nothing. I really can't figure it out. . ." She paused, then cautioned. "That doesn't mean that you're off the hook regarding the review of Mary Jo's lease. Where did you get the sequence of commands?"

I evaded the question with an assurance that even though she found that the commands meant nothing, I would provide Mary Jo with legal advice. She handed me the paper and I left her office. As I headed down the hall, I realized that I did not have Mary Jo's number or last name, so I retraced my steps to Jacki's office and without knocking, I opened her door. It was clear to me that she had entered the sequence of commands and was in the process of printing them out on her printer. She looked surprised and a little embarrassed.

I did the best I could to pretend I did not notice what she was doing. I asked for Mary Jo's last name. Jacki informed me that Mary Jo would call me for an appointment. I said goodbye again, trying to be nonchalant. It was hard to gauge whether she realized that I had seen her save and print the commands.

I know that Jacki loves a mystery, but I was suspicious of her actions, and I thought it best not to divulge any more information. In fact, I considered feeding her false information to see if she was supplying data to the police. I rejected this as not being worth the trouble, and I made a note to ask Erika about the command sequence.

My next stop was Joelle Smithson's office. Joelle remembered me and seemed glad to see me. I was flattered and wondered whether I was wearing a new, unspotted tie and had shined my shoes. I asked if she would testify about the events of the evening of April 15th. She said that she would be happy to do so, but she no longer had a copy of the tape and her log had been requisitioned.

My immediate thought was that the police had discovered the tape and took it.

"The police?"

"Oh, no, nothing quite so exciting as that," she replied affably. "Someone from special events came over and got it."

"Special events?"

"You know, the people who put on these dinners and things for the big wigs. To impress contributors, you know."

Upon further inquiry, she could not remember exactly who came for the log and tape. I asked her to describe the person. She said that a man had called inquiring if there was a tape of the event. Later, a young woman in her mid-twenties picked up Joelle's copy.

"What about the log?"

"Well, someone called from the finance office. They were doing a spot audit of our budget . . . it was my first one. They asked me for any time records I kept to substantiate the hours our office was in operation, to justify the budget or something. I have nothing to hide. It proves that we're are all above board . . . not like some departments, if you know what I mean. I'm happy to cooperate."

"Joelle, did they specifically ask for the time records for April 15th?"

"Yes and what luck—every minute of that whole day is accounted for."

"Joelle, this is important. Did you get the call about your log before or after the woman came over to get the tape?"

"They came and got the tape, then the finance people called about the log."

When I questioned the time delay between the two events, Joelle reported that the tape was requisitioned in the morning and the log in the afternoon of the same day. When I asked if they signed a receipt for both the log and the tape, Joelle seemed offended that I might think she was not doing her job.

She made copies of both receipts for me. As I left, I received her assurance that she would testify in court about the videotape of Judge Wibbleton's party. I congratulated myself on my foresight in making a copy of Joelle's log. I did not remind her that I had done so.

Later in the day I received a call from Jacki Snow. She had rerun the sequence of commands and was convinced that without additional commands in the sequence, the computer would produce nothing. Ten minutes later, Mary Jo called for an appointment.

34

I felt better about Jacki Snow. I chastised myself for being so suspicious of her. But I was puzzled. I could not think of any reason why Harley might have saved a list of computer commands that were meaningless.

I was sitting at my desk at the end of a long day thinking about this when Marie appeared in my doorway. I posed the question to her.

"It's easy. Those computer commands are a marker."

"Marker?"

"Marker. A red-herring. Erika put that paper in the hiding place. Her logic was that if you discovered it while searching Harley's office, you might not let her know what you found. Especially the love letters. But you might ask her about the sequence of computer commands. That would tell her definitively that you or the police found the evidence she planted to convince you that she was framed by Harley."

I thought about it for a moment.

"You see," she continued, "if Erika put in regular commands, she couldn't know for sure whether you had found the evidence she planted in Harley's office. But if it was garbage as Jacki Snow said it was, albeit carefully arranged garbage, Erika could be certain that you had found the evidence when you asked her about the command sequence because no one could recreate the same garbage sequence."

Marie's observation made sense. After Jacki could not decode it, my first inclination was to ask Erika about the sequence of commands. Perhaps Erika figured she might be one of the first persons I would ask to interpret the commands. This whole line of thought again brought to the fore my concern that Erika might be guilty of the crime.

"Marie, why should it matter that I disclose in advance that I had possession of the evidence from Harley's office? She would see it soon enough at trial."

"Sometimes I wonder about you," she said, the seriousness in her voice and smile on her face reflecting how incredibly naive I sounded.

"You see, if you hadn't found the evidence before trial, she'd have to direct you to it or produce other evidence for you to use in court to show that she was framed. She couldn't risk that you'd get her off, notwithstanding your considerable abilities. She just couldn't take the chance — her freedom would be in jeopardy."

"Why couldn't she just tell me where the evidence was? Why go through all this?"

"Don't you see?" Marie said with a healthy dose of reproach in her voice.

I was baffled at her insistence that I see her point.

"My God! Don't you see?" she asked again, "It's you. She knows you're an honest man. You've told me yourself a hundred times when you were preparing for trial. You always say that out of our greatest strengths spring our greatest weaknesses. She didn't dare bring you into her confidence. She knew that if you believed that she was guilty it would affect your performance. You'd be forced to be dishonest with yourself. You would feel uncomfortable . . . falter. Your conscience would be at issue. You would hedge. On the other hand, if you truly believed that Erika was innocent and framed by that son-of-a-bitch Harley, your efforts would know no bounds — pardon the eloquence — but it's true."

"Marie, I've represented guilty people before. You know that it is the job of the D.A. to prove guilt beyond reasonable doubt. It's not our job to prove that they are innocent. They must produce the evidence of guilt. That's all I do — hold the district attorney to that standard — same as any attorney."

"No," Marie interjected. "You're not the same — you're different. You say you do that, and you do when the client is guilty . . . and they have him dead to rights . . . it was written all over them. Oh, okay, you impeached a witness now and then. You found the police's error at the arrest . . . you know, some technicality like the Miranda warning — or better yet, you had your client confuse the jury with honest-sounding, heart-rending sob stories, but none of them were the same as Erika . . . none of them . . . they were all different, and you know it."

I did know it. Neither of us spoke for a few minutes.

"Look," she said softly. "You know I've stuck with you through good and bad. And you've stuck with me with all the turmoil I've had in my life. That's what I admire about you — your standards . . . they're your great strength. But you know that they are also your great weakness. Your standards set this law office apart from all the rest. But the future of this law office has definite boundaries."

'Definite boundaries' is the term Marie uses when commenting to others on my future prospects as a lawyer. It haunts me still.

"If you were different, we would be in a law firm making more money, and neither of us would feel as good about it."

Marie knew that she had said enough. She gave me a reassuring smile and bid me goodnight. I heard her footsteps retreat down the hallway. I heard the chime at the door sound her departure.

The women in my life, Marie and Sallie, understood me well — better than I understood myself. I was concerned that the other woman — Erika — knew me just as well.

I tried to put personal considerations behind me and focus on the issue at hand. It was possible that Marie was correct. Over the years I have learned to trust Marie's instincts. But we tend to see what we want or expect to see in the people and events around us. Marie did not like Erika. And, despite Marie's considerable powers, she was not right all the time. I think what raised my doubts about Marie's view was that Rick Place had said it could never be assumed that we would find the evidence because it was so well hidden. No matter how clever Erika might be in baiting a trail, she couldn't assume that we would find it. Bait, by its very definition, must be visible or easily discoverable to be useful.

I hated to think of myself as Erika's prey. I preferred to think of myself as her attorney. I generally feel obligated to disclose all information to a client that might influence their decisions in the course of litigation. However, in criminal cases, I am not as forthright with the clients. Often the situation dictates that I develop my own game plan without disclosing the specifics. I justify this by telling myself that a surgeon does not discuss the fine points of the operation with a patient. The patient cares only about the end result. I don't really keep anything from clients. I merely spare them the gory details of the development of the defense. I realize, however, that this rationale stands on shaky ground.

The next morning Erika was in my office when I arrived. She was concerned about the progress of her defense.

"Erika," I explained, "it is only natural that you might be anxious. After all, we are looking at a jury trial that will be splashed all over the papers."

"All I can think about are those television camera crews poking their lenses in my face. I suppose that for their sake, I am obliged to pull my coat up over my head. The eleven o'clock news looks better that way. Or maybe I should look defiant, acting nonchalant makes you appear arrogant and guilty . . . or maybe I should. . ." Her voice trailed off.

I sat for a moment not knowing exactly what to do. I resigned myself to facing the issue.

"You need not go to trial, Erika. You could plead guilty to the charges. Naturally, we would make a deal before you did that."

[139

"Do you think I'm guilty?"

I sat looking at her for a minute. When I said nothing to her question, she smiled.

"Well, at least you did not use the obligatory lawyer's statement like in the movies: 'Erika, my dear, it is not my job to judge your guilt or innocence, that's for the judge or jury to decide'... thanks for sparing me that indignity."

I could not gauge her mood or the reason of her visit. She seemed overwrought and disturbed. This was uncharacteristic behavior for her.

"Erika," I began, "there are times when one should think about the risk-reward ratios. I have represented criminal defendants who pleaded guilty when there was a substantial chance of a successful result at trial. Trials are very stressful for defendants. The script plays out according to the rules of procedure and both the district attorney and the defense counsel pretty much know the strengths and weaknesses of the Commonwealth's case and the defense's plan. But, you see, though the drama is played out according to the rules and with the opponents knowing each other's cases, the ending is never certain. There is always enough uncertainty to make any case a sizable gamble. I have gone in with nothing but a clean shirt and a smile and come away with a hung jury. I have also gone to court with a good defense and had the jury find my client guilty. The litigants can never know the ending of the drama until the jury writes it."

"If I may ask the point?" she responded impatiently.

"If you are guilty, I want to know it. I've been unable to find any evidence that can prove you are innocent of the charges except, of course, your own testimony that you did not commit the crime as charged."

Without appearing to do so, I carefully watched her for any reaction. I knew in my heart there would be none. She did not disappoint me.

"I do not intend to plead guilty."

I nodded. From that moment forward I knew that we were going to trial.

35

I had not been in contact with the district attorney's office during my entire investigation. This was not unusual, since the district attorney felt it was a sign of weakness to be the first to broach the subject of a plea bargain with defense counsel. He would let the defense attorney come to him first with a proposal. It is my policy to avoid going to the district attorney at all except in the most extreme circumstances.

I learned long ago that the reputation of settlement is an attorney's weakness. Many attorneys fear trial and prefer to settle either a civil or criminal case rather than take it to trial. The uncertainties of litigation play havoc with the psyches of all but the most hardened veteran trial attorneys. Soon an attorney's hesitancy to try a case becomes apparent to other attorneys who then exploit this tendency by forcing the case to trial. I know the identities of these attorneys, and I rejoice each time I have a case with any of them as opposing counsel. I know that if I push hard enough, they will sell their clients the settlement I dictate. The harder I push, the harder they push their clients to settle. I know that I will win the case on the courthouse steps, not in the courtroom. Of course, I am always careful to let opposing counsel believe that my case is weak, settlement is my idea, and that they have squeezed the last dollar from my client's pocket. It serves no useful purpose to do otherwise.

Early in my career, I was advised by a grizzled old veteran to take to trial a hopeless civil case every so often. He explained that even though I would lose the case, the other attorneys would soon learn that I would take any case to court — even a loser — rather than settle. The veteran explained that as hired guns, bluffing is preferable, but we are only effective if others know we are willing to pull the trigger when the time comes. I followed his advice. I believe that I have gotten more favorable settlements from other attorneys because they know I will go to court, no matter how grim the prospects for victory.

I received a call that day from the district attorney's office asking if it might be convenient for me to meet with him in the next several days on what was described as "procedural matters" involving the Williams case. I expressed my willingness to discuss anything. The secretary responded that the district attorney knew that my sensibilities might be offended by his request that I go to his office, so he suggested that I meet him for coffee at the "Rise and Shine" coffeehouse. I responded with a remark that I also knew better than to invite him to my office where his appearance might be viewed as a case of the "mountain coming to Mohammed."

"Mr. Bricker said you'd say something clever like that. That's why he suggested morning coffee. Tuesday at 8:00?"

"That's fine. I'll be there," I responded.

"Good," she said, "Mr. Bricker also said you'd not be one of those attorneys who had to posture by insisting on naming the date, time, and place for the meeting."

I was not sure whether her statement was meant to be complimentary.

I was fairly certain that this discussion was not intended as a forum for the district attorney to extend the olive branch. In the past, Bricker had been courteous at all meetings, but he always had a purpose. As a prosecutor he feels that he has to make a point. He frequently uses such meetings as opportunities to try to impose a plea bargain that I cannot live with. Like all good prosecutors, he prefers a plea bargain to trial even when he stands a better than even chance of obtaining a conviction on a lesser-included offense.

Most criminal code violations include less severe criminal acts, depending upon circumstances that might mitigate or excuse a higher degree of guilt. For example, if the defense offers proof that the victim or other factors have impacted upon the defendant, the jury may find that a less serious crime was committed. There could also be a failure of proof that might change the jury's view of the elements of the crime. For example, with the Williams case, embezzlement is a felony in the second degree. It requires that the district attorney prove all of the elements of embezzlement. If he is only able to prove that Erika took money that she knew was not hers, a lesser-included offense might be receiving stolen property, or failure to make required disposition of funds. The jury might find that she was not guilty of embezzlement but was guilty of receiving stolen property or failing to make required disposition of funds.

Plea bargains may involve the negotiation between the prosecutor and the defendant of a lesser crime with a lower level of punishment in exchange for a guilty plea. Or, the negotiations may require a guilty plea to the crime in exchange for a recommendation of a less severe sentence. This latter form of plea bargain is more risky for the defendant, because the defendant pleads guilty and the prosecutor can only recommend a sentence to the judge. The judge is generally not bound by any plea bargain involving the sentencing authority of the court. Therefore, the defendant cannot be assured of a lesser sentence in exchange for a guilty plea.

I approach plea bargains with a reduced sentence recommendation in the same manner I approach skydiving. The risks are not worth the reward. I try to bargain the guilty plea for a less severe crime. The criminal code specifies the penalty for the crime expressed in terms of a maximum sentence and a minimum sentence. By bargaining for a lesser crime, I still have a chance at the sentencing hearing to argue circumstances which would favor a lesser sentence for a lesser crime. If I exchange a guilty plea for a recommendation of a lesser sentence, my options for gaining the best bargain for the defendant are limited.

The district attorney may attempt to plea bargain if he thinks he has a weak case, or if the case is one in which he runs a legal risk. For example, certain defendants may be guilty of a crime, but the prosecution of that defendant is unpopular. For example, an abused spouse seriously maims her husband, but the community sympathy toward her might make prosecution difficult and unpopular. Most good prosecutors know not only that the jury must find that the defendant committed the crime but also that the defendant's record will be permanently blemished by the conviction. The jury might feel that the guilty verdict is unjust in light of the circumstances surrounding the crime. Often these considerations include the identity of the victim. If the victim was not a good person or if the victim had it coming, there might be some justification or an excuse for the defendant's crime. The jurors must believe that the defendant was either a bad person or a good person who acted badly without justification or excuse for committing the crime.

Political considerations also can affect a potential plea bargain. A prosecutor would not knowingly bargain away a chance to make political hay. And, although justice might be better served by a child molester's indefinite confinement in a psychiatric hospital, a trial might be mandated in order to serve the public need for revenge.

In Erika's case, I did not favor a plea bargain before a jury was impaneled. Since this has been my practice in the majority of criminal cases I've defended, I was certain that the district attorney knew my habit and that talk of a plea bargain was premature.

36

Ed Bricker greeted me courteously when we arrived simultaneously at the "Rise and Shine". The small restaurant specialized in different coffees and various breakfast treats including my favorite—cranberry walnut muffins. We went to the counter and ordered coffee, paying separately. I chose a full roast Mexican fina altura coffee. Bricker was not used to having a selection of coffees and seemed puzzled by the variety offered.

"I've never seen such a choice of coffees. I mostly drink minimart coffee out of a styrofoam cup with artificial cream and artificial sugar. I suppose the coffee is artificial, too. The only thing I seem to taste is chemicals leaching from the cup," he explained.

Ed Bricker is a man in his late thirties. Although he is physically fit and has a good strong countenance, his presence is not intimidating like that of many trial attorneys. Despite being neatly dressed, he cannot escape possessing the aura of a government bureaucrat. His job involves a substantial amount of administrative and management skill. He has installed a system for handling hundreds of cases, and his office and staff are models of efficiency.

Administrative and management skills which require attention to detail and sensitivity toward subordinates are somewhat incompatible with trial attorney skills which place a premium on a dramatic and strong personality. Although Bricker is a skillful and tactically competent trial attorney, he doesn't threaten to overpower opponents and sway juries with the force of his personality.

When he served as assistant district attorney prior to his election to his present position, I tried two robbery cases against him as defense counsel. Neither of us really won the cases, and we came away with a healthy respect for each other. I know Bricker to be an honest and forthright prosecutor who would not take advantage of a situation to gain a conviction that he does not deserve. In that sense, he represents the best tradition of the prosecutor. He serves both the Commonwealth's interest and the high ideal of justice for all. I could expect no quarter and sought none from him. I hoped he felt the same way about me.

He opened the meeting with small talk about the University's football team. I listened politely to this socially useful introduction to our discussion. When I was young, I didn't fully appreciate the benefits to be gained from small talk. Over time, I have learned that small talk enables others to adjust to the unfamiliar surroundings. It also gives me an opportunity to sell myself to clients and to adversaries alike as a competent and thoughtful person. It also allows me to assess personalities. If someone seems uncomfortable or intimidated I change my approach to ease any doubts about me as a person.

Presently, Bricker asked which coffee I had chosen.

"Mexican fina altura . . . Clark's shop sells it to this place."

He nodded, took another sip, and launched into the purpose of his visit with me. "We go back a long way. I know that you are defense counsel of substantial ability, and I must say that your program at the University on criminals and defense was fascinating. I have carefully considered what you said that evening on more than one occasion."

He was referring to the program I gave during a symposium on campus two years before.

"I think we should get right to the point. You know it's not my style to talk plea bargain. If I were you, I wouldn't talk plea bargain with the prosecutor, at least until after I'd seen how I might do at the jury selection. Hell, I'd do exactly what you're doing."

I nodded.

"And I'm not talking plea bargain now. I have nothing to offer, only an ear. I'm telling you this because we're getting a lot of pressure to see that your client serves time. We think that we have a strong case, although we both know that anything can happen at trial. I'm just saying that if you want to talk, it will have to be soon — within twenty-four hours. I don't have my customary leeway. There is too much pressure from certain sources that want Williams punished."

He watched me closely for a reaction. I tried not to disclose anything other than an interest in his proposal.

Bricker continued. "We know about the alibi defense. I'll write you a letter acknowledging it to save time and trouble."

He was referring to the rule of criminal procedure that required the criminal defendant to disclose to the prosecutor the particulars of a defense where the defendant claimed to be at a location other than the scene of the crime at the time the crime was committed. Any alibi defense would have to be employed during the defendant's case after the prosecution presented its case against the defendant. The rule requiring disclosure was designed to eliminate the unfair advantage of the defense surprising the prosecution with an alibi that could not possibly be verified as the trial neared its conclusion.

I nodded.

"All I am saying is that as a courtesy to you and to save us both a lot of trouble, if you want to talk about a plea bargain, I have some discretion, but it is limited. Soon it will be eliminated altogether. But I need to know. Do I make myself clear?"

He again searched my face for any reaction that might indicate that I viewed this last statement as a threat.

"I hope I don't sound threatening . . . that's not my intent. I know I can't browbeat you. I might go for a lesser-included offense—something like failure to make required disposition of funds. And I might be in a position to bargain on the sentence. They want her to serve time," Bricker explained. "We could work something out. You see we have the money . . . she has been suspended from her job. We would want her cooperation to clear up some things with the computer."

When I remained silent he continued.

"I know your views on bargaining over sentence—lack of control—you explained that at that program. I would permit you to protect Williams and withdraw your plea. But time is short and I must know."

He paused for a moment. I could tell that the conversation was nearly over. His face betrayed his disappointment that I hadn't responded to his initiative. Although he did not achieve his objective, I could tell that he was satisfied that he had conveyed a message to me.

"Well, next time I think I'll try the Kenyan blend. I'm coming back for some more real coffee for sure."

He stood up and smiled. I thanked him for being candid with me and promised that I would give him an answer the next day. We shook hands and he departed.

After he was gone, I went to the counter to refill my cup. I wanted to allow the dust to settle before I began analyzing such an important meeting. I returned to the table with my cup and stared out the window, watching the people pass along the sidewalk and into the library across the street. I wondered again why my fantasies with Eben Jones involved only Petrikin and not Charles Perrow. I had presumed that it was because I trod the same ground as Petrikin, albeit more than a century and a half later. I also knew a little of the history of Petrikin the man. The little biographical data I had been able to discover allowed me to construct a framework upon which to hang mental images of the man as father, politician, and country lawyer. I could only guess about Perrow's character. He most certainly was not a civil rights activist if he lived in rural Virginia and wanted to eat regularly.

The only evidence of Charles Perrow's personality was revealed in his letter to Petrikin. I cautioned myself not to expect the curtains to part between the handwritten lines disclosing Perrow the man. After all, my letters as a lawyer were specifically drafted to achieve a desired result through the force of the written word. The purpose of Perrow's letter was the same. Perrow was careful not to frame his request in social or political terms, and he did not appeal to an anti-slavery sentiment because he could not know for certain if any existed in Petrikin at that time.

All in all, the letter revealed only the skill of the writer in requesting the cooperation of its recipient. My fantasy was left to its own devices to conjure up the image of Perrow. My fantasies did not disappoint.

The large elm trees provided some relief from the hot Virginia sun as Perrow sat on the front porch of his house.

"Pray, brother, why must you persist in seeking the freedom of that slave held these many months in the colored prison?"

"Ah, I have long awaited your inquiry in that regard," said Perrow to the younger man. "You see, though I am committed to the maintenance of our life here in these mountains, I am duty bound as a lawyer to see that justice is done."

"A noble statement of a lawyer's purpose. Ah, but a negro . . . and slave at that. It can serve no socially useful purpose but to encourage our slaves to run off to the North. When other runaways are captured and returned to Virginia they will want competent counsel to seek their freedom by legal means when they have failed as runaways."

"Brother, you, like many here, mistake my motives. I do not seek the freedom of Eben Jones — that is the negro's name — for his sake as a person. I only support the laws of our Commonwealth which provide the procedures for testing the legality of the sheriff's action."

"If you succeed, many will run away. You will be viewed in this community as not favoring of our way of life. I have already heard such talk."

Perrow thought for a moment. "It is my job as a lawyer to make my plea on behalf of this negro. If the judge should decide that he should be free, that judgment will be upon our esteemed judicial authority and not upon me. I serve only as advocate, not judge. Freedom and slavery are not my provinces."

"Brother, I understand your logic. I have read law, but others like Farmer Colleton have not. Colleton believes that your conduct is unforgivable. You threaten our way of life because of your well-known abilities to plead a case. In that regard you appear to be an instrument of evil to the society that Farmer Colleton knows. It is not enough to excuse yourself by blaming the judge for setting the negro free. Many will believe your plea led the judge inexorably to that decision. And do not forget that the judge and Colleton are cousins."

"Then Farmer Colleton should understand, Brother. You have nothing to fear. Eben Jones shall have his day in court and I shall make his plea, just as I would make yours."

The last of my coffee had been drained from the cup. Thoughts of Perrow and his brother sitting in the shade of an elm tree receded and the reality of Erika Williams' impending trial reasserted itself. Perrow, Petrikin, and Eben Jones would have to wait until another time.

37

Back at my office, I tried to review the salient points of my meeting with Ed Bricker. I was particularly taken with the remark he had made about his having attended the program I had given about crimes and criminal defense. I tried to remember the content of my talk but could not, though I did remember the event. I had been asked to speak by the Department of Administration of

Justice about crimes, criminal law, and criminal defense. The featured speaker at the symposium was to be a well-known criminal defense attorney from the state capital, he had a last-minute conflict. Several local defense attorneys were approached but deferred for various reasons. I was their sixth or seventh choice for speaker. I have never rejected an opportunity to talk uninterrupted for fifty minutes, so I accepted.

I retrieved my notes from the program to refresh my memory. I had spoken about my experience as defense counsel. One of the major points I emphasized was the failure of criminals to prepare adequately for the crime. In my judgment, in criminal cases that are planned in advance, the criminals conceived very good plans. But in each case, the planning fell short. Most considered all of the necessary elements of completing the crime but failed to continue the plan beyond the point where they hoped to enjoy the fruits of their wrongdoing. Any complete plan should have included a viable defense to be employed at trial.

Most criminals assume that they will not be apprehended. This may be a hope, but it should never be an assumption on which to construct a successful plan for a crime. As part of any such plan, the prospective criminal must assume that the long arm of the law will prevail and the crime and the criminal will be uncovered. When that happens, the criminal must have ready access to a defense to be employed at trial. I cited sample defenses for the audience including insanity, self-defense, duress, and the like. The criminal should always plan for eventual discovery of the crime, capture, and trial.

I noted that people were especially attentive when I raised these issues. I remembered feeling a little queasy later about disclosing so much information to such a diverse audience. I did not want to appear to be soliciting the commission of a crime which is, in itself, a crime. Afterwards, I received a number of favorable comments about the program's content and delivery. My ego was inflated and, as a result, my queasiness soon was forgotten.

Bricker had stated that our meeting was not for the purpose of discussing a plea bargain arrangement because it was not his custom to initiate such discussions, although it seemed clear to me that Bricker wanted to make some sort of deal. The first incentive for seeking a plea bargain was the weakness of the case. Although I had spent considerable time developing a theory of the prosecution, I was not convinced that the prosecutor had as air-tight a case against Erika as he would have led me to believe. The strength of the prosecution's case was based upon the discovery of the money in an account in Erika's name; the presence of the secret codes hidden in her office; and the fact that it was Erika's computer that ordered the funds transferred. The problem was that anyone who could have masterminded the theft of the money most certainly would have covered his or her tracks more effectively. Why go to the trouble of committing a crime and then place the money in an account with one's own name and social security number? After all, Erika had computer access to the names and social security numbers of thousands of female university employees and students. She could have opened an account in any of their names without arousing suspicion. They would not have known anything of the matter until at least a year later when the Internal Revenue Service matched the interest paid as reported by the bank with the failure of the unsuspecting victim-taxpayer to report that interest income on their tax return. By then, Erika would have been long gone.

Another possible motive for the meeting initiated by Bricker may have been to discover whether I intended to employ an alibi defense. He mentioned as an aside that he would acknowledge it in a letter. He may have wanted to judge my reaction to his statement to confirm that the defense was intent upon proving alibi. I remembered that I had only nodded to each of the things he said.

There were actually two alibi defenses. The first occurred at 7:30 P.M. when Erika stood by Polly Morrat's desk while Polly retrieved a diagnostic diskette from the computer substation. The other was Erika's presence at the dinner in honor of Judge Wibbleton at 8:31 P.M., the approximate time that Erika's computer directed the university computer to make the transfer of funds. It was possible, though not likely, that Bricker was willing to accept an alibi for the 7:30 P.M. time because he knew that the crime actually was committed an hour later. Was it possible that Bricker did not know that Erika had an alibi for the actual time when the crime took place?

I remembered Joelle Smithson had indicated that someone claiming to be from the Office of Special Events came and took her only copy of the videotape of the dinner. Someone from an auditor's office also came on the same day to obtain her time log for April 15th. It was too much of a coincidence for both items to be requisitioned from Joelle on the same day. I assumed it was the police who directed that the evidence be recovered. I was pleased that I had followed my instincts and had copied both items for use at trial.

My only concern about using the videotape was the nine minute period when the lights were out during the showing of the video tape. It could not be verified that Erika did not leave the room during that period. Nine minutes was not enough time for her to go to her office, but it was ample opportunity for her to trigger her computer by phone and complete the crime. I was disturbed by the gap in her visibility on the tape. I decided that I would wait until I received the letter from Bricker before further considering the alibi defense.

Bricker may also have been attempting to induce me to disclose some of the points of my defense. In theory, any settlement of a civil or criminal case should reflect the relative strengths and weaknesses of the respective parties' cases. As part of the settlement process, attorneys attempt to enhance their bargaining position by using the strength of their case as leverage. All other factors being equal, a plaintiff with a very weak case cannot hope to obtain a substantial settlement. A defendant with a weak defense on the issues of liability and damages cannot escape with a minimum settlement. From a practical rather than theoretical standpoint, other factors may play a role in the settlement process. These include the relative economic power of each party, the experience of the parties' attorneys, the pressure upon either or both of the parties to have a resolution of the matter, and the costs in dollars and emotional energy of continuing the litigation.

If Bricker hoped to draw me into a discussion of my case, he should have been more forceful about the strength of his own case.

Then I would counter with a strong point of my own case. This process would continue until I had disclosed my entire case. But he never exposed the strength of his case. He understood that I was too experienced to fall into any such trap. Although my thorough review of the meeting helped place matters in perspective, I resolved that my inquiry into Bricker's motives for the meeting was not likely to bear fruit. I decided to report the conversation to Erika Williams.

38

I was always cautious about talking with Erika on the telephone for fear our conversations could be overheard. I suggested we meet at the same little coffee shop where I had met with Bricker, and she joined me there for afternoon tea. It was the first time I had been out with her in a public setting, and I felt a little self-conscious. Was I concerned that Sallie or one of her friends might see me? In any case, I felt a little uneasy when Erika joined me. She chose caffeine-free raspberry-apple tea and I had darjeeling. She remarked about being seen with me in a public place and questioned whether someone might be suspicious.

"Of what?" I asked. She looked embarrassed for having raised the issue. I congratulated myself on this brilliant response. Then I realized that I was playing power games with her and cautioned myself to concentrate upon the business at hand. I felt embarrassed and must have looked so.

"Well, we're both playing a game that serves no useful purpose," she commented.

I allowed her remark to pass and began the business portion of the meeting without engaging in any small talk. I discussed my meeting earlier in the day with the district attorney and disclosed my thoughts about his intent. I asked if she had any comments.

[153

"Well . . . no, I have already made clear to you my position on a plea bargain. I'll take my chances unless you tell me that the risk is so great that there is no viable alternative."

I assured her that nothing had changed since we last discussed the matter and asked if she had any other thoughts that might assist in her defense. She sat silently for several moments. I sensed that she was weighing a decision rather than searching her memory for an important fact.

"There are letters—letters I wrote to John Harley—love letters."

I asked what bearing that might have on the case.

"I'm not sure. What do you suppose he did with them? You are a married man. What would you do with letters received from your lover? Would you read and re-read them? Would you treasure them as a woman would, or would you destroy them? Remember, you are a man."

The fact that she had to remind me of my sex was a little disconcerting, but I thought about it for a moment. I believed that such a decision might be influenced more by personality than sex, and I expressed this belief to Erika.

"Based upon what you know about Harley, do you think he kept the letters intact?"

I pondered the question. I felt that Harley would not be influenced by sentiment to retain the letters. Once they were read and re-read his ego would have been satisfied and he would have destroyed them. However, if the letters might serve some potential alternate purpose, he most certainly would have retained them.

"But would he have ever taken them home?" she asked.

"No. Never," was my response. It is not the moral imperative of the marital vows that deters many men from having affairs. It is the fear of the consequences of discovery which causes men to toe the line. Harley would not have taken them home under any circumstances. I told her I felt that if he had kept them, they would be hidden in a location other than his house or his car. He would have to be sure that his wife never set eyes upon them or he might suffer severe consequences. I shuddered at the thought of such letters falling into the hands of a unsuspecting wife.

"Erika," I asked, "what has any of this to do with our defense?"

"Well, I was so much in love then, and today I feel like a fool for having written them at all. I keep thinking that he really might have wanted to get rid of me. There was so much emotion in those letters that he must have believed I would direct my passion against him if he rejected me. There could be a motive for his setting me up to take a fall. Even if I am not convicted, I will be forced to leave here under a cloud. Either way, he is rid of me."

I could not judge with any certainty the purpose of her raising the issue of the letters. My first reaction was that Marie would have shot an "I-told-you-so" look in my direction because Erika was trying to discover whether the evidence had been recovered from Harley's office. I let the matter of the love letters drop and asked if there was any other matter helpful to the defense that came to mind.

She began to summarize the case against her. "It seems that the strength of their case is that I had both opportunity and motive for committing the crime. The motive is money. The money was recovered in an account in my name with bank statements in a rented post office box in my name. I had access to the secret codes to transfer funds and the crime was committed using my computer. The codes were recovered in my office. But still, there is no 'smoking gun.' No one can testify that I actually pulled the trigger. The evidence is all circumstantial. I have an alibi for both 7:30 and for 8:31 — whichever time the crime was committed. Do they really think I would commit the crime then put the money in a bank account in my own name? Do they think that I would assume all that risk for a measly fifty-thousand dollars?"

I wondered whether her question was meant to be rhetorical.

"Erika, in the case of embezzlement, only the tip of the iceberg is visible. If they believe that you stole fifty thousand dollars, they may suspect that you stole ten times that amount but they have not yet discovered the loss or traced it to you. It may very well have been that the district attorney was hoping that by pressing on with this case, he could solicit your cooperation to disclose other thefts or else get a conviction and put you out of business. Even if he loses the case, you will have to move on. The University will be rid of you. You said so yourself."

Erika sat in silence sipping the last of her tea. She seemed suddenly depressed and, by habit, my desk-side manner manifested itself.

"Look," I said trying to sound sincere, "please try not to worry. I think we have an excellent chance without having to deal with Mr. Bricker."

She said nothing and stood up. "Thank you for the tea. Call me when you want me."

And she was gone.

39

Over the years, I have tried to pay closer attention to my physical, emotional, and mental reactions to the events happening around me. I believed that this was clear proof of my maturity. I was shocked when I discovered this was not maturity but middle age overtaking me. I realized that my physical and emotional energy were finite and that without pacing myself, I risked losing my edge.

I usually become anxious during the preparation for any court case, and I could feel the stress of Erika's impending trial overtaking me. At times like these, even my fantasies do little to relieve the pressure. When I arrived home that evening, Sallie noticed that I was preoccupied. She has weathered my moods in the past as I prepare for trial. Her plan of attack is to make sure that I am properly fed. If I want anything more from her, she knows that I will make those wishes known. Otherwise she leaves me alone.

That evening she had prepared stuffed pork chops with browned potatoes, peas, and cornbread twists. At first, I hardly noticed the special effort she had made in preparing such a delicious dinner after having worked all day at the bank. Fortunately, my instinct for self-preservation was still intact and I complimented her on the meal. She beamed with satisfaction at my remarks. Like most people, I tend to restrict my praise but give criticism freely. This character trait is a definite liability in both my professional and personal lives. Immersed in the grind of daily living, I seem to forget the inner rewards derived from making others feel good. Sallie's smile reminded me of how much I miss by reserving kind words and saying nothing when I could so effortlessly brighten someone's day.

"Sallie," I asked as I dried the last of the pans from dinner, "suppose you were having an affair with a married man."

I knew that would attract her attention, and it did. She looked at me not knowing what was coming. "And, you had written him some very steamy love letters. The affair ended . . . for whatever reason except discovery by a spouse . . . would it matter to a woman whether she knew what happened to the letters or not?"

Sallie looked at me skeptically.

"It's a hypothetical question, Sallie," I reassured her, trying not too sound defensive or serious.

"That wasn't why I looked at you that way . . . we're talking about Erika, right?"

I nodded.

Sallie thought about it for a moment. "Well, you're asking me as a woman. Hmm. . . . I don't think a woman would be very concerned about having written the letters. Women are a lot less sensitive about letting their feelings show, and I doubt that a woman who wrote letters like that would be ashamed of them. I think if the opportunity arose, a woman might destroy them. But I don't think a woman would perceive them as a threat—unless the woman were married herself. In that case it would be a matter of absolute necessity to make sure that her husband didn't see them. And since a former lover could not be trusted to return them, the situation is fraught with danger of the most serious kind."

I thought about Sallie's comments for a moment and, not wishing to press my luck, I remained silent. But Sallie knows me too well. She knew I had not completed my investigation.

"And . . . go on, you're not finished," she prodded.

[157

I chuckled. "Of course, you're right, there's more. As a woman, what would you do if you found out that your husband was having an affair with Erika?"

Try as Sallie might to sound clinical and objective in her response, I could tell she had something in store for me.

"Well, it would depend on how I found out. For example, if my husband admitted it, I would have a different reaction than if, for example, I saw him cozying up to her, holding her hand under the table at the "Rise and Shine" coffee house this afternoon at about 3:37 P.M. to be exact — and he didn't even see me come in and get a pound of New Guinea coffee for his breakfast."

She caught the surprise on my face and could not control her laughter. She pounced on me, knocking me to the kitchen floor, and playfully poked me in the ribs. "I would do this to my husband who had coffee..."

"...tea," I gasped.

"...with Erika."

Sitting on my stomach, holding me to the floor, Sallie reached up and unbuttoned the top buttons of her blouse revealing her breasts. I have always admired them, and she knows it. She stroked them gently with her fingertips, arousing herself and me as well. Then she leaned over and kissed me passionately.

We showered together afterward, washing, then drying each other. We continued the discussion lying in each other's arms on the bed.

"I think I know what you are asking. If I found love letters from Erika, I would be much more angry — though no less hurt — than if you admitted you were having an affair with her. My anger would be directed against you, not Erika ... though I would scratch her eyes out if given the chance. On the other hand, if I were having an affair and you found out, I think your anger might be as much directed against my lover as me. I think it is one of those male-female differences ... though I know you had that unfortunate incident happen years ago. Am I allowed to ask the purpose of this line of inquiry?"

My resistance level was low so, in possible violation of my attorney's vow of client confidentiality, I explained the purpose of my questions. I justified my conduct by assuring myself that I was not betraying a client's confidence. I was doing essential research into all aspects of her case and was merely soliciting an independent view of the facts surrounding the love letters. I had second thoughts later about having disclosed personal information about Erika to Sallie. In all honesty, I realized that I had told Sallie about Erika in order to protect myself, and that I was morally poorer for having done it. I knew in my mind that my conduct diminished an otherwise wonderful and memorable evening with Sallie.

40

There was an unmistakable note of excitement in Marie's voice as she buzzed the intercom and told me that John Harley was on the telephone. I had not spoken to him since he visited my office. Coming on the heels of Erika's inquiry about the love letters the day before, I should not have been surprised. I could not escape the nagging feeling that I was a character in a play who had not been made privy to the script.

Harley requested my presence in his office at my earliest convenience. We agreed upon an appointment for later in the day. I engaged in my usual routine, but found that I was distracted by thoughts about the reason for his insistence that we meet in his office. I could not imagine that he would discuss any facet of the case in his office where conversations might be overheard.

I arrived a few minutes before the appointed hour. I knew that he would make me sit in the outer office for a few minutes, but that he would appear within a short time of the appointed hour. As if on cue, Harley appeared from behind a closed door. He extended a hand to me and smiled.

"Thank you for taking the time to come to my office."

[159

He made a point of telling his attractive young secretary that he was not to be disturbed. I was sure it was standard operating procedure that he not to be interrupted during meetings. He had given those instructions so I would think that I was important and would have his undivided attention. I follow the same procedure in my office when I want to make the same impression on a client.

We entered his office which commanded a view of the campus. I thought it strange that he left the door open as he ushered me to a chair facing the large, polished desk. When I was seated, he walked slowly to the door and closed it. He surreptitiously studied my face as if he were searching for a clue to what I might be thinking. I had not been in his office, so I looked around as he seated himself. He watched my face as I observed the decor of the room and glanced at the large number of diplomas, certificates, and citations that hung on the walls as testimony to his academic success and community involvement.

Although I had not seen the room before, Rick Place had described it to me. Since Harley was watching me intently, I was careful not to glance at the spot where the evidence had been concealed. I wished that Place had not disclosed the location, lest I betray my knowledge. I knew that Harley was watching for any hint that I might know of the hiding place. I tried to relax.

I complimented him on the decor and commented about his desk being free from papers. I could tell he understood the importance of conveying the impression of being in complete control. A clean, well-organized office sends an important signal to a visitor.

"I know that you may not be comfortable in discussing Erika's case in these surroundings, or in any other location for that matter. And that is not the purpose of my request which you have so graciously honored."

I nodded and he continued. "You are Erika's representative, and for a number of reasons — appearances, requests from the authorities, and the unsettled nature of my relationship with Erika — I cannot speak to her directly. Therefore, I am pleased that you have come here this afternoon."

Again I nodded.

"Erika wrote me some letters — beautiful letters at the time when we had a . . ." he paused.

I was tempted to interject the words "an affair" but I held my tongue.

". . . special relationship. They were so well written and meant so much to me that I was indiscreet enough to have retained them. They were special, and I assumed that eventually Erika and I would be able to have an open relationship. When that happened, these letters would have no longer been . . ." Again he paused.

"A threat to your existing relationship?"

"Well said. The letters were secreted here in this office."

Again he studied me intently to see if my eyes betray my knowledge of their hiding place. I kept my eyes upon him, pretending to be totally absorbed with the conversation. He knew he had not sold me his line about the letters meaning so much to him.

"Well," he continued, "the letters were removed from this office by persons unknown and I have not seen them since. Please do not misunderstand my next statement, for I mean no disrespect to your honor personally or as an attorney, but my initial reaction upon discovering their disappearnce was that I might soon be hearing from you."

I knew that he was referring to his belief that I might use the letters to induce him into cooperating with Erika's defense. I was not sure that I wanted him to know that blackmail was my first reaction to his statement. I decided to take charge of the moment.

"I understand your concern. Let me assure you that I know that you cannot be blackmailed. You are not vulnerable to such tactics. Blackmail may be employed only in situations where the victim cannot think rationally. It is not likely that you ever would reach that point. In your case, the consequences of disclosure of the information would not be as terrible as your loss of control over your own fate."

I paused to allow Harley time to consider my statement. I thought about saying that I had never seen any letters and did not know their whereabouts. But Harley knew I chose words carefully. If I said anything, he would realize soon enough that I knew of the letters. He then would assume that Erika had discussed them with me and that they were in Erika's possession or she knew where they were. Erika would not be safe.

[161

He leaned back in his chair, considering his next move. When I did not continue, I think he realized that the conversation was over. I would disclose nothing more. He had verified that I understood that he was not vulnerable to blackmail. This removed that threat. But he was no closer to discovering what had happened to the letters. He had lost control of events, he was vulnerable, and more importantly, he knew it.

"I do care about what happens to Erika," he said without much sincerity as he stood up, indicating that the meeting had been concluded.

"I know that you do," I lied.

I sensed that he was engaged in a desperate game, the nature and extent of which I did not clearly understand. Perhaps my last comment sounded too shallow, for he shot me a distrustful look as I stood to leave. He opened the door for me, still watching my eyes. He did not shake my hand or acknowledge my departure. On the way out I smiled at his secretary. I noticed that she had red hair.

41

After my meeting with Harley I asked Rick Place if he would verify that the letters were still hidden in Harley's office. Rick's first reaction was that one of the purposes of the meeting might have been for Harley or the police to bait a trap for us. He cautioned me that Harley was very smart and that we risked more than we could gain by re-entering Harley's office. He questioned whether the letters had any bearing upon Erika's defense. I asked Place if it was possible that Harley had gone to the location while we had temporarily removed the letters. He responded that it was technically possible but unlikely. Place had marked the hiding place so that if anyone had entered before the material was replaced, the re-entry would have been disclosed. Rick Place certainly knew what he was doing.

Erika's mention of the letters followed by Harley's inquiry provided much food for thought. I decided to ask my resident expert, Marie to interpret the facts for me. That afternoon during a lull in the daily routine, I related Erika's comments about the love letters to Marie.

"It seems clear to me that the letters are part of Erika's plan, or she would not have brought them to your attention. That wasn't just idle chatter or intellectual curiosity on her part about how a man or a woman would react to the discovery of a spouse's infidelity. It seems that you are to become involved with the letters. Of course, you have not reached that part of the script yet."

"Or," I asked, "you think she would not have mentioned them?"

Marie nodded. I recounted the substance of my meeting with Harley.

"Well, it might be blackmail by Erika. But I know Harley's type. He would never stand for blackmail. Placed in that position, he could be unpredictable. I don't think Erika would play that game with him . . . it's too dangerous . . . and she's much too smart."

"But, Marie, what about the letters? Why tell me about the letters?"

"Good question. You didn't disclose to Harley that you knew anything about them. That was good. I'm not sure that Erika knows you're that smart . . . no offense, but we're talking about a woman who is not bound by the same constraints as you and I. You're not equipped emotionally, morally, or psychologically to face off against her. . . . For our sake, I hope you never have to."

"The letters?" I asked, trying to return Marie to the subject. It seemed to me that she was using every opportunity to plant the seeds of doubt in my mind about my relationship with Erika.

"Oh . . . maybe she thought that you would let it slip that you'd heard of the letters. After all, you said that you thought of doing just that when Harley brought up the letters. Then she would have conveyed the message to Harley — through you — that she had regained possession of the love letters. That's not exactly blackmail. As I said, Erika knows better than to attempt blackmail. It is better

[163

to give Harley the impression that the letters are in Erika's possession. He never would go after her or the letters unless he knew for sure that she had them. The risks would be too great."

"So?"

"Even though Erika did not contact him about the letters and make demands of Harley, he could not know for sure that they would not be used by her against him in the future. It keeps him off balance. He cannot become too aggressive in his testimony against her. There is the implied threat of retaliation through disclosure of the letters to his wife. It is kind of like the 'nuclear blackmail' of the Cold War. Neither side threatened overtly. However, there was always an implication of retaliation. It served a useful purpose. I think Erika knew that Harley would ask you about the letters."

"How so?"

"Well, she knew that Harley would be concerned about them. Harley likes to have every base covered. He discovered the letters were missing and he had to assume that Erika had something to do with it. If his wife had found them, he would have noticed immediately by her reaction. What wife wouldn't react? He could not contact Erika for the reasons he mentioned to you. You are the only person connected to Erika who might be able to shed light on the subject. After all, you said you almost told him that you did not know where the letters might be. A statement like that would have confirmed for Harley that you knew about the letters and that they were in Erika's possession. The letters have nothing to do directly with the defense."

Marie's explanation seemed a little farfetched. If Erika was using the letters to keep Harley under control, there must be a better way to convey the message to Harley.

"I know what you are thinking." Marie agreed. "I guess Erika could have conveyed the message about the letters to Harley anonymously. Of course, he might not have known that Erika had them."

I reminded Marie that we were not even sure who had the letters. In spite of Rick Place's warning about a possible trap, I called him and asked that he verify that the letters were still there. He agreed to undertake the assignment, but told me that I would have to wait. It was too dangerous to re-enter the office within such a short time after Harley had mentioned the disappearance to me.

The next morning there was an urgent message on our office answering machine from Rick Place. When I arrived at his office, he was all smiles. I assumed that he had re-entered Harley's office and had important news to report.

"Well, I have re-affirmed my faith in my instincts," he said as he led me to his lab. He loaded a tape in a videocassette recorder and played a segment for me. It showed the office building where Harley worked. The picture was distorted.

"Night camera... sees in the dark," he explained.

I asked what I was supposed to be looking for.

"See over there — up by Harley's window... there is someone hidden on the ledge looking in."

After I knew where to focus, I was able to clearly make out the figure of a man positioned to observe the interior of Harley's office.

"And look at the parking lot and in front."

I observed two automobiles one in front of the building and another near the parking lot at the side. Both vehicles were occupied.

"And a van in the loading zone."

"Yes," I replied.

"Police... a stakeout."

"When?" I asked.

"Last night from about 1:30 to — let's say — 4:00. I think they knew someone had been in the building. Each time I went in there it was at about 2:30 A.M. This could explain some of the things I encountered during my previous visits — like the sensor that would detect someone in the room. I'm sure Harley's office is bugged."

I did not quite follow Place's reasoning.

"It seems clear that a trap was baited for someone. They don't order a stakeout just for kicks. I thought it might have been me they were looking for, or possibly Erika. In any case, after they packed up and left, I entered the office. The seal to the hiding place was broken, the letters and all the other materials were gone."

I just could not understand how the letters and the police stakeout figured in Erika's case.

"From an investigator's point of view, there's a place on the puzzle board for every piece. And every little fact is important. But I must say that, aside from being evidence of the affair between Erika and Harley, I cannot guess how these letters might be important to Erika's case. We know they were hidden by someone in Harley's office, but they have nothing to do directly with the crime. Erika mentions them and later that day Harley calls you to his office to discuss them. That night the police post people to observe the office. Now, the location of the letters is unknown. The coincidence is too compelling. Obviously, those letters are important to someone," offered Place.

I obtained an assurance from Place that he would use his considerable deductive powers to pose a theory. There was too much going on for a simple case of embezzlement. There was too much intrigue. I could not imagine what was happening to involve so much activity. My comfort level with the whole case was diminishing rapidly.

42

Even my alter ego James Petrikin was having his doubts about his role in the Eben Jones case.

Petrikin walked slowly along the dusty street from his office, up the hill to the county courthouse. It was late afternoon and there were few people on the street that mid-week day. It seemed that the weight of the world bore down upon his shoulders. Over the last months his cough had sunk deeper and deeper into his chest. In the past, his cough did not become worse until late in the winter. This year, for the first time, the cough returned in late summer. He began to breathe harder as he reached the town square. He interrupted his trek pretending to himself that he was surveying the street scene, and that he really was not gathering his strength for a final assault up the remainder of the hill to the courthouse.

"The worst lies," he cautioned himself, "are the lies we tell ourselves."

Earlier that day he had obtained the census reports for all of the townships and municipalities in the county. He poured over every name reported to the county by the township supervisors and town councils for the years 1818 through 1821. Eben Jones was not listed.

In the years before government-funded welfare programs, each municipality was responsible for dealing with its own indigents. A group of men was appointed to deal with each person who appeared to have no visible means of support. These men, called Overseers of the Poor, had the power to order a person out of the jurisdiction by holding a hearing and filing a report with the court. They often ordered a person to leave, burdening a neighboring municipality's Overseers of the Poor who, in turn, acted to pass the problem on to someone else. Upon the chance that Eben Jones was a vagrant, Petrikin went through all the proceedings and reports of the Overseers of the Poor in the various townships as filed with the clerk of court from 1818 through 1821. Eben Jones' name did not appear on any of the lists of vagrants. It seemed that everywhere Petrikin searched, he could discover no evidence that Eben Jones had ever been in the county. Yet the information related by Jones in Perrow's letter indicated that Jones was familiar with places in the county and people who still lived there. The facts were too compelling to disregard.

Petrikin re-entered the courthouse intent upon searching the assessments record to see whether Eben Jones owned real or personal property. The fact that he had filed the lawsuit against Peter Karthaus was an indication that he had enough property to hire a lawyer to plead his case. The assessment clerk, an elderly man, listened intently as Petrikin explained the purpose of his inquiry.

"Well, Squire, I doubt that you'll find any assessment for this person. Most negroes have no property and most of the local assessors in the townships do not even bother to list their names. You see, if they list their names, then their property must be assessed or an exoneration from imposition of the tax must be filed with the county here in this office. Taxes can be exonerated for reasons of disability or military service, or of course, indigence. The county must ascertain the validity of each reason for exoneration. In doing so, we make inquiry of the local assessor. The assessor is paid prorata only on the taxes collected. They have little interest in verifying the status of someone they will not be able to assess and collect taxes from. They complain about having to remit reports supporting the exoneration for indigents even though it is their sworn duty to do so. After making time-consuming inquiries regarding these indigents, the assessors learn that it is not in their interest to list persons on the tax rolls who are excused from payment by reason of indigence. As a consequence, we do not receive reports that may include persons in the townships who are unlikely to pay their taxes."

Despite the warning, Petrikin began to search the tax rolls for Eben Jones. Soon it was apparent that the name was not to be found.

"Another disappointment," Petrikin commented as he handed the book of tax rolls to the assessment clerk.

"I am sorry, Squire. You seem so intent upon finding the name of this negro."

"I cannot understand how a man may have passed through this county and has recounted important points of his life here, but there is no evidence of his existence and no one seems to remember him."

The clerk thought about it for a moment. "Sir, with all respect, have you considered that the slave Eben Jones was not truthful with the attorney Perrow?"

"How so, Clerk?"

"It seems that you are taking as true the story recounted in the letter from your colleague in Virginia."

"But," replied Petrikin, "there is no reason why Attorney Perrow would wish to promote a falsehood with me. He has solicited my assistance in establishing the freedom of Eben Jones through a writ of *habeas corpus*."

"Mr. Petrikin, I am not suggesting that Perrow has imposed upon your good offices. Perhaps it is this Eben Jones who has misled Perrow. The account is not Perrow's. Your letter indicates that it is Eben Jones' story as recounted to Perrow and retold to you. As you men at the bar might argue before our judge, Jones' account as reported by Perrow is merely hearsay evidence. It may very well be that Eben Jones was not here in the county. He may have spun a yarn to persuade Perrow to take his case. After all, he had every reason to do so."

Petrikin thought about it for a moment.

The clerk continued. "You must understand that this negro is facing a life of continued slavery. Maybe he is a runaway. As luck would have it, during the time he was temporarily free, he may have been in the company of men . . . white or negro . . . who knew our county. He listened to the stories about life in Pennsylvania. When he was captured, the lawyer Perrow agreed for whatever reason to plead his case based upon this story. The unfortunate Jones knew that if he could be proved to be a resident and citizen of Pennsylvania, he might be freed. He recounted to Perrow the stories that he heard, making claim that they were *his* experiences while a resident here. Perrow took up the case and enlisted you to verify the information."

"Which I regret I have been unable to do," commented Petrikin.

"Exactly, Sir. You see, even if you were to find the name of Eben Jones in the record here in the county, or if you were to come upon someone here who remembered him, there is no justification for believing that the negro there is the same negro who passed through this county . . . or even that the negro there languishing in jail at Lovingston, Virginia, is Eben Jones. Someone here who knew the negro of 1819 must go there to verify that this negro is the same person as the one there. I have not read law, as you have, Mr. Petrikin. . ." The clerk paused, trying to choose his words carefully. ". . . but I wager that it does the lawyer Perrow little good to receive your affidavits about Eben Jones' citizenship or residency in our county, without being able to prove that the negro held there is the same person who was here. Your affidavits cannot do that. His writ will fail if he relies upon your affidavits alone."

Petrikin had not fully considered the issues raised by the clerk and a look of disappointment crossed his face.

"Squire, do not be discouraged by this. Your charity and sense of duty and honor are well known among the citizens here. You are well respected. This lawyer has asked of you what cannot be done."

"I am discouraged. Clerk, your kind words provide me much comfort and I am grateful for them. But I must believe that if I can produce the affidavits and forward them to Virginia that I may be of assistance to this unfortunate slave. The lawyer Perrow would not have asked something that would be of no consequence to the freedom of Eben Jones."

"I pray, Sir, that you are not being taken for a fool."

The clerk shrugged his shoulders, turned his back on Petrikin, and replaced the tax roll book on the shelf. Petrikin gathered his strength once again and left the courthouse to return to his office. He was troubled by what the clerk had said. Had he taken time to consider carefully the legal implications of Perrow's request, he might have had second thoughts about making the moral commitment to help Eben Jones. His legal training had been displaced by his moral opposition to slavery. Instead of thinking like a lawyer, considering the evidentiary requirements of a writ of *habeas corpus*, he had acted with his heart and not his head. He had nothing to show for the valuable time spent pursuing Eben Jones' elusive past.

By the time Petrikin arrived at his office, he had resolved to continue the search for evidence of Eben Jones' residency in the county. However, Petrikin realized that not all tasks undertaken as a lawyer bear fruit, no matter what the effort. Nobility of purpose may serve to motivate action, but it cannot guarantee results. The best that a lawyer can hope to achieve is to represent a client's interests to the best of one's ability.

I opened the door to my own law office with the same sense of purpose and resolve as Petrikin. I had been led astray by Erika's dominating personality and the web she had spun around the characters in this unique drama. I had permitted her case to overwhelm me, and I had lost sight of my role in the matter. Like Petrikin, I had forsaken my training as a lawyer in favor of my wish to unravel the mystery surrounding the parties involved and to save a damsel in distress. I was defense counsel, charged with mounting a defense to the Commonwealth's charges against her; I must now limit my efforts to that.

Jury selection was scheduled for the next morning. I had no time to squander.

43

At the beginning of my career with the law firm, the lawyers would gather in the firm library before an important trial to discuss the various facts of a case. From time to time I participated in these pre-trial planning sessions; they were one of the best aspects of being in a law firm. Typically, the most senior partner took charge. The assembled lawyers would brainstorm over the case's facts and law, and they would argue trial tactics among themselves.

Although I was never a football player, I have always felt that this approach to trial preparation was similar to a football game plan. All the assistant coaches gathered under the direction of the head coach. The relative strengths and weaknesses of the opponent's game were analyzed. A plan was formulated to counter the opponent's strength, and appropriate measures were instituted to exploit its weakness. The opponent's possible game plan was also scrutinized, taking into account the team's own strengths and weaknesses.

In the firm, the discussions and the decisions that resulted in a trial plan, like a football game plan, were a product of collective reasoning and discussion. I never ceased to marvel when one attorney would point out a flaw in the plan that had gone unnoticed by the group. In these discussions, the trial attorney who had charge of the case seemed less able to judge accurately the strengths and weaknesses of his or her own case and the merits of the various legal arguments. A senior member of the firm confirmed for me that it was for that very reason that these discussions were held. A fresh perspective was always important. Every participant brought his or her unique training, experience, and perspective to the meeting. During these discussions, egos were often bruised, and rivalries and animosities among the partners exposed. But, the end result was a well thought out and highly developed trial plan. When the trial was won, the whole firm shared in the success of the collective effort.

As a sole practitioner, none of this is available to me. There is no one to test my legal argument. The interpretation of the facts and the application of the law are solely my own, without the benefit of a second or third opinion. The trial plan was a product of one man's effort, influenced by my own prejudices and predilections and my strengths and weaknesses as an attorney.

I know that other attorneys are more experienced, smarter, and quicker than I. But I never perceive these to be disadvantages for which I cannot compensate as the need arises. However, I must do everything alone. When preparing for trial, this vulnerability plays havoc with my psyche. I vacillate between moments of extreme hope and excessive despair. Although I have been in sole law practice almost fifteen years and have gone through at least fifty major trials, I have never become accustomed to the anxiety of having to prepare for trial without the support of colleagues.

Having resolved to keep things in perspective, I asked Marie that I be left alone. She has worked with me a long time, so she knew that I would be focusing my energies on the defense. I sat alone in the office library and outlined my overall trial plan.

The case against Erika was all circumstantial. No one could testify that her fingers had pressed the computer keys ordering the transfer of funds. The Commonwealth's plan had to involve what I call "stacking" circumstantial evidence. Since no one actually saw Erika commit the crime, the jury would want to see a substantial number of pieces of evidence that indicated that Erika probably committed the crime. It is a human failing to believe that the more circumstantial evidence that is accumulated implicating a person in a criminal activity, the more likely it is that the person actually committed the crime. I believed that the district attorney would build a case against Erika piece by piece until the jury was faced with a mountain of evidence against her and as a result, the jury would believe beyond a reasonable doubt that Erika was guilty. Bricker and his staff were skilled prosecutors. They would assemble a string of witnesses. The district attorney's trial plan would not stop there. Not only would the evidence of wrongdoing have to be stacked heavily against Erika, the prosecutor would also attempt to convince the jury that Erika was capable of criminal behavior. Without tying the evidence to Erika's willingness and ability to commit the crime, the district attorney's case was vulnerable.

My trial strategy was to attack the Commonwealth's case from the start by questioning the evidence and the inferences to be derived from it. Since the D.A. would rely on the cumulative effect of a lot of evidence, I would have to meet each new piece of the puzzle and destroy its probative value as evidence against Erika. I could do this by attacking the credibility of the person who presented the evidence, or I could point out to the jury that the witness was an enemy of Erika's or had something to gain by her conviction. I could also undermine the assumptions upon which investigators or experts interpreted the evidence for the jury. If I were able to destroy or cast doubt upon most of the circumstantial evidence against Erika, I would undermine the Commonwealth's case. If evidence beyond a reasonable doubt was severely lacking, I could seek a dismissal of the charges before having to present a defense. This was the best-case scenario for me. But I know all too well that the best-case scenario and worst-case scenario rarely happen. Although it is necessary to prepare for both in a well-developed trial plan, even the best trial plan may not survive opening arguments. There are too many variables.

Each piece of circumstantial evidence did seem to indicate Erika's guilt. In undermining the mountain of evidence, I would have to argue that Erika was framed by someone. After all, how did her signature appear on the bank signature card or the post office box rental agreement? If Erika did not sign them, who did?

I felt that I had more than a fighting chance of casting doubt upon the validity of each piece of evidence that the prosecutor could muster against Erika. But juries are composed of humans. If I was going forward with a claim that Erika was framed, I had to produce a likely person responsible for doing so.

Establishing good rapport between the defendant and the jury is an important element of any defense. My job would be to cast a favorable light upon Erika so that the pre-conceived notion of a defendant's probable guilt would be mitigated. If the women on the jury felt threatened by Erika, or if the men found her attractive yet cold and calculating, the scales could tip heavily against her. On the other hand, Erika might be viewed by the jurors as a helpless female caught in a web of deceit masterminded by some heartless administrator at the University. My efforts to undermine the prosecution's case might then take root and the seeds of doubt about Erika's guilt might bear fruit.

This was a difficult assignment. Erika was beautiful. People are threatened by beauty even though they profess to admire it and seek it for themselves. My concern was that Erika's beauty would be perceived as unapproachable to men and threatening to women. Women did not like her. If men liked her, they certainly were not part of her life. I needed to portray her as the pretty "girl-next door" to the men jurors and as the good-looking, non-threatening "best friend" to the women jurors. I made a note to discuss this aspect of trial preparation with Erika.

The district attorney placed a high value on his staff. At trial Bricker would often have two or three deputy prosecutors with him. He might have his chief investigator at the table and a secretary to transcribe important testimony. Once, years before, after a jury trial, a juror had told me that the district attorney had so many people at the table with him while I had only the defendant that the jury felt I was the underdog and we received the benefit of many of the doubts in testimony. I knew that Bricker would have a table full at trial, and I resolved to sit alone with Erika to give the jurors the impression that it was just the two of us defending ourselves against the Commonwealth of Pennsylvania's overwhelming superiority in numbers and resources.

The final aspect of trial preparation was to remind myself that the key element of the jury's decision would be their interpretation of the evidence, and not the interpretation of the facts as viewed by the prosecution or defense. I must therefore examine the facts from the jury's point of view. Since absolute truth was not relevant to the jurors' decision, my job was to make our interpretation of the meaning of the facts more believable than the prosecutor's.

One aspect of trial work that continues to amaze me is the inability of most trial attorneys to keep things simple for the jury. The jurors want to see things as black or white, right or wrong, yes or no, guilty or not guilty. They take their job seriously and they conscientiously want to see cold, hard facts upon which to base a verdict. Trial attorneys tend to become so involved in the nuances of their cases that most of what is presented to the jury goes unnoticed and plays no role in the decision the jury is called upon to make.

At trial, I try to remember that the simplest questions are the best and that the jury is not there as an audience to view my clever cross-examination of witnesses, my repartee with the prosecutor, and my incisive legal argument to the judge. They are there to make a guilty-not guilty decision. I would structure my attack against the prosecutor's evidence to make it easy for them to see that Erika was framed. Once the jury knew what my argument was, I would tailor my approach to meet their expectations.

Based upon my past experience with the district attorney and his staff, I was not convinced that the prosecutors did this mental exercise of keeping things simple. They always seem to make complex arguments that are well structured and well reasoned as debating techniques, but were too difficult for the average, non-legally trained juror to comprehend. This fact gave me hope, and as the finishing touches were applied to my trial plan, I knew that I had reason for optimism.

44

It was my first evening meeting with Erika. Marie made a special effort before she left the office to remind me about her perception of Erika's character and to issue a special warning on my behalf. As I left the house after dinner, Sallie was also on the verge of saying something, but hesitated, smiled, and kissed me on the cheek instead.

At the appointed hour, I met Erika on the street and escorted her to my office. We entered the library and sat at the conference room table across from each other. She seemed relaxed and smiled pleasantly as I opened one of my files.

"I was thinking," she started, "about the kind of impression I should make on the jury. I know that you consider this to be an important element of the defense, so I have given it substantial thought."

It was true that I considered it to be very important, but how did Erika know about the premium I placed upon the defendant's appearance?

"I will wear my hair up and back, in a kind of ponytail. My makeup will be very muted and I'll wear a dress that resembles a jumper — and a pair of low heels. I won't carry a briefcase, but I will have a large, floppy, over-the-shoulder leather purse. I won't wear any jewelry except for a sports watch with a dark band and plain post earrings. This will give me a more youthful and innocent appearance. I've researched it, and unless you object, I plan on giving that impression."

I cautioned her that her wardrobe was only one aspect of the impression that she might create before the jury. I explained that her demeanor must also be appropriate. She should not actively engage other people in conversation, but should speak only when spoken to. When spoken to, she should be respectful in both words and tone of voice. She should not appear to be intimidated by the proceedings and the environment, but she should not seem comfortable with them either, lest the jury believe that she had been in court before.

"How should I react to the testimony of the prosecution witnesses?" she asked.

I explained that while she should not nod or shake her head to statements made by witnesses, it was inappropriate to refrain from all reaction. It is a human tendency to react negatively to false accusations, and the jury would expect her to react to direct accusations leveled by witnesses and the prosecutors.

"Erika," I instructed, "the jury will assume you have feelings and emotions. They instinctively know that this trial should be stressful for you. They will expect you to react . . . but not overreact . . . to events as they unfold. I must emphasize that they will expect you to be human."

". . . but you don't think I am?" she interrupted.

The question was rhetorical. Despite my wish to the contrary, I knew that Erika never cared what I thought of her personally. It was all strictly business to her.

"Erika, the important thing is that you act as if you are human. The jury must not be disappointed. Reality matters not — appearances and impressions do. I know you are capable of reacting appropriately as circumstances warrant. If a witness or the prosecutor says something hurtful to you, you can look hurt. To do otherwise would be unnatural. Just don't oversell. It is always better to understate your reactions. The jury will fill in the blanks."

"I can do it," she assured me.

I knew she could.

Over the next half hour, I explained to Erika the trial plan I had developed. When I finished, she sat pensively.

"Well, I must say that you've put a lot of effort into this. Conceptually, I like it."

"But?" I asked a little defensively.

"No 'but' really . . . but . . . the plan is only as good as your ability to execute it. I guess the reality of the situation — my future — this has squarely placed that at issue . . . is that . . ."

I knew that she was verbalizing the fear that her future was beyond her control. Although she might be called upon to perform, her fate had passed into another's hands. This situation was intolerable to a woman like Erika who so highly prized her self-sufficiency, independence, and invulnerability. Her stock in trade were competence and self-confidence. She displayed these attributes to everyone to create the image of herself as having to answer to no one. She could take care of herself without help from anyone. Yet here she was.

Not knowing what to do next, I just sat there. I felt that my own vulnerability would be revealed if I defended the trial plan or my ability as a trial lawyer. On the other hand, she was the principal and I was the agent. I owed her the duty of building her confidence and allaying her fears, lawyer to client. I feared that my reassurance would be rebuffed by someone who professed by her words and deeds not to need it. Like everyone else, when I speak words of kindness, I do not like to have them rejected.

She leaned back in her chair and placed her right index finger against her pursed lips.

"Well, Counsellor, no words of wisdom? I can see in your eyes that you have thought the words, but you have not shared them with me. Perhaps it is that you now believe that this is strictly business and your thoughts are not relevant to the transaction."

Try as I might, I could not believe that Erika's defense was "strictly business." It flew in the face of the vision of myself that I had established. Caring about my clients is what sets me apart in my own mind from my money-grubbing colleagues.

"No, Erika, it never is 'strictly business' for me. There are always issues of honor, dignity, and principle. These issues are very much a part of your case and they are important in terms of you as a person, too. It never is 'strictly business.'"

"Good. That is all I need to know." She smiled at me. I escorted her from the office to the street and said good-night.

When I returned to the office, the telephone was ringing. It was Ed Bricker, the district attorney. He apologized for calling me after hours, but he assumed that I too would be burning the midnight oil.

"I think," he began, "that I should make one last attempt to discuss one of the issues with you."

Such a pre-trial call from the prosecutor's office was unheard of. Suddenly it all fell into place for me. I now knew the reason for the coffeehouse meeting and this late night phone call.

"Ed," I said, "I know why you are calling, but I'd like to hear it from you."

"I don't think you do know," was his response.

We were engaged in a game, trying to bluff each other into disclosing the purpose of the call.

"Ed, it is you who called me. I did not call you. But, just to assure you that you have my cooperation — within appropriate limits and attorney to attorney — I know that you are calling to explore the possibility of a plea bargain to reduce the risk to me and to solve a problem for you."

"Solve a problem for me?" he asked, trying to prod me into disclosing more.

I remained silent.

"Of course you are right," he continued. "I am calling to offer you a bargain that I think will reduce your risk in going to trial. You know better than to tell me that you have minimal risk."

I knew better, but did not express this to Bricker.

"Well, I'll agree to reduce the charge to failure to make required disposition of funds — one count — a definite probation offense. I checked. Williams is clean, no priors, I could even suggest a suspended sentence . . . she resigns . . . leaves town. The case is over — a memory. The Commonwealth's interest has been served. Your client walks away, almost scott-free."

I knew that there are always two parts to any bargain.

"And the price?" I asked.

Bricker hesitated. There was silence. The prosecutor's experience with embezzlement had been the same as mine. They had found the fifty-thousand dollars, but they had not been able to discover any additional funds missing from the university accounts that may have been attributable to Erika. Either there was more money missing that remained undiscovered, or it was likely that Erika was framed and innocent of the charges. I knew this was the reason for the late night call.

When Bricker remained silent, I decided that it served no useful purpose to continue the intrigue any longer.

[179

"You want her to disclose where the rest of the money is and how she got it?"

"Right. I want her to come clean. I'll guarantee that there are no repercussions."

I knew that there could be no such bargain and I told him so. "I hope we are not both being taken for fools," he said as he hung up the phone.

45

Bricker's parting words echoed in my ears as I drove home that night—being taken for fools—the same words uttered to James Petrikin by the clerk after his fruitless search of the assessment records. Over the next several days Petrikin searched his memory for any evidence that Charles Perrow may have had a hidden agenda when soliciting Petrikin's help. Even if the clerk's point about the probative value of the affidavits were true, Petrikin could think of no other reason why Perrow might seek his help.

"There is no reason for Charles Perrow to engage me in gathering the affidavits other than to establish the freedom of Eben Jones," Petrikin reassured himself.

Petrikin sat in his office and re-read the letter from Charles Perrow. He had been unable so far to confirm any of the facts in the letter as they related to Eben's residency in the county. Inopportune as it may have been, he had made inquiry of Judge Burnside, but the judge indicated that he knew of no negro named Eben Jones. There was no indication of the lawsuit that Eben said he had filed against Peter Karthaus. The letter also made reference to a Mr. Reese and a Mr. Fleming as additional people who may have remembered Eben Jones. Petrikin knew no men named Reese or Fleming, but he resolved to check the census rolls again for their names. There was no practical method for verifying any of the other events recounted in the letter.

Petrikin's efforts to locate evidence in support of Eben's writ of *habeas corpus* had not met with success. Since his health was impaired, he needed to limit his efforts. He considered writing to Perrow and reporting his lack of success. If he did that, Perrow's enthusiasm as expressed in his letter might flag, relegating Jones to a life of slavery. Petrikin would not be pleased to have that on his conscience. He tried to place himself in Perrow's position.

Petrikin knew that the effect of an unfavorable response would depend upon whether Perrow had alternative legal theories in support of his petition for a writ of *habeas corpus*. Perrow's legal argument as disclosed to Petrikin was a constitutional one, based upon the fact that Eben Jones was a citizen of Pennsylvania and as such was not subject to the registration laws of Virginia. Jones was apprehended without proper papers which he need not have carried if he were a citizen of Pennsylvania. To support that argument, Petrikin must provide evidence of Jones' Pennsylvania citizenship. However, if Perrow had other arguments in support of his petition, the failure of Petrikin to obtain the affidavits would not necessarily be fatal to the prospects of the judge's issuing a writ to free Eben Jones.

"Perrow did not disclose any alternative theories in the letter," thought Petrikin. "But, were I Perrow, soliciting the aide of another attorney on humanitarian grounds, I certainly would give the impression that the whole case depended upon receiving the assistance as requested."

Petrikin decided not to inform Perrow that his efforts had thus far been unsuccessful. There was no point in discouraging Perrow if supporting evidence could ultimately be supplied. Satisfied with his decision to defer writing to Perrow for the time being, Petrikin busied himself with his regular clients and cases reminding himself to keep to his priorities.

I had to remind myself to temporarily abandon my fantasies in favor of the business at hand. I knew I was ready for trial because I could work my way through the trial plan linking all the elements. I also knew that the trial was imminent through the return of nightmares.

One of my recurring nightmares during my undergraduate and post-graduate days was the sudden realization that I had a final examination the following day and had neither attended class nor read the course material. I usually awoke in a cold sweat, remembering in vivid detail the sinking feeling in the pit of my stomach as I entered the examination room with no hope of reprieve. After becoming a lawyer, the nightmare changed to seeing myself in court and hearing the call of the court docket for a case where I was listed as counsel and had not prepared and did not know the client. In my dream, I approached the judge, my stomach churning and beads of sweat upon my forehead. My mouth was dry and my voice cracked with each word of explanation that I was not ready to proceed to trial. As the judge leaned forward to admonish me and recommend immediate disbarment, I would awake, sweating and clutching the mattress.

After a few of these episodes, I sought professional help. I was assured that these dreams involving a lack of preparation and the resulting humiliation were common. Although the psychologist's reassurance brought me some comfort, I have never become accustomed to these dreams. And no matter how much I might prepare for a trial, the dream always recurs.

The routine around our house also changes as trials draw closer. Sallie knows I will be preoccupied, so she makes a special effort to avoid confrontation. She once remarked that during trial preparations she misses the confrontations because they remind her that she is married. It is reassuring to know that one of the main purposes of our marriage is to maintain a higher level of contention and confrontation than she might otherwise enjoy if she were single. However, good judgment prevails, and I never mention this observation to her.

Sallie never knows exactly what her role should be during these periods of impending trial. She wants to be helpful, but she does not wish to interfere. Usually, if I need her assistance I request it. On rare occasions I seek her counsel regarding how the jury might react to a particular style or line of questioning. And at times I practice my opening or closing statement before her. Sallie has a good sense of what a jury might accept or reject. However, I am hesitant to expose my professional expertise to her and I do not consult her as freely and openly as I might. I can never decide just why this is so. I tell myself that my professional life is mine alone, not part of my relationship with Sallie. Not seeking her help is a natural response to jealously guarding my professional independence. However, my therapist assured me that I have a deeply seated fear that she will criticize me and that I might perceive her negative comments as rejection. So long as I keep my professional life to myself, there is no possibility of rejection and my ego as an attorney will remain intact. I do not know how many times over the years that I have failed to consult Sallie when it might have been helpful to my client's cause. Knowing this and practicing it are two different matters. Like my alter ego Petrikin, I know that the worst lies are those we tell ourselves.

In addition to the nightmares and the change in routine around Sallie during the pre-trial period, I am also subject to violent mood swings. My temperament varies between moments of supreme self-confidence and agonizing self-doubt. After so many years, I have come to expect this behavioral pattern. However, anticipating it and dealing effectively with it are two different matters.

As a young attorney, I asked a senior associate in the firm if he too suffered from self-doubt before an important trial. He informed me that he never doubted his abilities as an attorney. At first, I blindly accepted his assertion that he was not afflicted as I was. I began to question whether I had the fortitude to be a trial lawyer. I tried to observe other lawyers closely for tell-tale signs that they too had crises of confidence before trial. Part of the stock in trade of a good attorney is the ability to disguise true feelings and intent, and I never was able to observe evidence of this weakness in others. As I became more seasoned, I knew intuitively that such feelings are part of the psychological experience of most trial attorneys.

Shortly before I left the firm, a more junior attorney approached me with the same question. He admitted that he was suffering from depression and self-doubt as he prepared for an impending court appearance and wondered whether I had experienced the same feelings. He was a bright and energetic person. My initial reaction was to reassure him that such feelings were normal and that his inner fears should be allayed. But by then, I had begun to become inculcated into the power-oriented world of lawyers. I did not want him to know that I was vulnerable, lest he exploit that vulnerability as we clawed our way up the associates' ladder toward the prize of partnership in the firm. Just as the senior associate had done to me, I told him that the affliction was his alone. Shortly thereafter, he resigned from the law firm and went into a government office practice not involving trial work. I wondered later if my unfeeling and dishonest conduct had adversely affected his career. It was one of those events in life that I wish I had played differently.

Although my mood swings are apparent to Sallie, I never express to her the depths of the self-doubt I feel. Erika's case loomed larger for me than most criminal trials and my vicissitudes must have been more apparent to Sallie than usual.

"Whatever you do, dear, don't get down on yourself," she commented as she brought me a bottle of Yuengling lager.

She was just trying to be supportive, so I said nothing lest I discourage her unnecessarily. She pointed out that I was fortunate to have a job where there was an opportunity to prepare and perform under circumstances when the stakes were so high. She reminded me that my life's work was interesting and challenging. I would not be happy unless my abilities and psychological strength were periodically tested, just like the boxers I so admire. How fortunate I was not to have a nine-to-five job where I was shackled to a desk shuffling papers for some obscure purpose. She is indeed a wise woman. I am fortunate to have this job and also to have her with me at times like these. All seemed right with the world as I faced the test ahead.

46

"The defense is ready, your honor."

I stood at the counsel table facing the judge. Erika Williams was sitting on my right. As promised, her attire appropriately reflected youth and innocence. Before jury selection that morning, the district attorney and I stood in the courtroom as Erika arrived there. Upon seeing her attire, Ed Bricker approached and complimented me.

"You could probably have made Charles Manson look like a kindergarten teacher. Nice touch."

As is the defense's constitutionally guaranteed right, Erika had demanded a trial by jury. Under most circumstances the defense will request a jury trial. Unless the parties agree otherwise, the Commonwealth must have a unanimous vote from all twelve jurors in order to obtain a conviction. This means the defense has only to destroy the jury's unanimity in order to obtain a favorable ruling.

The Constitution guarantees a trial by a jury of the defendants peers. The jury panel consisted of a large pool of people whose names were chosen at random from among eligible jurors in the county. In order to assure that the jury was impartial and could render an unbiased decision, both the prosecution and defense had an opportunity to ask questions of prospective jurors. After the prosecution and defense exercised challenges to various potential jurors, twelve people were selected and empaneled as the jury for the case.

"Let the record show that both counsel for the Commonwealth and counsel for the defendant have indicated that they are ready to proceed."

The judge nodded to me and to the several attorneys who were seated at the prosecution's table. True to form, Bricker had surrounded himself with his staff at counsel table. I hoped that the jury might notice that the defense was undermanned and that we were the underdog in this contest of the Commonwealth of Pennsylvania versus Erika Williams.

The judge looked at his watch. The noon hour was approaching. The judge used the opportunity to explain to the jurors that they were to have no contact with any of the attorneys, litigants, or witnesses and that each was charged with the responsibility of reporting any contact. He then recessed the proceedings until after lunch.

I used the lunch recess to review my notes and assess what I had learned in the morning session. I noted the presence of several prosecution witnesses. They included the administrative assistant at the bank where Erika's account was opened and the postal clerk who had taken the post office box rental application. Also in attendance were a police investigator who I had cross-examined in court on other occasions and the young woman who gave me the information at the police station when I began my investigation. I assumed that these were the district attorney's first witnesses. The prediction upon which I had constructed my trial plan was correct. The district attorney intended to build his case against Erika piece by piece using a string of witnesses each of whom would heap a log on the fire being built around Erika's feet.

I did the best I could to look positive as Erika and I re-entered the courtroom. I said some words of reassurance to her, and she smiled at me. As we sat at the counsel table, she put her hand upon my arm.

"It is I who should be issuing the words of encouragement to you. Throughout this whole process I have not been very supportive of your efforts on my behalf. I just want you to know that I have confidence in you. I haven't been much help. I know that you must think that I am some kind of witch for being so uncommunicative. I'm sorry."

My first thought was that the epithet 'bitch' would have been more appropriate than 'witch.' I could not determine whether she spoke from the heart, or she was doing what she felt necessary to encourage me. This was no time to analyze her motives. I knew that there was no purpose in doing so. Even so, I welcomed her words and returned her smile.

A buzzer sounded and the judge entered the courtroom. We all rose. The judge nodded and we returned to our seats. The jury filed into the jury box. For a moment there was silence as the entire cast of participants in the courtroom drama settled into their pre-assigned places ready for the production to commence. For me, the only other moment of higher expectation in court is at the end of the trial when the jury foreman rises to report the verdict.

The district attorney rose to begin his opening statement. In a cool, even tone he informed the jurors that Erika had committed the crime of embezzlement. He said he was the first to admit that no one saw her do it, but the great weight of the evidence to be presented would clearly and unequivocally prove beyond a reasonable doubt that Erika committed the crime. He asked the jury to listen carefully to each witness, for each witness would provide a piece of the puzzle of how $50,000.00 was taken from the University and was found in the possession of Erika Williams. When all the witnesses had completed their testimony and all evidence was assembled, the puzzle would reveal a clear picture of Erika's guilt.

I was very impressed with Ed Bricker's presentation. As he spoke, I watched the jurors' faces conjure up the image of a jigsaw puzzle. Bricker's opening statement was powerful and to the point. He had clearly established the boundaries within which we were to test Erika's guilt or innocence.

The judge nodded to me. It was my turn. Sometimes I waive my right to make an opening statement at the outset of a trial and I reserve that right until I begin my part of the case after the prosecution rests. However, in this case, Bricker's statement had made such an impact upon the jury that I felt compelled to respond. I knew that my opening statement would be critical. With it I would establish the tone of the defense.

"Thank you, your honor," I said as I arose.

"Ladies and Gentlemen. The prosecutor..."

I never refer to opposing counsel in a criminal case as the 'district attorney.' 'District attorney' is a euphemism for 'prosecutor'. To me, the term prosecutor conjures up visions of a brow-beating, hard driving, person, intent upon punishment. I wanted to create the image of a persecutor of innocent victims.

"... has told you that he intends to provide you with pieces of a puzzle. When these pieces are gathered and assembled, he would have you believe that the image of the defendant will appear as the person guilty of the crime. At the end of the presentation of evidence by both the prosecution and the defense, you will be instructed by the judge that the evidence must prove beyond a reasonable doubt that the defendant has committed the crime. As the prosecutor presents to you a piece of his so-called puzzle that he referred to, I ask that you carefully examine that piece and that each of you ask yourself 'does this piece prove that Erika Williams, the defendant, is guilty beyond a reasonable doubt?' If you do that after all the evidence has been put before you — piece by piece — and the puzzle is assembled, I know that an entirely different image of the events surrounding this case will emerge. Remember, all I ask is that for each piece of the puzzle, you ask yourselves 'does this piece of the puzzle prove beyond a reasonable doubt that Erika committed the crime?' Thank you."

No sooner had I finished than the district attorney was on his feet. I could see frustration in his eyes.

"Your honor," he exclaimed in a sterner voice than he intended, "may we approach the bench?"

Bricker and I walked to the area near the judge and out of hearing of the jury. Such 'side-bars' are very common, but I knew that the presiding judge disliked them. He felt that they slowed the progress of a trial and promoted bickering between counsel.

The judge looked sternly at Bricker. "Well? This had better be important. I am not going to permit this case to get bogged down with a lot of wrangling between counsel. We have a jury here that has better things to do than sit while you two posture.... You've both been here before.... I know how you both operate — and you know how I feel about these little conferences."

"Your honor, defense counsel intentionally and unethically has misled the jury with his opening statement. Both the court and defense counsel know quite well that each piece of evidence does not have to prove the defendant's guilt beyond a reasonable doubt. It is the cumulative effect of the evidence viewed as a whole that must prove the defendant guilty beyond a reasonable doubt. Defense counsel has misstated the law. I request that the Court instruct counsel to desist from this, and I request that the Court speak to the jury to set the record straight with regard to the standard of proof required to convict Williams."

Before I could defend my opening statement, the judge interrupted. "Mr. District Attorney, it is you who opened the door by your allusion to evidence as, quote — pieces of a puzzle — end quote. It is true that defense counsel took some liberties with the law here, but I see nothing unethical and counsel's comments were within the rules. You may be assured that I will instruct the jury that the evidence must be viewed as a whole when measuring the standard of proof. And, if the district attorney wishes, he may request a special instruction to that effect after both sides have rested their cases."

He paused. "Meanwhile, I want both counsel to limit side-bars. I want this case to move forward. . . . Do I make myself clear?"

"Yes, your honor," we said simultaneously as we backed away from the judge and resumed our places.

My goal was to have the jurors become more critical of the evidence from the outset, rather than having them question each piece when they began their deliberations hours or days later. With the reference to an 'entirely different image of the events' in my opening statement, I did not commit myself in advance to produce a culprit if Erika was not the guilty party.

This was round one of the fight, and the district attorney had been on the receiving end of a very powerful punch, delivered when his guard was down. He knew very well that I had raised the jury's level of awareness of the standard of proof required to convict in a criminal trial. This would make my attack on each piece of evidence more recognizable to the jurors. They would expect me to attack. I would disappoint them if I did not. Bricker had made a tactical error and he knew it. I was pleased. I was already off to a good start as the prosecution called its first witness, Scott Wilson, one of the investigating officers.

For the next hour, the district attorney led Wilson through the crime. He explained the investigative process in great detail from the discovery that the funds were missing to tracing the funds to an account registered in Erika's name. From time to time Wilson was asked questions which may have been hearsay or speculative, but I felt that the district attorney was going to get his side of the story into evidence anyway. There was no point in raising objections to testimony that would ultimately be admitted. I would object only if I felt that a future right were being waived or there was a flagrant violation of the rules of procedure or the rules of evidence. Bricker understood that I didn't object to some of the questions or answers as a courtesy to him. He did not overstep the invisible boundary nor did he seek to take unfair advantage of the latitude I granted him. I expected the same courtesy from him. It was an unwritten law among the local attorneys that both Bricker and I honored by tacit agreement.

The first part of Officer Wilson's testimony was background on the crime itself. When he began to link Erika to the crime I became more vigilant. Basically, he testified that the transfer of funds was done with Erika's computer. This was known because each computer was given a "signature" and any transaction using a computer had to have the "signature" of the computer in order to complete the transaction. The order authorizing the transfer funds from the university account to an account listed in Erika's name was made by Erika's computer.

Wilson also testified that certain authorization codes were required in order to transfer funds from any university account. The codes were a series of letters, numbers, words, or symbols that were entered into the computer at the time of the transaction. The central data bank would not complete a transfer of funds unless the authorization code was entered properly. Only certain people within the finance office had access to these codes. Erika was not authorized to use the codes that were required in order to transfer funds in excess of $10,000. Erika had access to codes that could transfer sums up to that amount. He testified that a 3½ inch diskette was recovered from Erika's office. The data stored on the diskette included a listing of the codes then in use that could authorize the transfer of funds in excess of $10,000.

At that point, the district attorney produced a blue 3½ inch diskette and handed it to Wilson.

"Officer Wilson, I show you what the court reporter has marked as Commonwealth Exhibit #1 and I ask whether you can identify it."

Wilson explained that it was the diskette that was recovered from Erika Williams' office. In the company of a person from the computer lab on campus, he reviewed the data on the diskette and had it printed by the computer onto paper. Commonwealth Exhibit #2 was a print-out of the data which, according to Wilson, included a list of the codes which were in effect on April 15th, the date when the crime was committed.

Here again I gave the district attorney great leeway. I could have objected to Wilson testifying about the information on the diskette and the presence of the codes. It was clear that Officer Wilson had no personal knowledge of the data on the diskette and no personal knowledge that the letters, symbols, and numbers that appeared on the print-out were actually the codes that could authorize the transfer of funds. However, it served no useful purpose to make the district attorney bring forth a succession of witnesses. The result would be the same. The evidence would be before the jury. Bricker knew that I was expediting the trial. When he came over to counsel table to show me Commonwealth Exhibit #2 he thanked me in a very low voice.

"Thanks for letting me get through this using Wilson. I know you could have made me grand marshall of a long parade of witnesses."

We both knew that my intent was not to curry favor, for there was none to be had. A smooth and efficiently run trial was in our mutual interest.

47

The jury stared expectantly at me as I crossed the courtroom and stood in front of Officer Wilson.

My trial plans used to include seizing every opportunity to do cross-examination. I was convinced that I could make any witness break under my incisive questioning. Once, during a civil trial, one of the senior partners in my law firm permitted me as co-counsel to cross-examine a witness to an auto accident. The witness was an older woman, and I was convinced that her memory had been clouded during the six-year interval from the accident to the trial. I began my cross-examination with a simple question.

"Madam," I asked, "the crash took place almost six years ago and you certainly have a wealth of experience with life. Isn't it true that your memory — like everyone else's memory — fades over time?"

She answered in the affirmative.

"And," I continued, "isn't it just possible that after all these years that you may be mistaken about which direction had the green light at the time of the accident?"

Again she answered in the affirmative. The senior partner tugged on my suit coat sleeve. I looked at him and he nodded. I was so pleased with myself that I mistook his signal to quit for an instruction to continue. When I started to ask another question, he pulled harder on my coat sleeve, but I was undeterred.

"Now, Madam," I asked, "your earlier testimony was that the light was green in the plaintiff's direction. You can't really be sure of that after all these years, can you?"

"Yes, I can. In answer to your previous question I said that it was possible that I was mistaken. Notice, I said possible . . . but not very likely. Two weeks before that accident, my grandson was involved in a similar accident. I had just been to see him at the hospital, when to my horror there was a terrible screech of tires and a loud crash... another accident like his took place right before my very eyes. As the cars crashed, I immediately looked up to see what color the light was, hoping that no one was hurt like my poor grandson. The fact is that your client went through that red light. It is possible that I am mistaken about it, but I don't think so. That terrible moment will be with me forever, and I remember it like it was yesterday."

One of the hardest lessons for young attorneys to learn in the courtroom is that there are no points awarded for style. The case was lost, and I learned a lesson. I only cross-examine when necessary, and when I do, I keep it short and to the point.

Although I make limited use of cross-examination, I feel that it is important in a jury trial to ask some questions. In criminal jury trials I never attack the credibility of a police officer, even though the jury expects cross-examination. I may question investigative techniques, but I don't think it is wise to attack an officer's integrity. It is bad for the image I want to cultivate with the jury. When it came to Officer Wilson, I decided to attack only the testimony that tied Erika to the crime. I would not attack him personally, nor would I question his professional expertise. He had already testified against my client's interest.

"Officer Wilson..."

He girded himself for an onslaught of questions.

"You testified that in order for money to be transferred by a computer, the computer had to have a 'signature.'"

"That is correct," he answered warily.

"When you say signature, you don't really mean a signature like signing a check, do you?"

"No."

Officer Wilson had been carefully instructed by the prosecutor to answer only what was specifically asked on cross-examination. That is a primary rule of preparing witnesses for cross-examination, and Wilson was faithful to his instructions.

"Can you tell us what you mean by signature?"

"Yes."

He was carrying his instructions a bit too far.

"Please tell us, Officer."

[193]

"Well, you see, there is a security system. All the computers hooked into the network have a pre-assigned number. When a transaction is made by one of those computers, a file is created in the database. The file records the date and time of the transaction and the preassigned number of the computer which ordered the transaction as well as a lot of other information. It is that computer's number that I called the signature."

I stood silently for a moment so that the jury could absorb the concept as explained by Wilson.

"Officer Wilson, you testified that each computer has a signature, that is, a number. Is that how you knew that the order to transfer the money came from the computer in Miss Williams' office?"

I had decided to begin by referring to my client as Miss Williams. I did not want the jury to think that Williams might have been the name she acquired as a result of an unsuccessful marriage. I also wanted the jurors to know that she was single.

"That is correct," Wilson answered.

"You just testified that the so-called signature is a security device."

"Correct."

"Is it possible to have an additional security device installed in the system so that each computer operator in the network has his or her own personal identification number . . . just like an individual might have for using the automatic teller machine?"

One of the techniques I employ in court is making reference to the jurors' own experiences. I find that it enables them to become more comfortable with my style if I relate important points in terms that they can understand. Most of the jurors were familiar with identification numbers for using ATM's.

"Yes, it is."

"Officer Wilson, would a personal identification number enable the main computer to identify not only the computer that ordered the transaction, but also the computer operator who ordered the transaction?"

"Yes, it would."

"And, Officer Wilson, was such a computer-operator signature or personal identification number security device in place in the university's computer system on April 15th?"

"No, it was not."

"Since then, has one been installed?"

The district attorney was on his feet in an instant with an objection.

My point was made. "Your honor, I withdraw my question."

The district attorney resumed his seat. He knew immediately that he had made a mistake by objecting. His fast response to my question was a signal to the jurors that I had uncovered something important.

"Officer Wilson..." I paused for effect.

I wanted the jury to be conditioned to listen carefully to any question where I named the witness, then paused for a long period of time. I altered the tone of my voice slightly, and speaking very slowly and deliberately, I continued.

"Officer Wilson, are you telling us that on April 15th, the security system could not tell whether or not it was Miss Williams who actually ordered the transfer of funds?"

"Yes," said Wilson, following instructions.

"Does that 'yes' mean that it was Miss Williams who ordered the transfer of funds . . . or that you couldn't tell who it was that ordered the transfer?"

My question did not allow a 'yes or no' answer.

"We could not tell who was operating Miss Williams' computer when the funds were transferred."

"Thank you, Officer Wilson."

I turned my back on Officer Wilson and moved to a flip chart that was set up behind my counsel table in clear view of the jury and the prosecution. With a marker, I wrote near the top of the large sheet 'Wilson: We could not tell who was operating Miss Williams' computer when the funds were transferred.'

Then, I asked the court stenographer to read back Officer Wilson's last answer. She read back the exact words that I had written on the flip chart. In this manner, I was able to have the jury hear the words twice, once from Wilson and once from the court reporter, and I had a written record of the words on the flip chart before the jury.

I glanced at the district attorney. I had not employed this technique in a criminal trial before, and I could sense that he was not prepared for what I had done.

A conservative approach is generally better for cross-examination, and normally I would quit cross-examining while I was ahead, but Officer Wilson had tied Erika to the crime because the Commonwealth Exhibit #1, computer diskette, was found in her office. I had to attack that piece of the puzzle, too.

Officer Wilson had hoped that I was finished with my cross-examination. I could see it in his eyes. His face clearly reflected his disappointment when I positioned myself before him and continued.

"Officer Wilson, you testified that you personally retrieved the diskette marked as Commonwealth #1 from Erika Williams' office?"

"Yes," he said, immediately returning to his prescribed instruction of answering either 'yes' or 'no.'

"Did you find the diskette as a result of a general search of Miss Williams' office?"

"I don't understand your question."

"Let me ask it another way. At the time you found the diskette, were you going through her office with a fine-tooth comb, so to speak, as part of an investigative search, or did you look in only one place?"

"I looked in only one place."

"Officer Wilson . . . " I paused for heightened effect. Once again I lowered my voice and spoke very deliberately to gain the jury's attention. "Why did you look in only one place for the diskette?"

"We received a telephone call telling us where the diskette could be found."

Continuing my tone and pace, I asked, "Who called you to tell you where the diskette could be found?"

"I don't know. It was an anonymous call."

"And, Officer Wilson, based on the information you received from this anonymous caller, did you go to Miss Williams' office and retrieve the diskette?"

"Yes."

I moved to the court stenographer's table and picked up the diskette and held it up so both Officer Wilson and the jury could see it.

"This is Commonwealth #1. But it did not look like this at the moment you retrieved it, did it?"

"Yes, it did."

Moving my hand slowly, I reached into my coat pocket nearest the jury and withdrew a small plastic sandwich bag and a twist-tie. I inserted the diskette into the bag and closed it using the twist-tie. When Officer Wilson saw what I was doing, he added to his answer.

"Well, what I meant to say was that the diskette looks the same, but when I found the diskette it was enclosed in a sandwich bag secured with a twist-tie, similar to the one you have in your hand."

"I know that you are very thorough. Did you test the diskette for fingerprints?"

I was taking a calculated risk. I did not know whether there were any fingerprints on the diskette. If there were, I assumed that the district attorney would have made much of that fact on direct examination. It would be the next best thing to a 'smoking gun' in sealing Erika's fate. I doubted he would hold back, hoping I would ask about fingerprints on cross-examination. If he had the evidence, I knew that he would have presented it.

I hoped that Officer Wilson would stick to his instructions and provide a 'yes or no' answer. He did not disappoint me and he answered affirmatively.

"Were Miss Williams' fingerprints on the diskette?"

"No."

This exchange illustrated one of the disadvantages of instructing a witness to provide a 'yes or no' answer. Wilson neglected to disclose whether there was evidence that the diskette had been wiped clean of fingerprints before it was placed in the plastic bag. If Bricker wanted to make this point, he would have to do it during re-direct examination.

"You testified that you went right to the place where the diskette was hidden?"

"Yes."

"After you and the police found the diskette and learned what was contained on it, did you conduct a full search of Miss Williams' office?"

"Yes."

"And Miss Williams' car?"

"Yes."

"And Miss Williams' townhouse?"

"Yes."

"And after you conducted all those searches, was this diskette the only one you found that had the codes?"

"Yes."

"And some anonymous caller directed you to it?"

"Yes."

I walked back to the defense table and retrieved a box under it. I withdrew a potted plant, the same one in which the diskette had been hidden. I held it up so that the jury and Officer Wilson could see it clearly. Next I took some newspapers out of the same box and spread them over the table under the potted plant. I took the plant with me and approached Officer Wilson.

"Now Officer Wilson, can you tell us what this is?"

"Yes, it is a plant."

"And, would you say that this plant is the same or similar to the plant and pot that was located in Miss Williams' office at the time that you retrieved the diskette?"

"Well, knowing you, I guess you are going to tell me that this is the exact plant from Williams' office." Wilson was beginning to lose his patience. He glanced at the district attorney.

"Officer Wilson, is that a yes or no answer?"

"It looks like the same plant and the same pot."

I returned to counsel table and placed the pot on the newspapers. I turned and asked Officer Wilson another question.

"Officer Wilson . . . " I paused for effect, lowering my voice slightly and speaking deliberately, "is it possible that someone might hide the diskette for later use?"

I could sense that the district attorney was ready to object, and Wilson, an experienced witness was waiting for Bricker to do so. When he did not answer, I asked another question.

"Well, Officer Wilson, if Miss Williams was only going to use it once, there would be no reason to keep the data. She could have erased it or discarded the diskette, couldn't she?"

Wilson again hesitated, waiting for Bricker's objection. When there was no objection, he answered in the affirmative, not knowing exactly where I was taking him. I reached down and yanked the plant from the pot with my right hand lifting it into the air exposing the roots. Dirt flew all over the table and onto the courtroom floor. Then with my left hand, I reached into the pot and retrieved a diskette enclosed in a plastic sandwich bag secured with a twist tie. Then I replaced the plant in the pot. I took a whisk broom and dustpan from the box and cleaned the table and the floor, pouring the excess dirt in the waste can by the court stenographer. I brushed off my hand with my handkerchief and then unwrapped the diskette. The whole process had taken about four minutes to complete. I turned to Officer Wilson.

"Officer Wilson, would you say that the hiding place of the diskette was a convenient or inconvenient location if Miss Williams wanted to retrieve the diskette for later use?"

"Objection!" exclaimed Bricker.

I withdrew the question. Before the judge could warn me about continuing the line of questioning, I launched one final question at Officer Wilson.

"But if someone literally wanted to plant the diskette in Miss Williams' office, then tip you off that it was there, it was an equally good hiding place from Miss Williams is that. . ."

Bricker became very animated. "Your honor, I object strongly to this line of questioning. It includes matters not covered on direct examination. It calls for a conclusion from the witness. It is speculative. And, counsel is testifying — not asking — proper questions."

I said nothing, but the judge looked sternly at Bricker and then at me. With his hand, he signalled us both before him out of hearing of the jury. When we arrived at the bench, the Judge looked first to me.

"Look counsel, I have given you plenty of latitude. This is a criminal case and you are entitled to defend your client. But, and I mean BUT, I will not have you violating court procedure with your questioning. You're not wet behind the ears... you know the rules and I expect you to follow them. And Counsellor, I expect you to clear my courtroom of all that dirt you spilled over there."

He turned to Bricker. "Mr. District Attorney, I know that it is early in the trial, but when you present such flimsy evidence as that diskette you leave yourself wide open to this kind of cross-examination. When you held back the fact that you were tipped off, what do you expect? You had it coming for presenting such evidence."

Then he spoke to both of us. "Look, gentlemen, we have a jury here. Let's get through this thing. The only one in the whole courtroom who is paid by the hour is defense counsel. Let's move forward. If the prosecution has the goods on the defendant, then let the jury see it. They'll decide. As for the defense, try to limit the carnival sideshows. This is not the courtroom television channel. You're not going to win an Emmy for your performance here in court—I guarantee it. Do we understand each other?"

We both nodded. I returned to the counsel table.

"No further questions on cross, your honor."

The judge looked at Bricker. Bricker stopped to consider whether he wanted to ask Wilson questions on re-direct. The damage had been done. There was no practical way for him to rehabilitate Wilson's testimony.

"No questions on re-direct, your honor."

Mentally, I scored round one for the defense.

48

After Officer Wilson's testimony, the district attorney called the postal clerk to the witness stand. The clerk testified that he had processed a box rental application with Erika Williams' name and signature on it. But on cross examination, he could not recall whether or not Erika had signed the card in his presence. I was able to elicit his admission that he could not say positively that Erika Williams had presented the application to him personally. Upon closer examination, he did not remember ever seeing Erika Williams at the post office even though his own signature appeared on the application as well. Finally, he said he could not testify whether the signature on the card belonged to Erika Williams.

The postal clerk could have been viewed as derelict in his duty for failing to require execution of the application in his presence and proper identification of the applicant. I did not want to embarrass him. I might one day find him sitting on a jury panel.

"Now," I asked him, "is it true that postal employees generally sign the bottom of the card intending to indicate that they have reviewed the application for a post office box rental and that it is complete?"

"Yes, Sir."

"And," I continued, "there are literally hundreds of applications for post office boxes. It's not really your job to ask for identification of each person who places an application for a post office box, is it?"

"No, it is not," he answered, relieved to save face before those in the courtroom.

The final prosecution witness for the day was the customer service representative at the bank. Her testimony was that Erika Williams' signature appeared on the account signature card and that the account was registered in Erika's name. She produced a printout of the status of the account showing the opening balance of twenty-five dollars and a deposit via wire on April 16th in the amount of $50,000. The current balance included the opening deposit, the wire transfer of $50,000 and interest accrued since April 16th was $51,345.67.

The bank's representative was an exceptionally warm and personable young woman with a winning smile. Her voice was pleasant, and she responded respectfully to the district attorney's questions. I could tell that the jury liked her very much. When a jury attaches itself to a witness, it is important to tailor cross-examination so that the witness does not appear to be in danger of embarrassment, intimidation, or ridicule at the hands of a slick-talking, heartless lawyer. It would do no good to elicit admissions from her if the jury thought that I had taken unfair advantage or used unscrupulous methods to obtain them.

Even experienced lawyers often do not appreciate the necessity of tailoring cross-examination delivery to suit the witness. When cross-examining Officer Wilson, I used a colder, calculated, professional tone of voice. For the postal clerk, I used a more matter-of-fact tone, but I retained a business-like manner. For the young woman, I decided on a friendly, yet non-ingratiating approach.

"You must serve hundreds of people as a customer service representative at the bank. In your earlier testimony, you did not say specifically whether you remembered Miss Williams coming into the bank and opening an account and signing that card in front of you. Do you have a specific recollection of Miss Williams opening that account and signing the card?"

Again I had taken a risk. It was a substantially larger risk than the question I had asked Officer Wilson about fingerprints on the diskette. It was possible that the district attorney had set a trap for me by not asking her the question, hoping that I would. If the witness remembered Erika signing the card, her response would have a greater impact on the jury if it came on cross-examination. It would also be a badly needed moral victory for him. Bricker sacrificed little by laying the trap. He could ask her the same question on re-direct if I did not rise to the bait. I almost withdrew the question, but before I could do so, she answered.

"You are correct. I have opened hundreds of accounts and met a thousand people in the course of my employment. I do not have a specific recollection of Miss Williams in the bank. The district attorney showed me photographs of her and I saw her picture in the paper and on television, but I do not remember her at the bank. But . . . she could have been there and signed because my initials are on her account card."

I knew that her testimony would not survive cross-examination. The fact that the witness's initials were on the card was not proof that Erika was in the bank. However, I was hesitant to attack her testimony directly because of the special relationship she enjoyed with the jury.

I wanted a clarification from her that "could have been there" was not the same as "definitely been there." I had to take another calculated risk.

"You just answered that she—that is, Miss Williams—could have been there because your initials are on her account card. Does that mean that you know that Miss Williams was at your desk because you saw her there?"

"No, I don't remember seeing her there, but somebody must have given the card to me personally, because my initials are on it."

Continuing the questioning I asked, "I certainly do not want to put words in your mouth . . ." I regretted my choice of words immediately. I was afraid that it might sound too tricky. When someone says they are not trying to 'put words in your mouth' that is exactly what they are doing. But it was one of those memorable days that happen so infrequently—my stars were in perfect alignment.

"I think I know what you are driving at," she added quickly in a pleasant voice trying to be helpful. "This is a court of law, and I am supposed to be precise. And I'm sorry if I confused you. I do not remember Miss Williams being in the bank and signing that card. But someone must have given me the account card, because my initials are on it. I think what you're asking me is whether I can say for sure it was Miss Williams who gave me the card. It might have been, but I cannot say that it was. I do not remember who gave me that card."

"No further questions on cross, your honor." I made a mental note to purchase a lottery ticket on my way home.

Bricker rose to ask questions of the witness on re-direct. I thought that his next witness might be a handwriting expert who would testify that the signatures on the post office box rental application and the account card were Erika's. It was essential that he find a way to link Erika to the account card with this witness. Just as things had gone my way that day, the opposite was true for the prosecution.

Bricker asked the witness whether proving the signature on the card belonged to Erika Williams also definitely confirmed Erika Williams' presence at the bank.

It was a risky question that should not have been asked. He

[203

should have known better, and I knew deep down that he did. It was my first indication that the prosecution was desperate. The witness was doing her level best to be cooperative, but I could tell by her previous answers that she would not speculate on what may or may not have happened. She would state only what she knew.

"Mr. Bricker," she answered, "I cannot say that. People often bring me bank account cards that are signed elsewhere. It is not my job to verify the identity of the person presenting the card as being the same person who signed the card. The fact that Miss Williams' signature is on that card does not prove that she was in the bank. Anyone could have given me the card. All I did was initial it."

There were no questions on re-cross. I stood up and wrote on the flip chart "Bank Employee: The fact that Miss Williams' signature is on that card does not prove that she was in the bank." When I finished, Bricker stood to voice an objection. But he had been bloodied by her testimony, and he realized that the objection would serve only to re-emphasize what she had said. He resumed his seat.

I mentally awarded round number two to the defense.

I have never become accustomed to the stress of being counsel in court; for the Williams trial, the stress and strain seemed to increase ten-fold. When court recessed at 4:00 P.M., I could only describe my emotional state as resembling a squeezed lemon. It was as if all psychic energy had been wrung from my being and nothing remained save a little pulp and a lot of rind. I did my best to look positive and confident for the jurors as they filed out of the courtroom. For the benefit of the prosecution staff, I pretended to have a vast reservoir of energy; I busily pushed papers here and there on the counsel table and re-loaded my briefcase. They tried to appear optimistic, but I could tell that they understood things were not going well. Beneath the calm assured manner of the district attorney, I knew his stomach juices churned. I had been in his shoes on numerous occasions, and I had empathy for him. Now that the defense's strategy had been revealed and the weaknesses of his case had been exposed to the jury, he would spend the night restructuring his trial plan. I was sure that he took heart in the fact that he would have ample opportunity to inflict the same devastation on my defense.

I waited with Erika as the courtroom emptied. After the prosecution staff departed, only the court stenographer remained, marking her exhibits and packaging her transcripts. During the proceedings, Erika had said little to me. I preferred it. Too often clients try to be helpful, tapping me on the arm, trying to talk. It distracts me. The level of concentration required to follow the trial closely leaves little opportunity to coddle the client.

"Well, counsellor..."

Inevitably, at the end of the day, citizen-type defendants make excessive demands upon me for reassurance about the progress of the trial. Tired as I usually am, I enjoy re-hashing the events. I girded myself for the onslaught of questions about every aspect of the day's session.

"Yes, Erika?"

"You certainly performed brilliantly today. Is there anything you want me to do tonight?"

I shook my head.

"Very well. See you here tomorrow at 8:30?"

I nodded. She stood, smiled, and left the courtroom.

I was exhausted, but my exhaustion could not mask my concern. I was again haunted by my recurring questions about Erika. Her conduct continued to be unprecedented in my experience. Every citizen-type criminal defendant I have ever represented wanted to know the minutest detail — my assessment of the jury, the trial plan — in short, they were relentless. Not so with Erika. The day's successes in the courtroom seemed to be of little consequence to her. It was as if she had just put in a normal day's work and was going home to do her laundry, watch a video, and soak in the jacuzzi before retiring. She acted as if the trial were a trivial event, with little or no relevance to her own life.

In all honesty, I know that I enjoy the client's hanging on my every word as I analyze the day's events in court. It gives me a sense of importance. I therefore could not judge accurately whether my concern about Erika was genuine or whether I was disappointed that she did not exhibit the same obvious dependency as my other clients.

When I am emotionally tired, I know that I am very vulnerable.

All of my personal foibles weighed heavily upon me as my original concerns about Erika resurfaced. I told myself that there was no point in worrying about them for there was little I could do.

The courtroom was empty. I gathered my belongings. Taking the whisk broom from the box, I knelt under the counsel table. As I did so, I looked toward the doorway. There stood the judge, watching me as I swept the carpet of the dirt that had fallen there early that afternoon.

49

My footsteps echoed in the hallway as I left the courtroom. The head maintenance man at the courthouse once told me that the building was erected in 1801 and these were the original marble floors. That meant the marble flooring was 18 years old when Eben Jones brought his lawsuit against Peter Karthaus and 26 years old when James Petrikin was sifting through the various lists searching for evidence of Eben Jones' residency.

"Almost two centuries of lawyers have passed down these hallways," I thought.

I wondered whether James Petrikin's courtroom experiences were as emotionally draining as mine had been that day. I have difficulty relating to law practice as it may have existed in 1827. In those days, lawyers had to plead their civil cases according to the remedy being sought. For example, if a lawyer wanted to sue for breach of contract and seek monetary damages, the pleadings would be in *assumpsit*. If a client sought the return of an item of personal property in the possession of another, the lawyer would bring the case in *replevin*. These were the ancient "forms of action." A lawyer could not plead alternative causes of action. A choice had to be made. If the wrong form of action was pleaded, the lawyer's case could be thrown out of court. I find the forms of action very intimidating and I am thankful that the modern day rules made pleadings more forgiving. Cases are no longer filed according to the form of action. It is now possible to plead inconsistent legal causes of action and to seek alternative remedies.

In my fantasy world, I was certain that James Petrikin was comfortable with the legal world in which he found himself in 1827. If he could not accustom himself to the pressures of pleading the proper form of action, surely he would have become a blacksmith or a carpenter. In 1827, he was still a young man and could have changed careers, but the court dockets revealed that he did not. He continued practicing law until his death. Returning to reality, I knew I was only fantasizing. As James Petrikin walked this very corridor on his way from court, win or lose, he felt trapped by his profession. And, in our highly specialized society, I found myself a prisoner of my occupation as well.

My fantasies are recreational in nature. I justify them to myself on grounds that they are therapeutic and have no adverse effect upon anyone. I never approached the Eben Jones matter as a real case. If I had, I would have spent my energy trying to discover why the letter from Perrow to Petrikin had survived so many years. I knew that the riddle of Eben Jones would not be solved unless I was able to learn the secret of the letter's survival, or unless I traveled to Lovingston, Virginia, and discovered the result of Perrow's petition for writ of *habeas corpus*.

Once I was outside the courthouse building, I left my thoughts about Eben Jones behind, and I felt better. This was no time for fantasy. I drove home, arriving just as Sallie was putting the finishing touches on a special shrimp and scallop casserole.

"I knew you'd need fortification of body and soul. . . How'd it go?"

This was more than a polite inquiry. Sometimes when Sallie would ask that question, her tone of voice would betray her lack of interest in learning the answer. Early in our marriage, I resented her lack of interest, but I realized over time that it was not a manifestation of her lack of concern for me. She had her own life. What matters are the parts of our lives that we share and Sallie is always interested in that.

I used the opportunity to explain the day's events, reviewing them in my own mind in order to gain some sense of the progress of the trial.

"Sounds like you should be pleased," she offered.

I was pleased, except for the inopportune resurfacing of my nagging concerns about Erika.

The television shows and movies do not accurately portray an attorney's existence. They focus upon office intrigue, trial preparation, and the highly dramatic events unfolding in the courtroom. They convey the impression that an attorney can devote all energies to one client and one case. The reality is quite different. When I returned to the office after dinner that evening, I found a mountain of mundane matters, all of which required my immediate attention. As I forced myself to undertake the tasks associated with my law practice, I was sustained by the truth that it is the routine matters that put bread on the table. I spent the next several hours drafting letters and memoranda, paying bills, returning telephone calls to clients I could reach in the evening, and doing general office work. There was nothing glamorous or interesting in ninety-eight percent of what I did. As I worked my way through the pile of material, I consoled myself with the hope that the remaining two percent would provide adequate compensation for my laboring in the vineyards of a generally uninteresting vocation.

It was well past nine o'clock when I turned my attention to Erika's case. I tried to anticipate the following day's events in court. I knew that the district attorney would have to authenticate the signatures on the post office box rental application and the bank signature card as being Erika's. He would do this through the handwriting expert who had done the original investigation. If my luck held, the prosecution had not discovered that the two signatures were duplicates.

Trying to place myself in my opponent's shoes, I ventured that the next witnesses would place Erika at the scene of the crime at the exact instant that the crime had been committed. Since Erika had an alibi defense, I had to pay special attention to the exact times as they were elicited from the witnesses.

Up to this point in the case, I felt I had met and successfully undermined each piece of the puzzle being proffered by the prosecution. But I knew that there was danger lurking in the future. We are all shackled to our past tendencies, and Bricker's was to save the best part of his case for last. I could only assume that the last piece of the prosecution's puzzle would be John Harley's testimony.

I could not think of a specific piece of evidence that he could provide that would have enough impact to seal Erika's fate. Here again, I began to sink into the depths of a serious depression. I was bound by the limitations of my own pre-established framework of reality, hampered by my own familiarity with the facts surrounding the case. I had no second or third opinion available.

I had a vision of being in a boxing ring, flawlessly defending myself from this jab or that right-cross delivered by the district attorney. Occasionally, I would slip a punch between his gloves, making his nose bleed a little, raising welts above both eyes. I knew that he had a powerful knockout punch somewhere in his arsenal, and I could not escape its full fury unscathed.

Rather than despair further, I called Marie, awakening her. After expressing my apologies for the intrusion, I explained my dilemma.

"You woke me up to ask me that?" she said reproachfully. "Sometimes I wonder about you."

It was all part of her standard repertoire, so I did not take offense.

"The answer is simple if you think about Harley's personality," she said.

"So?" I asked.

Usually at this point in the conversation, Marie lectures me about my inability to see the forest for the trees. She makes the most of such opportunities to display her superior insight. In this case, I was not treated to the standard fare, probably because she was sleepy.

"He'll swear to tell nothing but the truth, but he'll commit perjury. He'll lie. Simple as that. Now, let me get back to sleep. I have to run your office tomorrow while you and Erika are out having a good time. I need my rest."

I thanked her. She said goodnight and with a tone of encouragement in her voice she wished me luck.

Marie was correct. Whether or not Harley had framed Erika, he would stop at nothing to ensure that she left town either under a cloud or in a van transporting her to prison. He could provide no documentary evidence of Erika's guilt. He could, however, say anything. With his highly polished style, he might successfully testify that Erika admitted to him that she had committed the crime. He might say that she begged him to assist in a cover-up, but he refused to do so. I shuddered at the thought of the endless possibilities available once he committed himself to perjury. This might be the prosecution's knockout punch, and I had no defense ready to meet this formidable challenge.

I abandoned the search for an answer and went home before I became more discouraged. Sallie had a Yuengling lager waiting for me when I arrived. She had stayed up long past her bedtime. We made small talk across the kitchen table until the beer was consumed and the day's events were behind me. She reached across the table and patted my hand, telling me it was time to get some rest.

50

A trial plan is never completely finished until the trial is over. It needs constant revision to take into account changing circumstances as they occur in the courtroom. On the way to the courthouse, I decided that the previous day's events had taught me the value of being able to demonstrate my points to the jury. With this in mind, I brought with me a fresh supply of tricks. I hoped these would enhance my performance as a teacher before the jury and would further undermine and confuse the prosecution.

After the *dramatis personae* had gathered in the courtroom, the judge entered. We all responded with the proper show of respect.

The judge reminded the jurors of their duties. By his manner and facial expression, he seemed to be in a better frame of mind. He called Bricker and me before him out of hearing of the jury.

"Gentlemen, good morning."

We both mumbled a response.

"Now, is there anything either of you want to tell me before we get started?"

Bricker and I looked at each other. We both answered in the negative.

"Fine. Then let's try to get through this. I hope the prosecution can finish its case today. Do you see a problem with that, Mr. Bricker?"

This inquiry put a significant amount of pressure on Bricker. He was unsure how the defense might respond to his witnesses and did not want to make any commitment to complete his case.

When he did not respond, the judge prodded him for an answer.

"I'll try your honor," was the best promise the judge could elicit.

Then the judge turned to me. I knew he sought a similar commitment from me.

"Counsel?" he asked.

His attempt to push the lawyers was typical of the judges I encountered over the years. In my experience, many judges are more concerned with getting cases off their trial dockets than with serving the litigant's legitimate interest of having a judge or jury decide the case and bring the dispute to a resolution. In civil cases, judges pressure counsel incessantly to reach a settlement before trial. In criminal cases, judges let it be known that they expect defense and prosecution to have explored a broad range of plea bargain possibilities before trial. Each judge has his or her own style, but the import is always the same. An out-of-court settlement counts on their record the same as a verdict in a court proceeding. They prefer to dispose of a case without having to don their black robes.

Judges keep "book" on attorneys. They learn very quickly which attorneys can be trusted and which play fast and loose with the rules. It was essential that I do my best to maintain good relationships with judges.

On the advice of a senior member of my first law firm, I attempt to limit my trials to those matters where settlement is not a reasonable possibility. In addition, I never make frivolous objections in court and the legal arguments I present are carefully drafted and well reasoned. I never argue for the sake of argument or delay, nor do I permit clients to use the courtroom as a forum for political or social statements. I try never to blame or criticize judges or participate in the trial attorneys' standard practice of judge bashing. However, I always stand up to the judge at a side-bar or in the privacy of chambers when I think the judge is wrong or when I feel that the judge has misused authority. Preserving the dignity of the court is in my interest as a practicing attorney. I would never knowingly present a matter to the court that did not merit fair consideration. Like Bricker, I did not want to bind myself to a timetable. Based upon my best assessment of what lay ahead, I told him I would move along as fast as I could.

Not having obtained the commitment he wanted from either of us, the judge resorted to flattery.

"Well," said the judge, "I guess I am fortunate to have you two arguing this case. You both do a good job . . . and I know that I can count on you to keep things moving."

As we turned away from the judge, Bricker asked if I knew what he meant when he wondered if there was anything we had to tell him. I replied that I did not have the foggiest notion. Not knowing what to make of it, I dismissed the judge's inquiry.

The prosecution called its next witness, the handwriting expert. While the witness was being sworn in, one of the assistant prosecutors busied herself setting up a screen and an overhead projector in the area closest to the witness and in full view of the jury.

Mindful of the judge's instructions, Bricker proceeded rapidly. In court, a person who is qualified as an expert witness can testify about hypothetical situations and express conclusions based upon their expertise. Witnesses who are not qualified as experts cannot offer such testimony. The qualification process involves a demonstration to the judge that the witness has appropriate training and experience in the field of expertise. Normally, in order to expedite matters in court, I would stipulate or agree that a person had the requisite training and experience to be an expert witness, thus relieving the prosecution of the task of qualifying the witness as an expert through lengthy testimony. This time I decided not to cooperate.

Bricker qualified the witness, Officer Earl Horner, as an expert by having him list the specialized courses he had taken and the number of samples of handwriting he had analyzed over the years. After Bricker moved that Horner be permitted to testify as an expert witness and I did not object, the court ruled that he was an expert in handwriting analysis.

Officer Horner testified that he had examined the post office box rental application and the bank signature card and compared them to authenticated samples of Erika Williams' signature.

I raised an objection, demanding that he produce the samples he used for comparison purposes. Once, in an earlier criminal trial with Bricker, I had handwriting testimony stricken because the samples used for comparison were not available in court. A smug look crossed the district attorney's face as he produced them for the witness.

He flashed onto the screen a transparency of a sample signature from a receipt signed by Erika in the course of her employment. Next to it he showed the post office box rental application with Erika's signature. He testified about the form of the signatures, noting seven similar characteristics of her handwriting and how they appeared on both signatures.

"Now Officer Horner," Bricker asked, "based upon your examination of the two signatures—one of which has been authenticated as having been signed by Williams—what is your expert opinion about who signed the post office box rental application noted as Commonwealth Exhibit #13?"

Horner testified that Erika had signed the post office box rental application.

"Officer Horner," asked Bricker as he replaced the transparency of the application with the transparency of the bank signature card, "I show you the comparison of the authenticated signature with the signature that appears on the bank signature card marked as Commonwealth Exhibit #14. What is your expert opinion about who signed the bank signature card?"

Officer Horner again testified that using generally accepted techniques in the field of handwriting, there were a number of telltale characteristics that appeared on both signatures and that it was his professional opinion that Erika Williams had signed both. In order to emphasize his point, Bricker asked one final question of the witness.

"Are you absolutely sure that Erika Williams signed both the bank signature card and the post office box rental application?"

"Yes, I am absolutely sure."

Bricker turned the witness over to me for cross-examination. Based upon Rick Place's investigation, I knew that both signatures were duplicates. I concluded that the district attorney did not know that the two signatures were the same. Otherwise, he was committing fraud by introducing evidence that he knew was false. Such conduct was not Ed Bricker's style. Although the universe is expanding at millions of miles an hour, I felt that for the second day in a row my stars continued to be in perfect alignment. Luck was still on my side.

"Officer Horner, you testified that it is generally accepted in the field of handwriting analysis that you identify seven similar characteristics from one signature to another. Is that correct?"

I had emphasized the word 'similar' and he answered affirmatively. I hoped to open the trap door so that he would fall in on his own. "And why is that, Officer?"

"Well, even though one signature is identifiable as a person's signature, people do not sign their signatures exactly the same each time."

I wanted to give him the impression that I was going to point out the dissimilarities in the signatures between the authenticated one and the others.

"But, Officer Horner," I asked, "there are dissimilarities, are there not?"

He took the bait and became very aggressive with his testimony totally disregarding his standing instructions to give short 'yes-or-no' answers.

"Well, Counselor, I think I know what you are going to try to make me say. You are going to tell me that there are dissimilarities in the two signatures, but dissimilarities do not automatically indicate forgery. People never sign their names the same twice. Even if you try very hard to use exactly the same signature, it just cannot be done. The trained eye can unmask it. Let me assure you that the odds of a person signing their name exactly the same way two times are about a million to one. Just because there are some dissimilarities does not mean that the defendant did not sign both the application and the bank card."

I could tell he felt very proud of himself for being so definite and squashing my theory of dissimilarities. I glanced over at the district attorney who displayed a chagrined expression. He knew me well, and he knew something was coming.

I lowered my voice and paused. Speaking deliberately and evenly, I asked, "Officer Horner... No two signatures are alike. Is that your testimony?"

"Yes."

By now my teaching technique had taken hold and the jurors looked at me expectantly. I went to the projector and taking the transparency of the post office box rental application and the bank card, I placed one atop of the other so that Erika's signatures were superimposed. They matched exactly.

The district attorney was on his feet. He came to the projector and looked in disbelief. In a low voice he said that he had no idea that they were both the same and he did not intend to mislead anyone.

"I know you didn't, Ed," I assured him. I knew that he felt bad about introducing testimony that could be construed as being false.

"Now Officer Horner," I continued. "Just for the record, I have placed Commonwealth Exhibit #13 over Commonwealth Exhibit #14 so that the signatures purporting to be those of Miss Williams are aligned one atop the other. Can you tell me what you observe?"

"Yes. They appear to be exactly the same."

"And did you testify a minute ago that the odds were a million to one that a person could make exact duplicate signatures?"

"Yes, I did."

"Officer Horner, I could go through a long line of questions here relating to your earlier testimony in the affirmative that you are absolutely sure that Erika Williams signed both cards. Based upon the developments revealed here in court just now, do you now wish to change your testimony?"

Horner looked helplessly at the district attorney for guidance. Normally, Bricker would maintain a stoic face in such circumstances, but because he did not want to give the impression that he had tried to conceal the truth, he nodded his assent for his witness to cooperate.

"Well, since a person cannot sign the same twice, it seems clear that the defendant did not sign both the rental application and the bank card. Now that I think about it, from an investigative standpoint, I believe that it would be unlikely that the defendant signed either card personally, although I am convinced it is her signature. I think someone probably got a copy of her signature. With the technology now available using scanners and computers, it is likely that someone transferred a valid signature onto both documents. Based on what I've seen here in court, it is my opinion that the defendant did not personally sign the application or the bank card."

I went to my flip chart and wrote: Officer Horner: "The defendant did not personally sign the application or the bank card."

"No further questions of this witness on cross, your honor."

Bricker had no questions on re-direct. I could tell he was discouraged, but that he was committed to continue the fight.

"Round three to the defense," I thought.

51

A wise old veteran of the courtroom wars once told me that as attorneys we are never as good as we think we are when winning a case, or as bad as we fear we are when losing one. With that bit of wisdom in mind, I tried to maintain my perspective about the successes I enjoyed during the first phases of Erika's trial. The judge had called a brief recess after Officer Horner's testimony, and I used the time to prepare for the Commonwealth's next witness. Erika excused herself and I sat alone at the counsel table reviewing my notes.

Throughout the proceedings, Erika displayed to the jury an interest in what was happening around her, and she made notes from time to time on a legal pad. Between witnesses or during breaks in the courtroom action she might say something to me or ask a procedural question. I still had a nagging impression that she was showing an interest only for the benefit of the jurors.

My concerns about Erika bubbled to the surface again. Normally, this far into a trial, most of my citizen-type criminal defendants manifest serious signs of losing control. The accumulated stress plays havoc with their emotional stability. I often feel more like a babysitter than defense counsel as I constantly reassure them about the progress of the trial and act as a source of psychological support. Although it interferes with the level of concentration required of courtroom work, I enjoy the role of protector. The responsibility toward the client is a heavy burden, but it gives me a feeling of power to have others depend upon my professional expertise at such a critical juncture in their lives.

It was not so with Erika. She denied me the pleasure of being her savior. She expected a favorable result, but she did not seem very concerned with the manner of my performance. It was as if I had been hired to do a tune-up or front-end alignment on her car. She exhibited the lowest possible level of personal involvement

[217

with the job I was doing. I tried to tell myself that it was because she had total confidence in my ability to win her an acquittal, but this explanation did not ring true.

My musings were interrupted by Erika's return to the counsel table for the resumption of the proceedings. I thought briefly of expressing my concern, but I discarded the idea as being inappropriate. I was now virtually certain that the district attorney would make a last desperate attempt to convict Erika with the testimony of John Harley.

The trial resumed. The next prosecution witness called was the police officer present when I reviewed the police case file at the outset of my investigation. Officer Annette Park was a woman in her early thirties, with a pleasant voice which was soft in tone but self-assured in delivery. Like the bank employee, her manner was totally friendly and cooperative. I reminded myself not to threaten her in any way and to tailor my questions so that the jury would not think that I was harsh or unreasonable.

I was surprised when one of the junior prosecutors stood to elicit her testimony on direct examination. I had not seen this young assistant district attorney in action. Under the watchful eye of Ed Bricker, the prosecutor began his questioning.

The apparent purpose of Park's testimony was to establish the exact time when the crime was committed. She explained in great detail about the operation of the central computer database and the functioning of its internal clock, using technical jargon such as 'clock driver', 'default file', and 'internal memory'. The assistant prosecutor's lack of experience became apparent when he failed to interrupt Park's testimony to provide plain language explanations of key points for the jury. Every trial attorney at one time or another must introduce boring evidence through testimony of equally boring witnesses. The trick is to vary the speed and pitch of the delivery and to inject examples that illuminate complex concepts to enable the jury to understand the points being presented. Officer Park's testimony was comprehensive, but one glance at the jurors told me that they had lost interest in her as a witness. After the drama and excitement of the previous witnesses, the boring details of the computer's internal timekeeping mechanism taxed the jury's power of concentration beyond any reasonable expectation. They heard Officer Park's testimony but did not listen carefully to it.

For over an hour, the assistant district attorney droned on and on, taking the witness through an endless series of questions about the computer. I looked at the judge who pretended to be giving the case his undivided attention. In reality, I knew that he was doodling or making notes for his law clerk, paying little or no attention to the events taking place in the courtroom. Like the rest of us, he preferred drama and excitement.

The young prosecutor excused himself from the witness and went into conference with the district attorney at the prosecution's table. While he did so, the judge interrupted, saying that the jury had had enough for one sitting. The young assistant looked embarrassed by the judge's comment. The judge showed no remorse, and he recessed the trial for lunch.

As the courtroom emptied, I sat with Erika, reviewing my notes. I knew that I had to keep my wits about me for it was likely that I would be facing the testimony of John Harley that afternoon.

"I think that the judge has just about had his fill of the prosecution's case," commented Erika.

It was the first time that she had displayed any hint of interest in the proceedings. I nodded.

"Well, if this is the best the prosecution has to offer, I don't think it will be necessary to mount a defense."

I was taken aback by her observation.

"Erika, you may be correct that it has not gone as planned for the prosecution. But I am sure that we have not delivered the knockout punch. In other cases I have tried with Bricker, he has saved his best evidence for last. As he gets more desperate, he will be taking more chances. He is on the run, but he is by no means finished. What makes you think Bricker is ready to toss in the towel?"

"I did not say Bricker was ready to surrender. He most certainly is not. I was watching the judge. He is removed from the background of this case. It's just another long, boring, tedious jury trial to him. Both you and Bricker have made professional—and emotional—investments in the case. The judge hasn't. He is trying to decide when to intervene and throw this case out of court. I've been watching him. I know what he is thinking."

I had not been paying attention to the judge. In jury trials, I tend to focus on the jurors. They are the triers of fact, and the ultimate decision whether to convict or to acquit is theirs. The judge is merely a referee, present in court to make sure that the rules are followed. I expressed this to Erika.

"A referee can take the decision out of the hands of the judges at ringside. In boxing, he can stop the fight. I'm going outside to get some air. I'll be back at one-thirty."

She left me wondering what she was trying to tell me. I was convinced that everything she did had a purpose. For almost two days she had remained aloof, never sharing her thoughts or asking questions. She did not seem concerned in the least about the possibility that the district attorney had a surprise in store for us. She seemed convinced that Bricker was powerless to reverse the tide that clearly was flowing heavily against the prosecution.

When court resumed, it was apparent to all assembled that the young assistant prosecutor had received a lunchtime lesson in direct examination. He moved crisply through the remaining technical evidence, pausing here and there to elicit appropriate explanations from the witness in language understandable to the average citizen-juror.

Annette Park then testified that the crime probably took place at between 8:31 and 8:37 P.M. on the evening of April 15th. From my point of view, this testimony was pivotal. Erika was attending the dinner for Judge Wibbleton at that hour. The only issue was whether the prosecution knew of Erika's whereabouts at the time of the crime. If Bricker knew Erika was not at her computer at the exact moment when the money was taken, how did he propose to prove that she was guilty of the crime?

The young prosecutor halted abruptly, turning the witness over to me for cross examination. As I stood to begin my cross examination, I noticed that the jurors shifted in their places and gave me their complete attention. I had a momentary rush of satisfaction as

I realized that my technique had taken hold completely. I glanced at the judge who had also moved forward in his seat to listen.

"Officer Park, I notice in your testimony that you have determined that the crime was committed with Miss Williams' computer at between 8:31 and 8:36."

"Excuse me," she interrupted, "8:37."

I smiled at her and at the jury. "I just wanted to make sure that you were paying attention, Officer," I said with a smile. There was a general chuckle throughout the courtroom. It was the first bit of humor that I had injected into the proceedings.

"Officer Park, in the course of your investigation, did you happen to gather evidence about Miss Williams' whereabouts on the evening of April 15th?"

"Yes."

"And were you able to pinpoint her location during that evening?"

"Yes," she answered keeping to her instructions to answer yes or no to each question.

Next, I asked whether she knew a person by the name of Joelle Smithson who worked as a video technician at the University. When she replied that she did, I asked whether she had obtained a video tape from Joelle Smithson of a dinner in honor of Judge Wibbleton held at the Inn on campus on April 15th.

"And, Officer Park, did you have an opportunity to view that video tape?"

"Yes."

"Officer Park. . ." I paused, changing the tone of my voice slightly and speaking very deliberately. The jury responded by leaning forward to hear my next series of questions. "Did that videotape show that Miss Williams was in attendance at the dinner on the evening of April 15th?"

"Yes."

"And, Officer Park, were you able to correlate the time that the video was recorded with the actual time on the evening of April 15th?"

"Yes."

"And was Miss Williams at the Inn in clear view of the video camera between 8:31 and 8:37 P.M. so that her presence there was captured on tape?"

"Yes."

"Knowing what the video recording has revealed, is it your conclusion that Miss Williams was not at her computer in the finance office across campus at the time the crime was committed?"

"There is a period of about nine minutes when the lights were lowered so that a video could be shown to those in attendance at the dinner. During that interval Williams was not visible on the videotape."

It was desperation on the part of the witness to avoid answering the direct question that could exonerate Erika. It was a hopeless attempt. I had taken hold of the truth. Annette Park knew I would not let go. I looked sharply at her. She sighed.

"I guess I did not respond to your question. The video shows that the defendant was at her table in the Inn attending the dinner you spoke of between the times of 8:31 and 8:37 P.M. Obviously, she could not have been in two places at once."

"No further questions on cross, your honor."

"None on re-direct, your honor," said the young prosecutor.

The courtroom fell silent. I felt proud that I had delivered such a blow to the prosecution's case. I was sure that the prosecution was on the canvas taking a mandatory "eight count." If Erika was correct, as referee of this contest, the judge should step in between combatants and stop the fight.

I looked expectantly at the judge. I tried to interpret his facial expression. At first, he appeared puzzled and then, as if an answer had been revealed, he smiled and nodded. Then he did something absolutely unprecedented. With two hours of open court time available that afternoon, he recessed the trial, asking the jurors to return at 9:30 the following morning. He then instructed the district attorney and counsel for the defense to meet him in chambers at 8:30 A.M.

52

The courtroom emptied of people and I was sitting at counsel table alone when it happened. At first, because of my overwhelming success with the case, I felt that maybe I really was as good as I thought I was. But then a sudden uneasiness overtook me, similar to the feeling in the pit of my stomach when I realize that I have locked my keys in my car or left my wallet on the bench in the men's locker room at the gym. It consisted of one part embarrassment, one part helplessness, one part "how-could-I-have-been-so-dumb," and one part "I hope no one noticed." Although I had been working on Erika's case for several months, I finally realized what had happened.

I had examined the question from all sides, but I had never viewed it from the top. Why would someone go to unreasonable lengths to frame Erika for a crime and then commit it when she had a perfect alibi? The answer was that they would not. It was now obvious and the embarrassment I felt was extreme. I had so deluded myself into thinking that Erika was a damsel in distress and that there was nobility in my cause, that I had forsaken my training as a lawyer. I knew then, as I probably had known deep down all along, that Erika was guilty as charged.

As I sat there in the empty courtroom, I cleared my mind of all my preconceived notions about the case. I went over the evidence piece by piece. Within a minute, I knew what had happened. The answer was on the videotape.

A rush of excitement coursed through my body. Hurriedly stuffing the accumulation of papers into my briefcase, I left the courtroom. As I passed down the hallway, I wondered whether anything like this ever had happened to James Petrikin. I cautioned myself that this was no time for fantasies. I drove to the Inn on campus. There I explained to the banquet manager that I was working on a criminal case and wanted to examine the room where the banquet for Judge Wibbleton had been held. The manager knew me, and he said the room was open and I could browse to my heart's content.

The room was set up in a manner similar to the configuration that existed on the night of the banquet on April 15th. I occupied Erika's seat facing the podium. Timing myself, I left the table and went into the hallway through one of the side exits. About fifty feet down the hallway, I found the pay phone. I called my office. When Marie answered, I said hello. Then, I pushed several numbered buttons, said goodbye and hung up. I returned down the hallway, retracing my steps to the table and retook my seat. The excursion had taken almost four minutes.

I sat there for a few minutes lost in thought. When I heard footsteps behind me, I assumed that it was the banquet manager and I called out that I was just about finished. When there was no response, I turned around. It was Erika. I was not surprised to see her.

She came over to the table and I motioned for her to sit. For the longest time neither of us spoke.

"You understand," she said calmly and reassuringly, "that it was nothing personal . . . it was strictly business."

I nodded.

"It was my sincere hope that you would not find out until after the trial."

I was nervous and upset, and I felt victimized by her, but I knew deep down that I had allowed it to happen. "All along, I had the feeling that I was a character in a play performing a script I had not been shown. Was I so easily programmed?"

"Not so easy, but like most people, you are a prisoner of your personality, training, and principles. After the court recessed, I saw you linger at the counsel table. It was then that I realized that you had figured it out. This was confirmed when you hurried from the courtroom and I followed you here."

"And I was chosen because. . ."

"You have many good qualities and you are a person with principles. Actually, in some ways you are the father of this venture and you are responsible for its success. I attended your program at the

University about crimes, criminal law, and criminal defense. It is you who reminded me that a sound criminal defense must be part of any plan for crime. I just took it a step further by incorporating use of the defense counsel a part of the plan for the crime. I knew that you had to believe that I was innocent. Someone framed me. It is a part of your personality that you revealed during the program and many times since. I knew that you would never ask me whether or not I was guilty. You didn't really want to know the truth, the whole truth, and nothing but the truth. I might have said that I was guilty. You would not have wanted to hear that."

"And I was also the right person on the back end of the deal. You knew that my principles would not allow me to. . ."

"Blackmail me?" she interrupted. "Yes. I knew that you would never up the ante or want a percentage after you found out. I did not have to worry about being forced into a partnership or your getting greedy. You have your principles. They preclude your doing anything like that. You know, your personality is really not suited for your being an attorney . . . maybe 150 years ago, but not in today's no-holds-barred, greedy world. You are competent and honest. Definite disadvantages."

She could see that I was distressed.

"Please. . ." she said softly, demonstrating some sensitivity, "it was never my intention to hurt you. I only used what you willingly gave. It was strictly business — nothing personal. You've performed brilliantly."

"According to the script you had written for me."

She nodded.

"I may have written the script by planting the evidence and prodding you, but it did not detract from your performance as a trial attorney. You planned and executed everything with the highest level of competence. Please understand that choosing someone of your ability was a risk, but you stuck to your principles — most unusual among attorneys, I might add."

My principles mandated that I would not abandon the case at this stage and that I could be trusted to preserve the attorney-client privilege. I could see she wanted to ask something of me, but did not know how to do it.

[225

"You were going to ask me how I found out."

She chuckled. "Yes, I can see that your part in the play is over and we are now on equal footing. Where did I make my mistake?"

"For one thing when you observed me in the courtroom, I realized that I had never satisfactorily answered the question of why you were framed when you had an almost iron-clad alibi. I knew how you did it when I re-examined your alibi. You see, when the lights went out at the banquet, you were not visible. I stopped the frame of the tape at the exact instant that the lights went out. Then, I did the same for the frame on the tape when the lights were restored. You hung your purse on the right side of the back of the chair when you sat down at the start of the banquet. It was that way when the lights went out. However, when the lights were restored, your purse hung on the left side. I concluded that when the lights went out, you took your purse and exited stage left and went down the hallway. You called your computer on the phone, punched in a command to run the diagnostic program that you loaded earlier followed by the commands to transfer the money. When you returned, you hung your purse on the side closest the exit. The diagnostic program ran for five minutes or so. Then the computer executed the next command you had given it. At the instant the crime was committed, you were back on camera for the alibi. Your mistake was that when you re-entered from stage left, without thinking, you hung your purse on the other side of the chair as you retook your seat."

"We're all fallible," was her response. "Your question?"

"Why?"

"Private enterprise. The secret funds did not belong to the University. John Harley was in the employ of others. His job here was a cover. He was using the multi-million-dollar mainframe computer for private purposes. The university knows nothing of these funds . . . and it is better if you don't know anything about them either. There will be no repercussions for you as a result of this. I will see to it, but you must let go now. I cannot protect you if you persist. I do not enjoy such power. You see, it had nothing to do with the fifty thousand dollars."

"Why tell me about the secret funds in the first place?"

"I had to be a victim for you to take up my cause. I did not think that you would accept a frame-up based upon Harley's trying to discard a lover. Although you are a romantic, you would know that Harley would not frame me because he feared disclosure. You might buy-in if you thought that Harley was getting rid of me because I knew about the secret funds. I wanted you to believe that John Harley was a criminal who was out to get me. It worked. Mr. Harley will not testify against me. You see, the play . . . as you call it . . . is not yet over."

She paused and stood to leave. "I know your principles. You are bound irrevocably to them — not by me but by your own history — and who you are. Tomorrow when the trial is over, I will not thank you for what you have done. It might be perceived as an insult. Although you have done your job well, you believe that a serious miscarriage of justice has resulted from your efforts. It flies in the face of the code you live by. We both know that for you it was an unintended result . . . and I hope that you will not think ill of me for leading you down the path, or be too hard on yourself for following it."

53

Ed Bricker and I stood in chambers before the judge who was sitting behind his oversized mahogany desk. He had not yet indicated that we should be seated. It was his custom to make attorneys stand like misbehaving school children before the principal until he made his point. If anything remained to be discussed after he made his point, he would then permit the lawyers to be seated in the uncomfortable side chairs in front of his massive desk.

Early in my career, an audience before a judge was a terrifying experience. Just as dogs recognize by instinct the more powerful animal, judges know intuitively which attorneys they can bully and which they cannot. I was so concerned about making a favorable impression that invariably I did just the opposite, and I became an easy mark for them. With experience, I took a different approach before the judges. I was always respectful, but I understood the limitation of their power to impose their will upon me. The judges could sense that they held no special psychological advantage over me. At that point, my relationship with the various judges improved.

"I'll not beat about the bush with either of you." The judge's opening line did not sound as promising as I had hoped. Both Bricker and I shifted uneasily as we stood there.

"It seems to me," he continued, "that the prosecution is either sandbagging — holding back — or should not to have tried this case in my courtroom in the first place. Do you have the evidence to convict, Mr. Bricker, or don't you? I want an answer."

"Not any longer . . . if I had it at all," answered the district attorney.

"What is that supposed to mean?"

"Your honor, a witness who may have been able to shed some light on the case was critically injured in an automobile accident late last night. His wife was killed. He is not available to testify and may never be."

"Harley?" I asked.

The district attorney explained that there was a one-car accident on the bridge along the by-pass. Mrs. Harley had been driving their car at a high rate of speed when she apparently lost control of the car and it shot through the railing, over the edge of the bridge and crashed onto the highway below. The police think that alcohol might have been involved. She was killed outright, and Harley was not expected to recover.

I was shocked by this news, but having had my world turned upside down by Erika, I should not have been surprised by her powers. It seemed that she was in the process of playing out the last scene of the drama she had written.

"As for the defense," the judge said, turning to me, "fortunately your reputation has preceded you in my court so that I do not ascribe anything questionable to your behavior, Counselor. However, I was not born yesterday. Your case is much too pat. I know very well that your client probably framed herself and then built herself an air-tight alibi. I also know the crime of embezzlement—not personally, of course—but professionally, from my days as district attorney. With embezzlement there is always more. Apparently, the University has not discovered any more money missing. Is that right, Ed?"

The fact that the judge had called Bricker by his given name was an indication to me that the judge no longer sought to enforce his authority over us. His tone of voice and demeanor had changed. From past experience, we knew that we were to turn our energies from the adversary nature of court proceedings to negotiating a satisfactory conclusion of the matter. The judge motioned for us both to be seated.

Bricker nodded. "Judge, we've looked and looked. We just can't figure out what she had up her sleeve. Of course, it is possible that she actually was framed, possibly by Harley, the man who was injured. But we knew from the outset that no one would frame her with such carefully planted evidence, then permit her to have a perfect alibi when the crime was committed. Judge, like you, I don't ascribe anything to defense counsel . . . I think you were fooled, too, weren't you?" he asked, looking at me.

Without hesitation, I nodded, knowing that my assent would confirm for them the fact that Erika was guilty. They both seemed relieved. Bricker's action in bringing charges against Erika even though not proven in court was justified. He could not be accused by the court of bringing false charges, and his conscience was salved. When I would not discuss plea bargain with him, he had no alternative but to go forward with the case. There was a pause as we all considered what to do. We all knew that Erika was guilty, but she was now beyond the reach of the criminal justice system.

The Judge turned to me. "Counselor, I think it might be appropriate for you to come up with a solution — after all," the judge said with a smile, "you were pitching a no-hit shut out there in the courtroom—pretty close to a perfect game. You can't tell us that you weren't suspicious."

"Not until yesterday."

I was not about to reveal the depth of my feelings. It was better that they think we were all duped by this cunning woman.

"Williams will disclose nothing to me . . . or to you. She will resign her position at the University and leave town. The University has all its money . . . it has lost nothing else. Within the limits of the knowledge available to me, I can assure you of that fact. If the University will reinstate her and pay her regular salary plus benefits through today, Erika Williams is prepared to tender her resignation immediately. If you wish to conclude this matter, Judge, I would request that the court direct a verdict acquitting Erika Williams — or order a dismissal so she cannot be tried again. I think all parties will accept that . . . and I know the prosecution does not want this to go any further. Right, Ed?"

I could tell that the judge was satisfied with my suggestion. The dignity of the court was preserved, and the University was rid of Erika. The fact was that they all wanted Erika out of the jurisdiction, and I wanted this chapter of my life to end as soon as possible.

They may have thought that Erika was a loser, because she lost her job and had to leave town without any money. I was sure that as a prosecutor bent on uncovering crime and punishing criminal behavior, Bricker thought that justice was served. Only I knew that Erika was the winner. Only I knew how well Erika had compensated herself for her trouble.

"It's a deal," said Bricker.

He really had no alternative. He understood that I could have insisted on much more by continuing the case to acquittal. Since I knew that Erika's intention was to leave, I could be magnanimous in victory by enabling Bricker to tell the University that he had succeeded in having Erika resign her position and he could assure the powers-that-be that they would find no funds missing because of her. He understood that I had not held his feet to the fire when I had every opportunity to do so, and after we left the judge, as we passed down the corridor he thanked me for my cooperation and complimented me on my courtroom work.

His comments restored a small measure of self-confidence which had been seriously damaged when I realized how easily Erika had manipulated me.

I went immediately to the courtroom and found Erika sitting at the counsel table waiting for me.

"The judge is going to direct a verdict of acquittal. You will be free to leave. You have been reinstated and will receive full pay through today . . . when you resign your position. Is that satisfactory?"

She nodded.

"Now, tell me, Erika, how did you arrange to get Harley out of the way?"

She hesitated. I was afraid that she would withhold the information from me. And having already learned some of the truth of what had happened, I was not convinced that I really wanted to know more about the power of this dangerous woman. But, I was curious and like all successful people, Erika had an ego that needed to be fed. What good was the perfect crime unless it was shared with another? Pride of authorship consumed us all and Erika was no exception to this rule.

"Within a few weeks, the University will become aware that John Harley embezzled a very large sum of money. They already suspect him and the police have been following him closely. This will exonerate me completely and place him in the chair where I sit today as defendant."

"There's more, Erika," I said with more than a little reproach in my voice.

"Yes, there is, but I want you to know — for what it's worth — that I had no intention of hurting anyone. But I am aware that when you play with fire like I did, the results cannot be predicted. I know that I set into motion the chain of events that led to injury, but I feel no guilt or remorse. It was strictly business."

She paused. I shuddered inside. She certainly lived by different rules than I. My reality was that absolutely no business could justify what had happened to Harley. However, as a lawyer — ill-equipped as I was in Erika's eyes — I tried to keep an open mind and not to render judgment upon Erika.

"The letters. Once when Harley was at my townhouse, I took one of his sport coats and hid it. He was distracted and never missed it. I recovered the letters from his office where he had

[231

hidden them in his desk. I placed a whole packet of them in the breast pocket of the coat and sent it through the dry cleaners. Then, yesterday I called the cleaner, saying I was Harley's secretary and that he was looking for a coat which he needed immediately. Did they have it . . . if so to call the number on the tag . . . his home number."

She paused in her explanation to provide appropriate background.

"As a test, I sent one of my own coats through the same dry cleaner with letters in the pocket. When I picked it up, I found that the cleaner stapled a large envelope containing the letters to the plastic wrap and hanger. I was hoping that Harley's wife would be curious and go get Harley's coat. You see it was her job to take care of the cleaning. She used another dry cleaning company. A woman would be suspicious of a husband who cleaned a sport coat on his own using a different company. When she did pick it up, she would most certainly open the large envelope — wouldn't you?"

I tried to conjure up a vision of Mrs. Harley. The telephone rang. The clerk at another dry cleaning company reported that the missing sport coat her husband's secretary had called about had been located and she could pick it up. Such a call would have been unusual. I was sure that Erika would not rely upon just that call. There was more that she did not disclose to me. She would have done other things to Mrs. Harley to sow the seeds of doubt about her husband's fidelity. Either as a favor for her husband, or out of curiosity or suspicion about her husband, Mrs. Harley went to the cleaner and picked up the coat. The large envelope attracted her attention. Mrs. Harley would have justified opening the envelope by saying to herself that the enclosure might be important, something that John Harley needed at work. But she was suspicious. She opened the envelope. I could not even imagine the scene that might have followed as this unstable woman read and re-read those passionate and descriptive love letters one by one.

It made my blood run cold to think about Erika's motives. Was it "strictly business," or was it partly the revenge of a woman who saw her lover's wife buying fresh vegetables at the grocery store on a Thursday evening?

"Why tell me about the letters? Harley would only be concerned about the letters if he knew you had them. You told him you had the letters?"

"Yes. I hoped that might be enough to dissuade him from testifying. But it was not. He was prepared to come to court and testify. His testimony would have been that I told him that I committed the crime. I had no alternative."

"Why hide the letters in his office?"

"You found them?" she seemed surprised.

"Yes, behind the baseboard."

"And you did not tell me?"

I could tell that she was offended.

"I knew the police would not search Harley's office. It was the safest place until I planted the seeds of his guilt with the police. By then they had been recovered."

I was about to ask another question, when the judge entered the courtroom. After the assemblage rendered the customary show of respect, he thanked the jury for their efforts, explaining that a judgment of acquittal was going to be entered as an order of court. He dismissed the jurors and they filed out of the courtroom. I could tell that the jurors were relieved to have the case behind them. But for many of them, the courtroom scene was high drama, and they were part of the cast. I knew that they too had made emotional investments in the case and were disappointed that they could not have learned more about the personalities and events surrounding the case. Then the judge read into the record of the case an order dismissing all charges against Erika and directing a verdict of not guilty in her favor.

"I wish to thank the district attorney and defense counsel for their respect and cooperation throughout this trial. Both attorneys are to be commended. This court stands adjourned."

I sat at the counsel table as the courtroom cleared. I had lost my interest in finding out more about Erika's crime. Perhaps, I was afraid that there was much more to the drama. After all, I was only one character and much of the time I was off-stage. So I asked nothing more of her.

I think my reticence surprised her.

"No more questions?" she asked, indicating that she was willing to oblige my curiosity. She seemed so proud of what she had done. It was as if she were using me once more, this time as a sounding board to recount her success. After all, I was the only person in the world she could tell without fear of disclosure. But at that moment I wanted to know nothing more about the actions of this incredibly calculating and dangerous woman. I shook my head, preserving for myself some personal dignity.

We walked together from the courtroom, down the hallway. My mind flashed briefly to James Petrikin, and I wondered whether anything like this had ever happened to him in his career as a lawyer here in the county.

Outside on the marble steps under the portico, a number of reporters and cameramen were waiting for Erika, gathering like pigeons in the park. Erika smiled for the cameras and then leaned over to me and gave me a hug. It was not a traditional, warm, meaningful hug that expressed gratitude or affection. She had not anticipated the presence of the reporters and she used the hug as an excuse to move closer to speak softly into my ear.

"I said I would not say 'thank you' and I won't. You will hear from Condor Trucking. I know you — you want this behind you — and it is. Goodbye."

She smiled again for the cameras.

"Please," she said sweetly to them, "My attorney will answer any questions you may have. Thank you."

Apparently, she was determined to use me once more. I had no alternative but to oblige. It was an easy scene to play and I knew the script by heart. I explained to the assembled reporters how grateful Miss Williams was that the judge had dismissed all charges. She had faith all along in the American judicial system and knew that once all the evidence was brought to light that she would be exonerated. Although she had been reinstated to her former position at the University, she felt that it would be better for all concerned if she tendered her resignation effective immediately. After a short vacation, she intended to pursue other opportunities as an accountant in another state. She bore no grudge toward the University because the evidence at the time the charges were filed did seem to indicate wrongdoing on her part. Once all the evidence was revealed, the University understood the truth. She thanked the news media for their consideration for her feelings throughout the proceeding by not seeking statements that she could not give. When I felt that the news people had been fed sufficiently, I personally thanked them and said that I would have nothing more to say about the case.

Without looking at me, Erika started down the steps. The crowd of reporters parted to permit her to pass. I stood there watching as she walked down the sidewalk to the street. I knew that I would never see her or hear from her again. The curtain had finally come down, and the play was over.

54

As the reporters wandered away to file their stories, I tried to define my feelings. Each time I serve as trial attorney, win or lose, I feel depressed when the case is over. I had always assumed this was because each case took so long to reach its conclusion. There are months of investigation followed by the laborious pleading and discovery process that could add months or even years to a case. Then, once a case is procedurally ready for trial, another delay is certain as it works its way to the top of the trial list. Once the trial starts, it seems that the climax of the case is always short and to the point. When the verdict is in, a terrible emptiness replaces the purpose and excitement that has dominated my life.

This was no less so with Erika's case. Not only had it consumed my physical and emotional energies for months, but the result exposed serious flaws in the principles that guided my personal and professional life.

Sallie is fond of pointing out that, for me, every event in life has

[235

meaning, whether it does or not. Of course, she is right. It is one area where Sallie and I have major philosophical differences. I seek meaning in everything that happens. Sallie is more willing to accept most events in life as random occurrences without her constantly having to re-define her place in the cosmos. I decided to allow time to pass before dissecting the case and the events surrounding it.

Marie greeted me with applause as I entered the office. It was an appropriate response considering that I had performed my role in Erika's play so flawlessly.

"Well," she asked, "how does it feel now that it's over?"

"I'm glad it is all behind us. Now we can go back to work in a boring, unfulfilling, meaningless, menial, mundane, and bland law practice," I answered with a smile. "I'm looking forward to it."

"And?" she prodded, "was Erika guilty?"

"Not as charged..."

"But guilty, nonetheless. Just as I said." Marie gloated. "I knew the case was over when I heard on the news this morning about that terrible accident with the Harleys. I don't know how she did it...."

"Marie, the case is closed—behind us. Erika is gone. I'm ready for the routine of our uninteresting existence."

"Right, Boss."

She uses the word "boss" when she knows that further discussion is futile. It is her way of telling me that she is complying, but that she is doing so only because I said so, not because there is a valid reason to terminate the discussion. It reminded me of the response I received when I questioned many of my mother's decisions. When all reason failed her, the response was "because I am your mother, that's why." To which I invariably replied "right, Mother."

"Don't count on it being too uninteresting. While you were in court this morning we got a wire transfer into our general account from a bank in Montana, I think—from a company called Condor Trucking. Eighty-nine thousand dollars. Last time we got a wire transfer, remember what happened? How shall I book it?"

I was not surprised that we were paid so quickly. Erika would have taken care of that detail as part of her plan. I was surprised only by the amount. I had not tendered a bill because the trial ended so abruptly. And, in the heat of battle, I had not even considered the matter.

My guiding principle of billing for legal services is that the fee charged should fairly represent the services rendered, no more, no less. I also try to bill immediately after rendering legal services. At that point, the client's gratitude curve is at its apex and the value of the services I performed for them is fresh in their mind. Beginning one day later, the client's gratitude curve begins a precipitous downward spiral so that within a month, the client has totally forgotten the value of my services. After even such a brief interval, collecting the fee is more difficult. Fee collection is one of the worst aspects of being a lawyer and I hate to call clients and ask for money. I find that clients resent an attorney who imposes on them by requesting payment of a legal fee even if when owed.

The funds we received were far in excess of the amount I might have billed Erika if I had taken the time to calculate the number of hours I had spent on her case and added a surcharge for the favorable result. It also occurred to me that the funds might have been part of the money that she misappropriated. On principle, I never accept tainted funds in payment for legal fees. But $89,000 — plus the retainer of $10,000 — was a lot of money that could be put to good use.

I assured myself that I could not refund the excess portion of the fee even if I were inclined to do so. Erika had given me specific instructions that I was not to contact her. She was a smart woman and the legal services must have had that value to her or she would not have paid that amount. She may have overpaid me as insurance that I would not try to locate her to collect more. I ended my rationalization of the matter by resolving not to test the fee received against my principles of charging fairly for my services and never accepting funds of questionable origin.

Later that day, I realized that I had performed brilliantly all of the necessary psychological gymnastics to overcome two of my principles of fee collection. Obviously, my experiences with Erika had begun to have a profound effect upon me.

"Book it to Erika Williams' account. Please call Rick Place's office and find out the amount we owe him. Pay him. Then take out a ten thousand dollar bonus for yourself. Write me a check for half of the balance as a withdrawal."

"Anything else?" she asked.

"Yes, get all of the things that require my immediate attention together for me to do the next couple of days. The mystery of Erika Williams is as solved as it's going to be. I am now turning my attention to my other mystery . . . the freedom of Eben Jones."

Marie gave me one of her familiar "are-you-sure-you-know-what-you-are doing" looks. But she had just been the recipient of a $10,000 bonus, so she smiled and did not press the issue. From her perspective, the larder was temporarily full and the wolf was no longer at the door. We now enjoyed one of those rare occasions when the business had a substantial cash reserve. Under those circumstances she must have felt that it was permissible to humor me.

I spent the afternoon catching up on routine matters around the office, but I was eager to share the day's experiences with Sallie and it was difficult to maintain my concentration. When I arrived home, I called out for her, but there was no answer.

"Strange," I thought. "her car is in the garage."

I went to the kitchen and there carefully arranged on the table were a can of vegetarian-style baked beans, a can opener, a sauce pan, an empty bowl with a spoon, and my pistol. Upon closer inspection, I found a picture cut from the evening newspaper showing Erika giving me a hug on the steps of the county courthouse. The caption read "Acquitted Defendant Thanks Her Attorney." Clipped to the picture was a note:

Make yourself a tasty last *supper then decide whether to attempt to explain this picture to me or commit suicide. Sallie*

P.S. The latter alternative will be easier and less painful. — S.

The clever little things that Sallie does from time to time are one of the features of her personality I love most.

"Two can play that game," I thought.

Pistol in hand, I went into the living room. I cocked the pistol chambering a bullet. Taking aim at the old sofa that we both hated, I pulled the trigger. There was a loud report and sofa stuffing flew everywhere. I quickly lay down on what was left of one of the sofa pillows. Upstairs I heard a loud scream and Sallie came running down the stairs. When she saw me draped over the edge of the wounded sofa, she screamed again. As she approached me cautiously, I reached out and grabbed her, taking her into my arms, wrestling her to the floor.

"You bastard," she whispered between kisses.

After the stress of the week's events, it felt good being with Sallie and we had a wonderful time together making love there in the living room.

"About that picture," she started, "the only thing that saved you was your grease-spotted tie. That told me that you weren't trying to impress anyone."

I showed Sallie the check that Marie had drawn for me. I thought she might be excited, but she was not.

"Your fee?"

I nodded. I was not sure whether she seemed upset because it was too large or too small, so I did not disclose to her that the check was less than half of the fee we received. Another of Sallie's lovable qualities is her ability to place money in its proper perspective. She categorizes money as an essential life-sustaining commodity like food. Money is essential, but if there is more than reasonably can be used plus a little rainy-day reserve, it could lead to gluttony and corruption. I am blessed to have such a partner.

"Why so down? There is even enough here to replace the dead sofa."

"I don't know whether or not it is a fair fee. I cannot judge that. I'm happy you were paid, but I was a little worried about you."

"And us?"

She nodded thoughtfully.

I thought of saying something reassuring. I might have told her that I knew what I was doing when I made the commitment to represent Erika. But Sallie knew better.

"We are lucky, Sallie. Erika is gone. She took advantage of me and my principles, but she never wanted anything more than I gave her. Nothing more was necessary to her plan. But I have no doubt that if she had put her mind to it, she could have had that, too."

Sallie thought about what I said. At first, I was worried that I had given her the impression that I wanted Erika. But, as always, I tend to underestimate Sallie's wisdom.

"You are a man and you were vulnerable. And she was a woman with a mission. You are right. Harley was the target, you were not. When I read the news today, I understood what had happened. I reviewed the video of Judge Wibbleton's dinner since that was the alibi. No one would go to the trouble of framing Erika for the crime and then neglect to ensure that Erika did not have an alibi when the actual crime was committed. It had to be Erika. Just had to. I knew it when she wore that bright dress to the dinner. Do you know what tipped me off?"

Sallie seemed so proud of herself that I hated to burst her bubble. But I did not want her to think that I was a total loss.

"The purse?"

Sallie pretended to be crushed. "How could you?" she whined. "I was so sure that I had unlocked the mystery for you."

Sallie and I laughed. No longer would Erika cast a shadow over our relationship. It was unspoken, but we both knew it and we were both relieved.

55

"He is our ghost," the woman explained as she ushered me into her office at the county historical museum.

"Ghost?"

"Why yes, his portrait hangs above the fireplace here in this very office. We believe that he haunts the museum."

I carefully examined the portrait of James Petrikin done in 1825 by an artist named Eicholtz. It was a traditional portrait of the period with the subject dressed in a formal collar and lace shirt.

Petrikin looked to be in his mid-twenties with a ruddy complexion and rounded facial features. I was surprised that his appearance closely resembled my vision of him. He was not handsome or rugged, nor did he appear angelic. To me he seemed to be likeable with a wry smile.

I showed the curator my letter from Charles Perrow. She read it with interest, making comments and nodding now and then. Lowering her glasses, she asked how I had come into possession of the letter.

"Do you have any idea why this letter would have been retained by Petrikin's descendants, or how it found its way into the collection of papers in the estate?" I asked.

I knew there would be no ready answer and I was not disappointed.

"It is a 'slave' document," she commented, "but on its face, the letter is not remarkable except for its age. Of course, it was not old when Petrikin died at age 35 . . . that would have been in about 1838. Not long enough after the letter was written to have historical value at the time. I don't think that it was retained for historical purposes."

"Well, someone made the decision to keep the letter and presumably safeguard it. Have you any idea why this might be so?" I asked.

She speculated, but none of the proffered explanations seemed to fit.

My next thought was that Eben Jones may have been one of the Negroes who was mentioned in the history book as having been captured by Virginians in the county and brought before the judge in November 1826. A search of the newspaper archives did not bear fruit. The issue cited in the history book was not in the archives, and a check of other references indicated that the University library did not have the issue either.

Although I was not able to uncover a shred of evidence about Eben Jones, I was able to find an undated article about James Petrikin bound into a book about early residents of the county. The history book had recounted some facets of Petrikin's personality, and the newly discovered article revealed others.

[241

The curator suggested that I re-check the assessment records as well as the Court of Quarter Sessions docket in the clerk's office. I walked up the hill to the courthouse pausing at the town square just as Petrikin had done so many years before. I looked down the hill to Petrikin Hall which stood on the west side of High Street on the site where Petrikin was born in 1803. In my mind, I could clearly picture this dapper young man standing by the street waving to the passers-by in 1827. He did not know then that in three years he would marry Mary Wallace and in eleven years he would be dead. I wondered what Petrikin might have thought of modern-day High Street with its omnipresent pick-up trucks roaring noisily up and down.

Petrikin's sense of commitment to the freedom of Eben Jones would have weighed heavily upon him. The article bespoke of a man of art and learning, not a man of worldly obsession for material things. The principle of freedom would have motivated him to continue the search for evidence of Eben Jones' residency in the county.

With renewed zeal, I resolved to continue my own search. I went again to the docket books of the court of quarter sessions for November term, 1826, to see if there was a record of the Virginians who captured the Negroes and paraded them through town. My search was interrupted by Attorney Oscar Brumbaugh whom I had encountered on my previous visit seeking information about the mystery.

"Continuing the search?" he asked politely.

Brumbaugh was much changed in the several months since I had last seen him. Although he wore his familiar Harris tweed sportcoat, it now fit him poorly. He had lost weight and was more stooped, as if he bore a heavy weight upon his shoulders. His color was ashen and his eyes lacked their former sparkle.

"Yes," I answered, trying to be polite, but not expressive enough to encourage him to linger. It was no use. He stopped and carefully lowered himself into a chair. I immediately felt trapped, but I chastised myself for the unkind thought.

"When we last met, you were about to ask me about James Petrikin. My secretary interrupted us. You see she takes care that I not bother people with my incessant chatter about the demise of the legal profession. The younger lawyers usually scatter to the four winds when I approach, lest they be accosted. I interfere with billable time, you know—modern lawyer alchemy—changing that illusive commodity, time, into that much sought after commodity, money. There is tremendous pressure upon our younger brethren to pay for their senior partners' Mercedes and, in time, to get one or more for themselves."

He looked at me curiously.

"And you, my friend, you have changed since last we spoke— you have a fresh tie, a new belt. This tells me that your attitudes have changed. I hope it was not the success of the Williams case that has affected you. I observed the case and was much impressed. You will be getting many calls for criminal defense, I think. And you will find that success is sometimes a curse—as you know, I am not so cursed . . . but I am pleased to see that you are continuing the search for whatever it is you are looking for in these ancient books."

I explained briefly the purpose of my search.

"Ah, the pursuit of knowledge about freedom and justice. Most noble—but not practical. You may end up like me."

"I could do worse . . . much worse."

He seemed pleased by my answer. But before he could say anything, we were interrupted by his secretary.

"Now, Oscar, there is work to be done in our office. You must dictate that letter—you promised," She said kindly.

It was apparent that she was his designated caretaker and that somehow he had managed to escape her watchful eye and wander across the street into the courthouse. Her thoughtfulness in the way she handled the situation was remarkable. I wondered if Marie would show the same compassion toward me.

"Well, continue the search for freedom and justice," he said with resignation in his voice. "You see, they have me tethered on a very short leash, and I must now be led back to the pound."

His secretary steadied him as they walked away. I could hear some younger lawyers in the outer office joking about him as he left. Once again the insensitivity of these young bucks betrayed

[243

their lack of understanding of the human condition. "Do they think, perhaps, that they will not suffer a similar fate in their old age?" I asked myself.

I resumed and concluded my search without finding a clue about Eben Jones. James Petrikin's name was spread widely throughout the record preserved in the docket books. Petrikin served as counsel in cases ranging from bastardy and fornication to collection of debts. But, there was nothing in any of the dockets and indices which indicated that Eben Jones ever had set foot in the county. And, there was no record of the Negroes who were presented in court in November 1826.

For the first time since I had obtained the letter at auction, I became discouraged, fearing that I might never know the ultimate fate of Eben Jones. It was possible that the mystery might remain so forever. This thought was anathema to my own belief that all things are possible. I knew deep down that Eben Jones was but a fragment of history, locked in the memories of Charles Perrow and James Petrikin, people who were long since gone. And Eben Jones was nothing more than a footnote in the history of those whose lives he touched if, in fact, he ever had been a resident. Nothing remained here of Eben Jones except for this letter and the musings of a frustrated lawyer more than one hundred and fifty years later.

As the dark clouds of depression began to gather over me, I reevaluated my own situation. Would I complete my career as a lawyer viewed by my colleagues in the same light as Oscar Brumbaugh, the butt of cruel jokes as I stumbled aimlessly through the clerk's office seeking a friendly face to talk to? Or would my colleagues feel that way today if they knew I was searching for information about Eben Jones, a black man who was dead and gone?

I have been through this many times, but it makes the depression no less painful. I consoled myself with the thought that it did not matter what the young attorneys thought of me. After all, it is my life, not theirs. If I choose to spend my time investigating events in the dimly lit past, that is my prerogative. I know, however, that I seek respect and acceptance just like everyone else. It does matter what others think of me. Rejection is as crushing a blow to me as anyone else.

I gathered my belongings and started from the inner vault of the clerk's office. As I left, the young attorneys who were gathered in the outer office moved slightly to the left or right to make room as I passed among them. Several nodded politely to me and I smiled benevolently at them. I read respect in their eyes. The Williams case had obviously raised my position within the legal community. The clouds of depression disbursed momentarily, and I was certain that—at least on this occasion—there would be no jokes behind my back after I departed. But fame is fleeting and illusory. Soon I would again be the subject of their speculation and cruel humor about why I serve my time as a sole practitioner and not as a senior partner in a law firm. The lawyer's heirarchy has no permanent place at the top reserved for me.

56

The Shenandoah Valley spread out before me like some magnificent painting as we drove south from Winchester, Virginia, on Interstate 81. Sallie dozed in the passenger seat. Ahead in Lovingston I hoped to unravel the mystery of Eben Jones.

It had been several weeks since the curtain had descended on Erika's drama, and I now felt better able to assess the events surrounding my involvement in her case.

I had been led willingly down the path in the belief that Erika's defense was noble. I had donned blinders that permitted me to see only what I had wanted to see. Erika obliged me and unknowingly, I had flawlessly performed my role in her carefully constructed criminal plan.

I had no remorse for having helped her abscond with an unimaginable amount of money. Her case had improved my standing among the other members of the bar, and though the judge sus-

[245

pected that I was a victim of Erika's criminal machinations, no adverse consequences were likely to follow. However, I did not count my courtroom success as a victory which I might place prominently on my resume.

I tried to re-examine my personal code to determine whether it needed readjustment. I knew that I was a prisoner of my personal belief that somehow my principles were more worthy and noble than my colleagues'. For me, nothing about the law is 'strictly business.' Yet I was more like them than I cared to admit. I turned a blind eye toward all the evidence that Erika was not the person I thought she was, convincing myself that she was a damsel in distress. And after the truth was revealed, I willingly accepted the generous fee and kept it for my own purposes instead of forwarding the excess portion to Amnesty International.

The beauty of the drive through the valley dulled my willingness to think seriously about these matters. My mind drifted back to 1827 where Petrikin sat at his desk writing a letter to Charles Perrow.

Dear Mr. Perrow,

With much care I have investigated the information supplied in your letter and I regret to inform both you and the unfortunate Eben Jones that I am unable to substantiate any of the claims made by him that he was a resident of our County in 1819. Therefore, I am unable to supply the requested affidavits to support the Writ of Habeas Corpus which you have filed in Nelson County. This is not to suggest that such evidence does not exist, only that I was unable to uncover it in any of the written records here in our county.

If other information is made available, I will do my utmost to make further inquiry in support of the cause of the establishment of the freedom of Eben Jones.

It is my sincere hope that other sources have been more successful than I. Until I hear further I remain

your humble servant,
Jas. Petrikin

Petrikin replaced his pen and re-read the letter.

"Nobility of purpose can motivate action, but it cannot guarantee the result," he thought. "I have done what I could on behalf of

Eben Jones. Perhaps others will have been able to provide what I could not."

Petrikin knew that it was unlikely that others would produce evidence to support the writ of *habeas corpus*. He needed to maintain an ego-saving lie that it was not his failure alone that would condemn Eben Jones to a life of slavery.

I left the main highway and wound my way through farmland on the road east toward Lovingston. It was difficult to imagine that these beautifully maintained farms surrounded by white fences employed an economic system which was based upon slave labor where people were bought and sold like John Deere tractors. It was a different world then. I wondered what Farmer Colleton and Charles Perrow might think of our world today.

Lovingston was a short distance from the main road which connected Charlottesville to the towns and cities of southwestern Virginia. I found it to be a small community very similar to many I knew in Pennsylvania. I speculated that the courthouse would be located on the hill above town and I was not disappointed. It was a small white stucco building situated on a small hill above the main street.

"We're here, Sallie," I said as I gently awakened her. She urged me to start my search and assured me that she would join me soon.

My excitement mounted. I was finally within sight of unravelling the mystery of Eben Jones. It seemed like such a long time since that November night when I lay in bed thinking about the letter and its significance to Eben Jones, Charles Perrow, and James Petrikin. Back then, I imagined that the spirits of the *dramatis personnae* and the memory of the events recounted in the letter had been cast adrift to float aimlessly in the vastness of history. Locked in a time warp of incalculable complexity, the letter and its contents awaited a chance encounter with a cosmic force and the memory of the people and the story they lived would be resurrected and retold. Notwithstanding the considerable ability of my fantasies to embellish fact, Jones, Petrikin, and Perrow were real people from the past. I felt that it was my destiny to unravel the mystery of the events and that it was my special mission to unlock and to set free this part of the history of their lives.

The front of the courthouse displayed the obligatory monuments to the Confederacy. There was also a monument erected in memory of the large number of citizens who perished when Hurricane Camille came through Nelson County during my own lifetime. Once inside, I was greeted by a deputy clerk who showed me the vault where the court and land records were kept. Old docket books lined the walls. Nelson County used an alphabetical index, similar to the one used in our own county, though our court and land records were kept in separate offices. In Nelson County, the Clerk of the Circuit Court performed the functions of recorder of deeds and clerk of court.

I began my search for the writ of *habeas corpus* filed by Charles Perrow. In the first index I examined I noted that, like James Petrikin, Charles Perrow was a general practitioner. His name appeared as attorney of record on all types of cases, both civil and criminal. About a third of all cases listed in the indices showed his name as attorney for one of the litigants. He had a booming practice.

The suspense mounted as I found the index for criminal and civil cases for the year 1827. My eyes darted quickly down the list, certain that I would see the name of Eben Jones. To my disappointment, there was no case listed in his name in the index for that year. I read the list more deliberately another time, but again my efforts were not rewarded. I continued the search in the indices for the years immediately preceding and following 1827, but Eben's name was not listed there either. Hoping that somehow the clerk in 1827 did not properly index the writ of *habeas corpus*, I began my search through the docket book one case at a time. Again, disappointment followed. There was no writ of *habeas corpus* listed in the name of Eben Jones or any similar name. Charles Perrows' name was prominently spread upon the record as he engaged in a busy law practice that year.

My disappointment must have been very visible for a man who had been working with the land records politely asked if he might be of assistance. If he had been typecast in a Hollywood production about a Southern country lawyer, this gentleman could not have looked more authentic. He introduced himself and I showed him the letter.

"Perrow . . . prominent name in these parts . . . think there are some Perrows practicing law in Lynchburg."

This country gentleman lawyer took up my quest. He busily pulled and examined docket books and land records. After exhausting the readily available resources he recovered from deep within the recesses of the vault a dusty old book listing slave marriages. After about forty-five minutes of effort with me following him intently, he turned and announced that if Eben Jones had existed, that existence was not recorded in Nelson County.

Discouraged, I thanked him for his efforts and went outside and sat in the shade waiting for Sally. The attorney must have observed me from inside the courthouse and he came outside.

"I think I know what happened. I've heard similar stories before. . ."

I nodded, eager to learn more.

Just then Sallie walked up the steps to the courthouse and joined us. I introduced her. Mustering all the southern charm available in his arsenal, he complimented her on her appearance. She blushed slightly and smiled. I made a mental note to be sure to use his line that she looked "as fresh as a dew drop on a magnolia blossom."

After the brief interruption, he continued with his story.

"Charles Perrow was not one of those early time American Civil Liberties lawyers. He ground out a living as a country lawyer and was dependent upon community support for his livelihood. Although he wrote about a writ of *habeas corpus*, there was none in the docketbook or the index. It seems clear that he did not file one on behalf of this Eben Jones. . ."

He paused.

"You see, most likely Perrow never intended to file the writ. You have to realize what it was like back then. Although Virginia was a slave state, there still was 'due process' here though not as we know it today. This was not an early day Nazi Germany. This runaway Jones was captured without proper identification. He claimed to be a citizen of Pennsylvania. Under the law, his story had to be verified. Perhaps the judge or someone else appointed Perrow to check the story. So, Perrow wrote to the attorney in Pennsylvania claiming to represent Jones and asking help in verifying the information. The Pennsylvania attorney believes that he can help win the freedom of a slave by doing his best to uncover the evidence for a writ of *habeas corpus*. The attorney in Pennsylvania..."

"Petrikin," I interjected.

"Petrikin, believing that his cause is noble, thus expends substantial energy looking for evidence to help establish the freedom of Eben Jones. In effect, he does the investigative work for the sheriff of Nelson County. He is used by Perrow to disprove the assertions of Eben Jones. Petrikin's inability to provide the evidence seals Jones' fate. He probably wrote back to Perrow that regrettably the evidence was not forthcoming. There was no writ of *habeas corpus*, nor was it Perrow's intent ever to file one. Petrikin's letter was the key that locked the chains around Jones' neck and returned him to a life of slavery."

He paused again. "Unless I miss my guess, you already have trod the same ground as this Petrikin fellow."

I nodded.

"And like Petrikin, you found no evidence that Jones was a resident there?"

"None."

"And no writ was filed here in Nelson County. But . . . it is an interesting story."

He smiled.

I thanked him for his time, we shook hands, and he went back into the courthouse to resume the lawyer's calling of turning time into dollars.

Sallie and I sat silently in the shade for a few moments. I was utterly disappointed that James Petrikin, my alter ego, may have been used unwittingly to obtain the result that he probably abhorred. Perhaps it was "strictly business" with Perrow, but certainly it was not that way for Petrikin. And sometimes others are able to take advantage of that kind of person.

Sallie looked intently at me, not knowing how to respond to my disappointment about the recent turn of events. She moved closer and put her arm around my shoulder giving me a squeeze that was two parts affection and one part encouragement.

"Well, that lawyer is right . . . it is an interesting story. Why don't you write about it?"

And so I have.

Lovingston, Nelson County, Va., September 4, 1827

Dear Sir:

I received your letter of the 7th July last, and am glad to find you willing to aid in this humane undertaking of establishing the freedom of Eben Jones. There is no statutary provision in this State for such a case as Eben's. Our statutes relating to runaway slaves can have no bearing upon his case provided we can satisfactorily show that he is a citizen or resident of another state. If he be a citizen of your state then our laws requiring free persons of colour to be registered here and to carry with them a certificate of such register of freedom with the County seal annexed thereto cannot operate against him; because he will stand protected under the first clause of the second Section of the 4th Article of the Federal Constitution. The question will then recur is he a citizen of Pennsylvania. If your laws do not disqualify him from the exercise of Citizenship, then if it shall appear that he was a free man in Pennsylvania he is a citizen thereof and stands completely protected under the Article quoted from the operation of our Laws relative to free negroes & mulatos & runaway slaves; if he be a citizen of Pennsylvania then the most speedy and safe course to pursue will be to apply to our Judge of our Circuit Court here at its next sitting which will be about the first of next month for a Writ of Habeas Corpus ad subjudiciendum, under the provisions of our Act of Assembly. In the proceedings before the Judge any evidence of a legal nature will be received; consequently the affidavit of Witnesses proving such circumstances as will be convincing that Eben Jones is a citizen of the State of Pennsylvania & a free man will be sufficient to procure his discharge. It is then of the first importance that such circumstantial evidence (if we can get none positive) as will affect the object be speedily obtained. I must therefore in the name of humanity and at the earnest solicitation of Eben request you to have all the facts, which I have communicated to Mr. Rankin and to yourself together with the facts hereinafter related and those which may suggest themselves to you proved and authenticated and transmitted as early as possible to me here. I have had all the letters written upon this subject

[251]

copied and kept here to make a link in the chain of evidence, and believe that if the facts related by Eben as stated in my former letters and in this be proved it will be sufficient to procure his discharge as the inference that he is a citizen of Pennsylvania & a free man will be too strong to be resisted.

I will now give you a further statement of facts related by Eben. He says that in the fall 1818 Judge Burnsides employed Mr. Rees to go to a Dutchman for a beef in Penns' Valley and that he went with Mr. Rees, but when they arrived there the beef was not gotten and Mr. Rees & himself went further up the valley and bought two, had them killed & imployed the seller (he believes a Mr. Wilson) to bring them home to Judge Burnsides. He thinks beeves costs about $40. He thinks the Judge Mr. Burnsides, Mr. Flemming or Mr. Rees must recollect some thing about this matter.

He says a girl by the name of Jenny Underwood lived with Mr. Burnsides & went from there to John Mitchels then went from Mr. Mitchels to her father's about harvest in 1819 and Mr. Burnsides had employed her, and Mr. Burnsides got him, Eben, to go to the half moon for her, he rode the horse & led another for her to ride, that he brought her down & she was living with Mr. Burnsides when he left Bellefonte just before Christmas he thinks in Dec. 1819.

He says when Judge Burnsides raised his house on Bald Eagle that he, Eben, & a young woman named Dalila & another named Polly, cooked dinner, he does not recollect the Sirnames of the young women and on the next day he received from Mrs. & Mr. Hughston 50 cents each.

He further says he brought a suit in Centre County against Peter Carthouse; and Lawyer Hale from Lewis Town & Lawyer Gretts, were his attorneys and it was tried before Wm. Petrikin esquire.

If such a suit is on record in your Court the record authenticated will be of very considerable importance here.

You will please consult your own Judgment as to what will be important to prove and let the Caption of the Affidavit state that it is submitted on behalf of Eben Jones a free man of colour to be used as evidence on an application to be made for a Writ of

Habeas Corpus to the Judge of the Superior Court of law for the County of Nelson & State of Virginia to release him from confinement in the jail of said County.

Your early & prompt attention will be thankfully received by the unfortunate Eben and will be highly gratifying to your humble servent.

Chas Perrow

If possible let the affidavits get here by the 1st of October, but if they cannot arrive by that time send them as soon as possible.

Lovingston Nelson County, Va. September 4th 1827

Dear Sir

I received your letter of the 7th July last, and am glad to find you willing to aid in the humane undertaking of establishing the freedom of Eben Jones. There is no statutory provision in this state for such a case as Ebin's. Our Statutes relating to runaway slaves can have no bearing upon his case provided we can satisfactorily shew that he is a citizen or resident of another state. If he be a citizen of your state then our laws requiring free persons of color to be registered here and to carry with them a certificate of such register of freedom with the County seal annexed thereto can not operate against him; because he will stand protected under the first clause of the second section of the 4th Article of the Federal constitution. The Question will then occur is he a citizen of Pennsylvania? If your laws do not disqualify him from the exercise of Citizenship, then if it shall appear that he was a free man in Pennsylvania he is a citizen thereof and stands completely protected under the Article quoted, from the operation of our Laws relative to free negroes & mulattoes & runaway slaves; if he be a citizen of Pennsylvania then the most speedy and safe course to pursue will be to apply to our Judge of our Circuit court here at its next sitting which will be about the first of next month for a Writ of Habeas Corpus ad subjiciendum, under the provisions our own Act of Assembly. — In the proceedings before the Judge any evidence of a legal nature will be received; consequently the affidavits of witnesses proving the circumstances as will be convincing that Ebin Jones is a citizen of the state of Pennsylvania & a free man will be sufficient to procure his discharge. If ——————————— as will effect the object be speedily obtained. I must therefore on the ground of humanity & ——— at the earnest solicitation of Eben request you to have all the facts which I have communicated to Mr Rankin and Mr ——— together with the facts herein after related and those which may suggest themselves to you proved and authenticated and transmitted as early as possible to me here. I have kept all the letters written upon this subject & copies I have kept here to make a link in the chain of evidence, and believe that if the facts related by Eben as stated in my former letters and in this be proved it will be sufficient to procure his discharge, as the information that he is a citizen of Pennsylvania & a free man will be too strong to be resisted.

I will now give you a further statement of facts related by Eben

He says that in the fall 1818 Judge Burnsides employed Mr Rees to go to a Dutchman's for a beef in Penns' valley, and that he went with Mr Rees, but when they arrived there the beef was not gotten and Mr Rees & himself went further up the valley and bought two, had them killed & employed the seller (he believes a Mr Nelson) to bring them home to Judge Burnsides, He thinks the beeves cost about $40. He thinks the Judge Mrs Burnsides Mrs Flemming or Mr Rees must recollect something about this matter —

He says a Girl by the name of Jenny Underwood lived with Mr Burnsides & went from there to John Mitchel, then went from Mr Mitchels to her fathers about harvest in 1819, and Mr Burnsides had employed her, and Mrs Burnsides got him, Eben, to go to the half moon for her, he rode one horse & led another for her to ride, that he brought her down & she went away with Mr Burnsides when he left Bellefonte just before Christmas he thinks in Decr 1819 —

He says when Judge Burnsides raised his house on Bald Eagle that he, Eben, & a young woman named Delila & an other named Polly, cooked Dinner, he does not recollect the sir names of the young women and on the next day he received from Mrs & Mr Hepsler 50 Cents each

He further says he brought a suit in Centre County against Peter Gerhard, and Lawyer Hale from Lewis Town & Lawyer Henry Gratz were his attornies and it was tried before Wm Potters Esquire

If such a suit is on record in your Court the record authenticated will be of very considerable importance here —

You will please consult your own Judgment as to what be important to prove — and let the Caption of the Affidavits tell that intended to be used as evidence on the trial of on an application to be made for a Writ of Habeas Corpus to the Judge of the Superior Court of law for the County of Nelson & State of Virginia to release him from confinement in the jail of said County —

Your early & prompt attention will be thankfully received by the unfortunate Eben and will be highly gratifying to
your ob. servt.
Chas Perrow

NB If possible let the affidavits get here by the 1st of October, but if they cannot arrive by that time send them on soon as possible